P9-DVV-077

Visual Awareness and Design

Philip Thiel

Visual Awareness and Design

an introductory program in

conceptual awareness,

perceptual sensitivity,

and basic design skills

University of Washington Press   Seattle and London

**Library of Congress Cataloging in Publi-
cation Data**

Thiel, Philip.
    Visual awareness and design.
    Bibliography: p.
    1.   Communication in design.
    2.   Visual perception.
I.   Title.
NK1510.T49   745.4'01   80-51079
ISBN 0-295-95712-3
ISBN 0-295-95786-7 pbk.

This book was designed by the author.

The text is 10 point Helvetica 3 point leaded,
and 10 point Caledonia 2 point leaded; set
on 27 picas. Notes and captions are 8 point
Helvetica 2 point leaded, and 9 point
Caledonia 1 point leaded; set on 13 picas.

Composition was done by the University of
Washington Department of Printing, on a Li-
notron 202 Phototypesetter.

Unattributed photographs are by the author,
and the calligraphy is by Midori Kono.

The inspiration for the approach to visual design presented in this book comes from Gyorgy Kepes. As teacher, friend, and mentor, he has provided both a creative insight into the nature of the issues and a convincing example, in his own life and work, of the integrative value of the artist's vision. Whatever virtues this book possesses are due to his influences; the deficiencies are entirely my own.

The development of the program owes much to the patience and dedication of my students, who, over the years of their trials and my errors, have demonstrated a remarkable fortitude. Thanks are also due Bill Curtis, Charles and Ray Eames, Dick Hoag, Jesse Reichock, Claus Seligmann, Victor Steinbrueck, and Bob Sommer for the lessons they have taught me and the advice they have offered. In addition, my colleagues in the departments of architecture at the University of California in Berkeley and the University of Washington in Seattle have contributed essential encouragement, and generous opportunities for experimentation.

Most specially I thank my wife, Midori Kono, for her indispensable and unflagging support. I dedicate this book to the memory of our son, Peter Akira.

CONTENTS

Preface

A Word with the Instructor

Vision is the principal channel of sensory information for our comprehension of the physical world. For this reason all of our interventions in the visual environment, whether incidental, accidental, or purposeful, are means of communication with others. The environment is an ever-present slate on which, consciously or unconsciously, we are continually writing messages to each other.

Any environmental scene is replete with messages: from nature to people; from people to people; and from people to nature. Implicit and explicit information on time, place, occasion, season, activity, usage, attitudes, roles, status, culture, technology, state, condition, conflict, change, and transition are copiously available and usually subliminally perceived. How many messages in what categories can you find in this scene?

For more on this subject see D. W. Meinig, ed., *The Interpretation of Ordinary Landscapes* (New York: Oxford University Press, 1979), and Jurgen Ruesch and Weldon Kees, *Nonverbal Communication* (Berkeley: University of California Press, 1956).

Those of us professionally concerned with changes in the physical environment for social purposes (architects, urban and regional planners, landscape architects, transportation planners, urban designers, civil engineers, interior designers, industrial designers, and environmental managers) have a public responsibility for both the content and the effectiveness of our implicit and explicit messages. The content is a matter of our head and our heart, but the effectiveness is a function of our visual literacy.

"When we use the word 'literacy' we mean an ability to read, to decode messages in a written language. If we are going to attach 'visual' to the idea of literacy, it would seem that we must be talking about an ability to decode nonverbal messages. What is a nonverbal message?

"In reality, we deal with such messages more than one might imagine. It is generally believed that a red flag is effective in irritating a bull. By common agreement we go on green lights and stop on red. Driving through an expensive residential district we get silent messages about family income, social status, class tastes, and the like, and if the trip takes us through a slum we get another set of messages, also nonverbal. 'Body Language' is supposed to be an entire communication system, all silent. Smiles and frowns are the same the world over. Some degree of visual literacy is expected of artists, designers, architects and others who work with forms and colors.

"Visual decoding takes place at a great variety of levels, and in this sense it is not basically different from the use of any language. When the Lone Ranger and his faithful Tonto stop at some scuff marks in the desert and conclude that a band of outlaws has passed that way, carrying a ravishing blond captive on a strawberry roan, and that the leader's horse had recently thrown a shoe, we marvel at their skill in getting so much information out of some disturbed earth. What these two would do if confronted by Picasso's *Guernica* is another question. Reading a painting takes another set of skills.

"Again, we can connect with the written language: an ability to follow the instructions for adjusting a carburetor does not necessarily guarantee that the same skill would take its owner through *Ulysses*. Furthermore, there are many written languages, and to learn any of them takes time and effort. . . .

"In visual reading, like verbal reading, the completeness of the reading relates directly to the quality of the reader's stored information. An FM broadcasting station produces an absolutely uniform transmission of information. If the broadcast is picked up in one case by a pocket transistor and in another by a high-fidelity system, there is obviously a tremendous difference in the quality of the message as received.

"Still another way of saying all this is to describe seeing as a *transaction* between transmitter (the sight) and receiver (the viewer). A cat may look at a king, as the old saying goes, but the visual message is more interesting if the onlooker also knows what a king is. Visual communication, therefore, is not unlike other kinds of communication in that it is broadcast and received and in that it uses a code or language which has to be intelligible to the receiver. . . .

"The questions that come up when visual matters are being discussed with almost any group except designers or artists almost invariably have to do with the possible value of being able to see. Does the visual literate have better taste than other people? Why should I learn how to 'read' buildings and steam irons? Will I understand art better? Do you mean that seeing is always a kind of detective work? Where do beauty and ugliness come in? Why do you talk about experience and performance and always ignore the aesthetic element? Can it help my career? How?

"It is very revealing that our entire social conditioning pressures us into looking for the exchange values of anything we acquire, whether property or knowledge. Never has anyone asked me if seeing makes life richer, or more entertaining. It has to be *worth* something.

"This is not the place to discuss the value of our values, but we might note in passing that if an ability to read words helps us get around, make a living, and add interest to our lives, so does seeing. *Why* one decides to learn anything stems from a broad range of motivations, and if one of them is a desire to help improve our physical environment, this is as good as any other.

". . . In a functionally blind society, the role of art is widely misunderstood. Art, for the visually illiterate, has some vague connection with 'beauty,' the 'finer things,' 'aesthetics,' and none at all with its real role of coming to grips with various aspects of perceived reality. In this sense, art is not that different from science, which is also involved in discovering ways of understanding reality. The difference lies not so much in the aims as in the method. Science insists on precise measurements and searches for laws which explain phenomena. Art tends to rely on an intuitive, visual approach. Even these distinctions are not absolute: many great scientists and mathematicians have worked intuitively; many artists show a strong intellectual approach in their work.

"In all cases, whether we read the findings of scientists or of artists, *we have to read*, which means we have to know the language. The language of vision uses light, shape, color, texture, lines, patterns, similarities, contrasts, movement . . . .

"A long-delayed question (I really should have brought it up much earlier) is, how does it happen that very young children, all of whom quite naturally absorb great quantities of visual information, grow up to be visually illiterate? The answer, as far as I can make out, is that this early capability is simply beaten out of them by the educational process."

—George Nelson, *How to See* (Boston: Little, Brown, 1977)

But visual literacy—competence in visual expression and communication—involves insights and skills no less disciplined than those required for proficiency in engineering and construction. A visual structure, like a physical structure, exists in terms of its own visual materials, perceptual elements, organizing principles, and social and economic contexts. Since any intervention in the physical environment ultimately manifests its own visual consequences, it is in the public interest that the education of those professionally concerned with this intervention should also include formal instruction in this visual discipline.

The process of visual design may be compared with that of structural design. In most cases, to serve the requirements of a given objective (the purpose) in a given situation (the context), physical substances (the materials) are formed into components (elements) and interrelated (in systems of organization) in accordance with their properties (attributes).

Just as structural design is based on a number of underlying *physical* principles which a designer neglects at the risk of the safety, utility, economy, and/or effectiveness of the design, so is visual design based on a number of *perceptual* principles, with similar implications for the performance, relevance, or suitability of that design.

The following comparison of structural design and visual design will make this more specific:

	Structural Design	**Visual Design**
Purposes, function, or use	support, enclose, contain, shelter, shield	communicate information, express idea or attitude, convey feeling or mood
Operating contexts	loadings, allowable stress and strain, technology, economy, culture, climate	spatial and temporal perceptual fields: cultural, social, situational sets and expectations
Materials	earth, stone, metal, wood, concrete, glass, plastic, fabric	modulated radiant energy 400 to 700 millimicrons in wave length (the visible spectrum)
Elements	slab, panel, beam, girder, joist, column, post, tie, strut	positive and negative basic pattern areas in the visual field
Attributes of elements	size, weight, shape, strength, stiffness, cost, durability	number, position, size, shape, direction, texture, color, surface quality, duration, brightness, motion
Systems of organization	arch, vault, post, beam, cage, panel, column and slab, truss, shell, dome	proximity, similarity, continuance, closure, rhythm, movement
Types of element connections	bearing, friction, weld, cement, rivet, bolt, pin, mortar, adhesive	identity, similarity, contrast, ambiguity
Design criteria	equilibrium, safety, durability, economy	legibility, expressiveness, coherence, order, balance, equilibrium

14

The program presented here has as its objective the inculcation of visual literacy. It has been developed over a fifteen-year period in interaction with large groups of undergraduates beginning their studies in environmental planning, design, and management. The program is concerned with the growth of competence in visual design, across the spectrum of conceptual awareness, perceptual sensitivity, and design-craft skills. The intention is to enable students to move from an assumed position of unawareness of visual structure and unfamiliarity with design terms, tools, and techniques, to a position of heightened appreciation of visual expression and communication, with a practical competence in visual design under supervision—all within the time span of one academic quarter.

The method used to accomplish this goal involves an integrated sequence of problems, exercises, readings, films, and quizzes. The problems and exercises are both graded and cumulative—that is, each provides a challenge within the capabilities of a beginning student, and each builds on the growth provided by the preceding work. Thus the student ascends a ladder of achievement, step by step, gaining in confidence and competence as a consequence of each challenge. Each problem is framed to focus the student's attention on a limited but increasing number of issues, so that he or she will develop both a capability in handling each one and the habit of being responsible for all of them.

These constraints also serve to characterize the learning activity as a "game." Designer Paul Rand, in an essay on "Design and the Play Instinct" (in Gyorgy Kepes, ed., *Education of Vision* [New York: Gèòrge Braziller, 1965]), discusses and illustrates the value of such problem limitations in education and art, and quotes the painter Georges Braque: "Limited means beget new forms, invite creation, make the style. Progress in art does not lie in extending its limits, but in knowing them better."

Furthermore, each problem involves the student in matters of conceptual awareness, perceptual sensitivity, and basic simulation skills, in proportions that necessarily vary from problem to problem. Implementation of these goals under any conditions, and especially in a short period of time, puts a premium on the use of language in mediating concepts, for, as the proverb goes, "The eye is blind to what the mind does not see." In this connection, experience indicates that we are obliged to devote some attention to the expansion of the students' working vocabulary. It must be remembered that our purpose is not just to encourage the students' production of artifacts which tickle the eye, but to transform the students at a fundamental level of their insight and outlook, integrating all levels of sensing, feeling, and thinking. As instructors, our "product" is specially qualified *people,* and our students' studio artifacts are significant only as signs of their growth. For this reason, all examples of student work are excluded from this presentation, since their presence here would implicitly encourage a superficial imitation of forms and a bypassing of the underlying issues. Such a procedure would eliminate an essential component of the student's developmental experience: the struggle to make his or her own cognitive resolution of each problem.

Because this program is directed toward the development of the students' ability to intervene effectively in the visual environment, each problem is a challenge in design synthesis. This involves both a conscious cyclical iteration of an explicit design process (identification, specification, hypothesis, simulation, and evaluation), and the development of the necessary simulation skills in a variety of media.

Woven into the text is a mini-anthology of excerpts from the writings of a number of key artists, designers, scientists, philosophers, and historians, included not only as a means for the optimal illumination of specific issues, but also to introduce the work of these experts and leaders as a source of information and inspiration. Since in this course some sacrifice of depth is made to gain a corresponding breadth of coverage, each problem also includes a discussion intended to open vistas of additional implications and challenges. Thus the program may be seen as a true primer: a wholistic introduction to an enhanced involvement with the visual environment, extending from an awareness of conceptual principles to an appreciation of sensory richness, and including the means to achieve a good measure of design competence.

The regimen set forth herein is certainly not the only way one may realize these developmental goals in this area of design. But, given a limited amount of curriculum time, it will encourage maximum student growth on a comprehensive front. The constraints of time and inclusiveness are of course the reasons for the disciplined structure of the program, and as in the case of similar intensive "total immersion" programs the students, self-selected for this area of study, in effect make a bargain with the instructor: maximum commitment for maximum growth.

The teacher's involvement with this program deserves further comment. Generally speaking, design courses are not very standardized, since each particular approach is properly the resolution of three factors: the interests of the individual instructor, the nature of the given student group, and the local educational program. To facilitate the use of this material by other instructors in different situations, the following notes are offered on the specific circumstances associated with the author's implementation of this curriculum.

As mentioned above, the program evolved from a repeated interaction with groups of twenty to thirty undergraduates in several areas of environmental planning, design, and management, as one of a series of introductory studio courses scheduled in their professional program at a large state university. A total of about 120 hours of class time and an equal amount of additional student preparation time is required for the course, with students spending from 240 to 300 hours in all on the work in the program. The material is presented at a brisk, involving pace during the ten consecutive weeks of an academic quarter, and the course is the major item in the students' program during that quarter.

In a group of this size, the instructor's time per student is rather low, but offsetting this is the inevitable diversity of such a group of students which provides a more-than-compensating advantage: when the program is administered on a noncompetitive, cooperative basis, the varied student backgrounds and professional aspirations will encourage student "interteaching." The students work on their own projects, but learn to assist each other as circumstances require, and thus gain by acquiring essential collaborative skills.

Communication between students can be stimulated and encouraged by positioning the individual worktables (minimum size 30″ X 48″) in a pinwheel arrangement of groups of four, so that each student is at a right angle with the adjacent person. The students have the exclusive possession of their worktable for the quarter, and as this is the first studio experience for most of them, they are encouraged to personalize the premises and make the studio their home away from home.

Initially the students are invited to make a free choice of these places in the studio, and thus to feel most comfortable in their location. About four weeks into the quarter individual strengths and weaknesses have become apparent, and in view of the generally increased self-confidence in the studio situation, some suggestions for relocation are individually proffered by the instructor as a means to achieve a balanced mix at each four-person cluster.

Other teaching facilities include wall space for the continuous eye-level display of both student work in process and final results, at a rate of not less than sixteen square feet per person (and preferably at twice that rate). Good natural lighting is provided, along with university-standard studio lighting (lamped, however, with deluxe cool white fluorescent lamps for better color rendering).

Adequate floor space permits gatherings for discussion of the wall display, both informally and at the end-of-the-problem meetings (the "Raspberry Club"), and for the weekly films and occasional slide projections. The presentation and discussion of the films and slides, integral to the program, is facilitated by the permanent availability of a screen and projection equipment, with shades to darken the room. There is also a large seminar table, doubling for use in layout work, a heavy-duty paper cutter, and lockable storage facilities for the students.

Facilities external to the above include the library, where all the references cited in the text are placed on reserve, and a photographic studio and laboratory where expert technical instruction is available to the students as part of the program. Administration of the photographic work in the program is aided by inventorying the students' camera equipment at the beginning of the quarter. This is done by means of a short questionnaire, which also provides an opportunity for the instructor to become better acquainted with the students' educational background, professional intentions, and possible conflicts between the demands of their academic program and part-time work.

To further reinforce the spirit of mutual assistance, the chilling competitive effect of university-required grading is minimized by avoiding any public mention of the instructor's opinion of individual student work, while asking the students to make an explicit evaluation of their own performance as part of their private "True Confessions" written after the discussion at the end of each problem. The instructor's estimate of each student's work is made simultaneously and also recorded privately, but with the results available to students individually on request anytime during the quarter, preferably in terms of a discussion of the student's performance and problems, and not as grades. By these means it is emphasized that as far as creativity is concerned the students are competing only with themselves.

The written quizzes, however, are handled somewhat differently. These are administered as a means of focusing the students' attention on the theoretical premises and basic principles which illuminate their procedures; emphasizing the essential integration of form and content as the prerequisite for significance in design; and enriching the students' inventory of familiar words as a coinage for this commerce in concepts.

Four quizzes are scheduled during the quarter: after Problem 1 (to quickly set the style), after Problem 8 (the halfway point), and after Problems 12 and 17. Announced a week in advance, they require about one hour of class time, and include four questions on material in the text and notes, and twenty of the words found by experience to be most unfamiliar to the students, to be defined in the context of the work.

These quizzes are graded and returned individually to the students, with a public display of the frequency distribution of all the grades. The class is advised from the start that the average of their three highest grades will constitute one-third of their obligatory final grade for the course. By this means it is emphasized that the students are members of and participants in a larger intellectual community.

Finally, it will be noted that the problems themselves are addressed to the students, with the presentation so explicit that the instructor is free to devote a maximum of time to individual students in critiques of their work in progress, and to group discussions of the results and implications of each problem.

It is expected that after some initial period of use, other instructors will choose to modify the program, in accordance with their own experiences and in adaptation to local circumstances—thus, in effect subsuming the present author's years of experience to their own. In this way they are engaging in a learning adventure with their students. Furthermore, the suggestions for additional studies, presented in the discussions of the problems, will inspire a subsequent variety of more specialized advanced programs. The author hopes that this program will in fact prove to be seminal for both students and instructors, and result in both personal growth and richer environments for all.

Visual Awareness and Design

Introduction  A

Courtesy of the Museum of Fine Arts, Boston

Vision and Environment

"A fish," it is said, "cannot discover water"—except, perhaps, when it is removed from its customary environment. In a like manner we may become more conscious of our visual environment if we attempt to speculate on the condition of our lives and the nature of our world without vision. Let us imagine for a moment that you became blind. The loss of sight would certainly cause a cataclysmic change in your life: gone would be the "rosy-fingered dawn" and the metamorphoses of the sunset, the shadows of clouds on the hills and the furrows of the wind in the grass. No longer could you see the smile on the face of your friend, or the look of wonder in the eyes of your child; and far less accessible would be the strange places you might have visited, the new books you might have read, and the films, plays, and exhibits you might have seen. Your sensory world would shrink to what you could hear, touch, taste, and smell, and you would thus be excluded from many of the richest human experiences.

Now, for another moment, suppose that the human species itself were blind and had evolved without the faculty of vision—but such a state of affairs is almost impossible to imagine. Perhaps people would be limited to a tactile, mole-like existence, crawling on the surface of the earth, living in burrows, and generally existing in a condition of culture lower than that of even a prehistoric society.

These exercises in imagination are suggested as a means for the post-childhood rediscovery of our visual environment. So pervasive is our adaptation to any sensory environment that it becomes almost "invisible" to us; it is habitually out of our awareness. Like fish, we move through it, not comprehending the full extent of its effect on us and unaware of our effect on it.

In this connection McLuhan and Parker suggest that the effect of all the arts, under all conditions, is to counteract the "invisible" character of the environment and thus heighten perception. "Any environmental form whatsoever saturates perception," they write, "so that its own character is imperceptible; it has the power to distort or deflect human awareness. Even the most popular arts can serve to increase the level of awareness, at least until they become entirely environmental and unperceived."

Thus, when art approaches the scale of the environment itself, in a sense of reciprocal isomorphism we may conceive of "the creative discipline of our visual environment," and say with Blake and the Palmist, "we become what we behold."

See Marshall McLuhan and Harley Parker, *Through the Vanishing Point* (New York: Harper and Row, 1968); and Edmund Carpenter, *They Became What They Beheld* (New York: Ballantine Books, 1970).

"In humans, vision is the master sense through whose afferent impulses and imagery, the person maintains almost continuous contact with the environment during the waking state. When a seeing person becomes blind, a large part of the content of consciousness is lost, and the person may suddenly feel demoralized and even disoriented until compensatory hyperacuity of other senses begins to compensate for the loss of vision. Hearing contributes the second most important sensory constituents of consciousness principally relating ·to speech and other modes of vocal communication but also contributing special esthetic experiences such as music, and background noise which many people ignore unless it becomes distracting or alarming because of some unaccustomed change. Cutaneous senses, kinesthetic or proprioceptive senses, and deep visceral senses contribute as everpresent and relatively un-changing background of sensations which contribute to feelings of Self. In states of anesthesia or paresthesia, the person may feel disembodied or not like 'one's usual self.' All these sensations are experienced against a background of feeling tone or mood which colors all of conscious awareness. Indeed, it is the feeling tone which largely determines the motivational quality of states of consciousness reactive to stimulation. Other contents of consciousness include memories, associations, images and creative thoughts in which new combinations of meaningful or nonmeaningful elements are presented."

—F. C. Thorne, *Personality* (Brandon, Vermont: Journal of Clinical Psychology, 1961)

"There is a general relationship between the evolutionary age of the receptor system and the amount and quality of information it conveys to the central nervous system. The tactile, or touch, systems are as old as life itself; indeed, the ability to respond to stimuli is one of the basic criteria of life. Sight was the last and most specialized sense to be developed in man. Vision became more important and olfaction less essential when man's ancestors left the ground and took to the trees . . . .

". . . The amount of information gathered by the eyes as contrasted with the ears has not been precisely calculated. Such a calculation not only involves a translation process, but scientists have been handicapped by lack of knowledge of what to count. A general notion, however, of the relative complexities of the two systems can be obtained by comparing the size of the nerves connecting the eyes and the ears to the centers of the brain. Since the optic nerve contains roughly eighteen times as many neurons as the cochlear nerve, we assume it transmits at least that much more information. Actually, in normally alert subjects, it is probable that the eyes may be as much as a thousand times as effective as the ears in sweeping up information . . . .

"The area that the unaided ear can effectively cover in the course of daily living is quite limited. Up to twenty feet the ear is very efficient. At about one hundred feet, one-way vocal communication is possible, at a somewhat slower rate than at conversational distances, while two-way conversation is very considerably altered. Beyond this distance, the auditory cues with which man works begin to break down rapidly. The unaided eye, on the other hand, sweeps up an extraordinary amount of information within a hundred-yard radius and is still quite efficient for human interaction at a mile."

". . . Not only is there a great difference in the amount and type of information that the two receptor systems can process, but also in the amount of space that can be probed effectively by these two systems. A sound barrier at a distance of a quarter of a mile is hardly detectable. This would not be true of a high wall or screen that shuts out a view. Visual space, therefore, has an entirely different character than auditory space. Visual information tends to be less ambiguous and more focused than auditory information."

—Edward T. Hall, *The Hidden Dimension* (Garden City, N.Y.: Doubleday, 1966)

All living organisms interact with their physical environment and affect it. But it is our technologically oriented human species, for better or worse, which is now the dominant force in modifying our planet Earth. All our environmental impositions, whether for sheltering and facilitating our personal and collective activities, or for providing, processing, and distributing the materials and services associated with our subsistence and operations, have massively and irrevocably transformed the globe, and we are obliged to accept their technological essence to remain human. Reciprocally, everything we do to the environment eventually has an impact on us, often

Landscapes in Japan: near Kyoto (left) and Nagoya (right)

incidentally or accidentally in ways other than those nominally intended. Although we are physiologically concerned with radiation levels and highway noises, with noxious atmospheric particles and well-oiled bathing beaches, we are also intellectually challenged and emotionally affected by the sight of clustered skyscrapers and acres of squatters' settlements, by ancient terraced paddies and newly strip-mined hills, by the shady fountain in the park and the neon drive-in strip, by the beer can by the highway and the geranium on the windowsill, and by the poignant funeral wreath and the happy bridal bouquet.

"The idea that human culture is dependent on its technological foundations is at first startling or even offensive, yet reflection will show this to be as obvious as it is undeniable. Chartres would have been impossible without the craft of the stonemason; the discoveries of Galileo, which revolutionized man's view of his position in the universe, could never have been made without the skill of the lens grinder; the glories of Bach would not exist save for the manufacturers of musical instruments. All human societies—their economics and political structures, and their intellectual cultures as well—are dependent upon their technological foundations . . . ."

—Victor C. Ferkis, *Technological Man* (New York: New American Library, 1969)

". . . the influences that affect human life most profoundly are not always the direct ones measured in such objective values as temperatures, chemicals, decibels, kinds of germs or numbers of people. Man converts all the things that happen to him into symbols, then commonly responds to the symbols as if they were the actual external stimuli. All perceptions and interpretations of the mind become so profoundly translated into organic processes that the actual biological and mental effect of a stimulus commonly bears little resemblance to the direct effects which could have been expected from its physiochemical nature."

—Rene Dubos, *So Human an Animal* (New York: Scribner's, 1968)

"It is not with tools only that we domesticate our world. Sensed forms, images and symbols are as essential to us as palpable reality in exploring nature for human ends. Distilled from our experience and made our permanent possessions, they provide a nexus between man and man and between man and nature. We make a map of our experience patterns, an inner model of the outer world, and we use this to organize our lives. Our natural 'environment'—whatever impinges on us from outside—becomes our human 'landscape'—a segment of nature fathomed by us and made our home . . . ."

Gyorgy Kepes, *The New Landscape in Art and Science* (Chicago: Paul Theobald, 1956)

26

But beyond such explicit and implicit signs and symbols there are the more subtle environmental messages inherent in the sensory patterns themselves. At a more fundamental level of our consciousness we are engaged with the richness or poverty of the range of colors presented to our eyes, with the order or incoherence of the forms that flow in sequence past us, with the variety or monotony of the rhythms we see before us, and with the freedom or constriction of the light-space in which we move. Thus at many levels our self-made environment sends a series of subliminal messages "to whom it may concern," and, consciously or not, in one way or another we are all concerned.

See Kevin Lynch, *The Image of the City* (Cambridge, Mass.: MIT Press, 1960); and Kevin Lynch, *What Time Is This Place?* (Cambridge, Mass.: MIT Press, 1972).

See also Juan Pablo Bonta, *Architecture and Its Interpretation* (London: Lund Humphries, 1979).

The environments we have made and saved and the environments we are now making offer persistent evidence of what is important to us and what we believe in. By these environmental means we continuously enculturate the young, orient both visitor and habitué in time and space, articulate attitudes, express feelings, and cue individual and social behavior. Our thoughts are nourished, our feelings conditioned, and our actions guided by our interpretations of the signals inherent in our surroundings. Our self-made environment is the soil supporting our culture and feeding its roots. In an infinite number of ways the visual environment serves as a universal channel of social communication, and through its use a commonwealth of denotative, connotative, and prescriptive images becomes established. This is a prerequisite to a cooperative social life.

"Our imaginative conception, or humanized envisagement of things, places, acts and facts, is guided by the steady development of our feeling toward the world around us. Feeling is native, spontaneous, instinctive; but feeling is also developed, formed and learned. This may seem to most people a strange proposition; how can feelings be learned? By what means are they formed and developed?

"They are formed as our ideas of the world are formed: by the influence of images which articulate them and exhibit them for our contemplation, so that their rhythms become clear and familiar . . . .

"Just as our vision is guided toward exact and intelligent perception of things by the way they are presented . . . our feelings are guided and shaped by the forms in which various artists have projected them. They fall naturally into those forms, and develop in ways prepared for them. Moreover, we learn feeling from seeing it expressed in art, because that expression makes it conceivable. A work of art is a logical projection in which feeling appears as a quality of the created object, the work. That quality is what good art has and bad art lacks; it is the artist's idea, inexpressible in verbal propositions, but clearly perceptible as the import of his presentation. To distinguish this sort of emotive expression from what is usually intended, we might call this expressiveness.

"Expressiveness may belong to forms that represent no objects or beings or events at all—to pure lines, to compositions in space and light and color, to proportions, contrasts—any and all elements of design . . . ."

—S. K. Langer, "The Social Influence of Design," in L. B. Holland, ed., *Who Designs America?* (New York: Doubleday, 1966)

"The city is a fact in nature, like a cave, a run of mackerel, or an antheap. But it is also a conscious work of art, and it holds within its communal framework many simpler and more personal forms of art. Mind *takes form* in the city; and in turn, urban forms condition mind. For space, no less than time, is artfully reorganized in cities: in boundary lines and silhouettes, in the fixing of horizontal planes and vertical peaks, in utilizing or denying the natural site, the city records the attitude of a culture and an epoch to the fundamental facts of its existence. The dome and the spire, the open avenue, and the closed court, tell the story, not merely of different physical accommodations, but of essentially different conceptions of man's destiny. The city is both a physical utility for collective living and a symbol of those collective purposes and unanimities that arise under such favoring circumstance. With language itself, it remains man's greatest work of art.

"The city, as one finds it in history, is the point of maximum concentration for the power and culture of a community. It is the place where the diffused rays of many separate beams of light fall into focus, with gains in both social effectiveness and significance. The city is the form and symbol of an integrated social relationship; it is the seat of the temple, the market, the hall of justice, the academy of learning. Here in the city the goods of civilization are manifolded and multiplied; here is where human experience is transformed into viable signs, symbols, patterns of conduct, systems of order. Here is where the issues of civilization are focused: here, too, ritual passes on occasion into the active drama of a fully differentiated and self-conscious society."

—Lewis Mumford, *The Culture of Cities* (New York: Harcourt, Brace, and World, 1938)

"Milieu can affect the standing pattern of behavior through operation of physical forces some of which are coercive (walls prevent passage), others suggestive (paths make walking easier than plowed fields); through physiological processes (temperature can control behavior tempo); and through physiognomic perception (smooth open places invite children's running, protected areas encourage social grouping). In such examples, milieu factors mold behavior to its shape or quality. Consider, however, the extent to which factors other than milieu operate to determine the final milieu-behavior unit. There is the imitation tendency (to sit as others sit, to show emotion congruent with the emotions one sees about him); there are social forces (the behavior in a setting can be influenced by authority, reward or punishment); there are facts of learning (children are taught how to use a school room; they may even be taught now to use parks and playgrounds); there are the facts that settings select persons and persons select settings; there is the final factor that behavior can create synomorphy by molding the milieu (cars parked on the curbless side street gradually encroach upon the grassy area; the area becomes hard packed and brown, thus encouraging an off-street space)."

—Paul V. Gump, "The Behavior Setting: A Promising Unit for Environmental Designers," *Landscape Architecture,* January 1971

"When Aristotle made his famous observation about men coming together in cities to lead the good life, he failed to add that, the moment two or three were gathered together in the agora, they would put up a pile of stones—roofed or unroofed—to shelter their concept of the good life. Such piles—be they the Stoa, the aisles of old St. Paul's or the Rockefeller Plaza—were an invaluable guide (and still are) to newcomers wishing to join the good life, to master its techniques and attitudes. But there has always been the risk that men would mistake the buildings for the life, the stone substance for the shadow in which the life was lived. In times of lost nerve, fetishism replaced functionalism, men bowed down to wood and stone instead of inhabiting them, and embalmed what health and sanity required them to destroy. The embalmed city is the necropolis of the insecure."

—Reyner Banham, "The Embalmed City," *New Statesman*, 12 April 1963

Here we arrive at the point of our present interest. We can now turn the situation around and argue that by paying specific attention to the visual consequences of all our interventions in the environment, and to both the implicit and explicit social implications of these consequences, we have a means for directly affecting our image of social reality. Our intentional use of the visual environment for the expression of feeling and the exemplification of attitudes, and for the illustration of ideas and the suggestion of responses, provides an opportunity to promote the growth of latent sensibilities and reconstrue old perceptions. By an effective use of the pervasive and durable communication channel that is the visual environment we can provide an impetus for both individual growth and social development. Since life imitates art, the art of living depends on seeing the environment as art.

The implementation of this process requires the services of both visually aware and demanding laypersons and visually competent professionals. Our specific interest here is the development of your visual literacy for either of these roles. But note that this development is a demanding matter involving the opening of both your eye and your mind, in a personal process of visual reeducation. What may not be so obvious at this point is that what we see (regardless of what is before our eyes) is determined by how we have learned to see. Our eyes are by no means merely open windows, admitting everything "out there" to our awareness or preconsciousness.

On the contrary, anatomically our eyes are a specialized part of our brain, constituting a visual *system,* which together with our other perceptual systems (auditory, olfactory, haptic, orienting) operates as an information-seeking and monitoring service. But this visual system has been culturally and occupationally programmed to decode and interpret the available latent environmental information on a probabilistic basis in very specific ways. Because the process of perception serves us so subtly, we must penetrate the barrier of unsuspected stereotypes and clichés in order that we may encounter at first hand the elements of visual form and the nature of visual organization and the expressive potentials of their use. By these means we may bring ourselves to the point of awareness at which we can discover what we might do to help ourselves. Since the ultimate test of knowing is by doing, in all this endeavor we require an exercise of the rich creative abilities you and every other person possess.

All revolutions result from a change in consciousness, and the essence of the human condition as an ongoing adaptive process is a continual growth of individual and collective consciousness. We are concerned here with such a change in your life through the expansion of your visual awareness and development of your creative potential, not only for the enrichment of your life as a layperson, but particularly for the possibilities it offers for implementing your vision of the better life, in your role as a professional or paraprofessional in environmental design.

See James J. Gibson, *The Senses Considered as Perceptual Systems* (Boston: Houghton Mifflin, 1966); and James Marston Fitch, "Single Point Perspective," *Architectural Forum,* April 1974.

"Whatever may be the language one happens to inherit, it is at once a tool and a trap. It is a tool because with it we order our experience, matching the data abstracted from the flux about us with linguistic units: words, phrases, sentences. What is true of verbal languages is also true of visual 'languages': we match the data from the flux of visual experience with image-clichés, with stereotypes of one kind or another, according to the way we have been taught to see.

"And having matched the data of experience with our abstractions, visual or verbal, we manipulate those abstractions, with or without further reference to the data, and make systems with them. Those systems of abstractions, artifacts of the mind, when verbal, we call 'explanations,' or 'philosophies'; when visual, we call them our 'picture of the world.'

"With these little systems in our heads we look upon the dynamism of the events around us, and we find, or persuade ourselves that we find, correspondences between the pictures inside our heads and the world without. Believing those correspondences to be real, we feel at home in what we regard as a 'known' world.

"In saying why our abstractions, verbal or visual, are a tool, I have already intimated why they are also a trap. If the abstractions, the words, the phrases, the sentences, the visual clichés, the interpretative stereotypes, that we have inherited from our cultural environment are adequate to their task, no problem is presented. But like other instruments, languages select, and in selecting what they select, they leave out what they do not select . . . ."

—S. I. Hayakawa, "The Revisions of Vision," in Gyorgy Kepes, *The Language of Vision* (Chicago: Paul Theobald, 1947)

Drawing by W. Steig; ©1968 *The New Yorker Magazine,* Inc.

Design and Designers

"For a number of reasons—good and bad—design is a confusing subject. Among the good reasons is the elusiveness of definition: a person who does a line of dresses for a couturier house and someone who draws a plan for a jet engine are both called designers. It is hard to see what they have in common.

"What both people share, I think, is the process; each starts with a problem, one related to the female figure and the other related to propulsion. Each arrives at solutions within a context: money limitations, materials available, skills and tools at hand, existing state of the art, competition, the nature of the market. In the end, each has designed an item that must work: the dress has to enhance the wearer; the engine has to drive the plane.

"A design may be very beautiful, but it is not art; a design has to do something. The artist works to make a kind of visual statement that has, for him, some important connection with reality as he perceives it. The designer needs a client to present a problem, and a factory to make his design in quantity.

"The scientist believes that problems can be solved with his intellectual equipment plus instruments. His answers are always quantifiable. The designer goes along with this to a great extent, but he also relies on the evidence of his senses and his intuition. So his work falls somewhere between art and science.

"A very bad reason for the confusion about design is the prevailing notion that it is a kind of frosting, an aesthetic overlay that makes humdrum objects more appetizing. No responsible designer believes this. In nature, organic designs (our best models) never show decoration that isn't functional, never show the slightest concern for aesthetics, and always try to match the organism with its environment so that it will survive.

"Misconceptions about design also arise because modern technology isolates so many people from the processes of designing and making. Considering how little we are taught about such things, autos and stereo sets might just as well grow on trees. Technological society has created the visual illiterate, a new barbarian who thinks people have eyes so that they can tell when traffic lights turn red or green, and who lacks the faintest idea of how his complex environment is put together."

—George Nelson, "We Are Here by Design," *Harper's*, April 1975

But what is design? What is it we do when we design? To answer this, we may say first that most generally design involves an act of purposeful planning, or the devising of courses of action aimed at changing existing situations into preferred ones. More specifically, design may be said to be a means of optimizing the use of limited resources of time and material in the realization of predetermined objectives, in circumstances where no satisfactory precedents exist. Since we are interested in the "best" way of accomplishing this goal, we face the necessity of originating and evaluating alternatives, and then choosing among them. To facilitate such choices, we logically estimate the probable consequences of each alternative, in effect constructing a model of the situation and testing each possible course of action in it before any action is taken in the real world. Design is thus an alternative-evoking and decision-rationalizing activity, involving a series of operations and decisions in an iterative process. The operations are:

1. **Identification** of the problem and its contextual constraints.

2. **Specification** of the goals and of the criteria for an acceptable solution.

3. **Hypothesis** or invention of possible alternative solutions.

4. **Simulation** or production of a testable representation of the proposed solution.

5. **Testing** or the application of the acceptance criteria to the simulation of the proposed solution by the appropriate person.

These operations are performed in this sequence, as shown in the accompanying flow-chart diagram. Failure on testing inaugurates the feedback loop to a rehypothesis and the generation of an alternate solution, and this process continues until all possible acceptable solutions are produced. It should be mentioned that these cyclical iterations also involve a continuing clarification and redefinition of the problem, as well as the consideration of a variety of means of simulation. That is, each cycle of the process increases our understanding of the problem, and implies the suggestion not only of alternative solutions but also of better means and ways to test them.

When all possible acceptable solutions have been generated, the process continues with the implementation and operation phases:

6. **Comparison** and rank-ordering of acceptable solutions.

7. **Implementation** of the most suitable alternative solution.

8. **Evaluation** of the implemented alternative, in use in the real world.

See H. A. Simon, *The Science of the Artificial* (Cambridge, Mass.: MIT Press, 1969), for a discrimination of "satisfactory" and "optimal" design solutions.

For more comprehensive treatments of the design process, see, for example: L. Bruce Archer, "An Overview of the Structure of the Design Process," in G. T. Moore, ed., *Emerging Methods in Environmental Design and Planning* (Cambridge, Mass.: MIT Press, 1968); J. Christopher Jones, *Design Methods* (London: Wiley-Interscience, 1970); Geoffrey Broadbent, *Design in Architecture* (New York: John Wiley and Sons, 1973); and Harold R. Buhl, *Creative Engineering Design* (Ames, Iowa: Iowa State University Press, 1960).

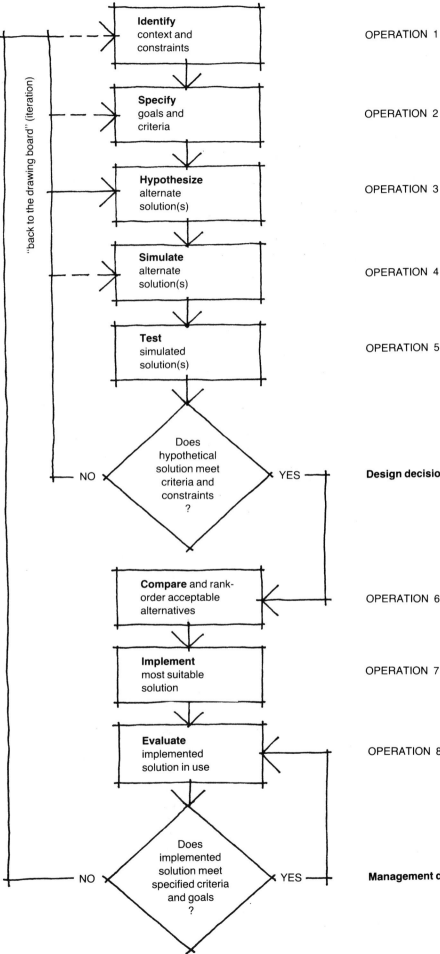

"back to the drawing board" (iteration)

Identify context and constraints — OPERATION 1

Specify goals and criteria — OPERATION 2

Hypothesize alternate solution(s) — OPERATION 3

Simulate alternate solution(s) — OPERATION 4

Test simulated solution(s) — OPERATION 5

Does hypothetical solution meet criteria and constraints ?

NO — YES — **Design decision**

Compare and rank-order acceptable alternatives — OPERATION 6

Implement most suitable solution — OPERATION 7

Evaluate implemented solution in use — OPERATION 8

Does implemented solution meet specified criteria and goals ?

NO — YES — **Management decision**

In this connection see Rudolph Arnheim, *Visual Thinking* (Berkeley: University of California Press, 1970), and Robert Sommer, *The Mind's Eye* (New York: Delta, 1978).

Heinz Von Foerster, "Logical Structure of Environment and Its Internal Representation," in R. F. Eckerstrom, ed., *International Design Conference, Aspen, 1962* (Zeeland, Michigan: Herman Miller, 1963)

We will discuss your use of this process in some detail in the next section; here we will only suggest that at all times all decisions you make involve some version of this process. If the process is carried on internally, the simulations are in the form of those mental representations called images or schemata, and the process is called "thinking." To externalize this process and communicate it to others requires a second presentation of the internal one by means of a conventionalized system of physical signals—vocal, gestural, or graphic. Such a "re-presentation" depends on a commonality from person to person in the attachment of the external sign to the internal presentation, and as Von Foerster points out, our consciousness of the environment and thus the nature of our intentional collaborative interventions therein are in fact limited to what we can communicate to ourselves and each other by means of these externalized representations.

This brings us to a consideration of the several *phases* of design, which are characterized by differences in the issues being studied, the decision makers involved, and the corresponding means of simulation appropriate to both the issues and the people. In general, five major phases can be identified. In order of occurrence they are:

A. **Preliminary Design:** in which those concerned with a problem, working mostly by themselves, use chiefly schematic and abstract representations to clarify the nature of the problem and to evoke some notion of whether a solution is possible, as well as some idea of the nature of the possible solutions. Subsequent stages of this phase involve more specific representations in analogic and iconic form for use in testing the tentative responses of others who are, or will be, concerned with the design or the consequences of its implementation.

B. **Detail Design:** in which, with the design constraints and criteria now more firmly established and the preliminary responses of all those concerned or affected being favorable, a more specific development of all details of the proposal is made with the aid of representations suited to the needs of those who will implement them.

C. **Approval:** in which the final reviews of all aspects by all concerned, including the public authorities, are undertaken, and, after any necessary revisions, authorization to proceed is obtained.

D. **Implementation:** wherein construction commitments are solicited and made (after possible recycling back to Phase B) and the actual modification of the environment occurs. Note that the design process does *not* end here but continues on to the next phase.

E. **Evaluation and Management:** in which the newly modified environment takes its place as part of the world. It is at this point that the whole design process is subjected to the final and ultimate test: in this real-world manifestation of the design hypotheses, are the predetermined objectives now realized; are the acceptance criteria satisfied? Furthermore, in this phase the environmental managers must respond to changes as they occur, within the time constraints of the real world—a process also involving new cycles of problem identification (in response to malfunctioning of an existing environment), solution hypothesis, environmental intervention, response sampling, and feedback for rehypothesis and reintervention.

"The architect knows, and his clients acutely feel, that his buildings do have empirical significance. His creativity could only be whole if he were to take account of it. People are currently so infuriated by the buildings they use, in part because they are the victims of the architect's hypotheses while he seems unconcerned about the users' reactions. Nor does he seem to know whether he wants to care about their reactions. It is not clear whether the practicing architect simply omits to verify his hypotheses by default, rather as the student does, or whether he does so deliberately through lack of interest in them.

"One implication of this argument is that the architectural profession should clarify the doubt. If there is a move today, as one would hope, toward more concern and responsibility for the user of buildings, architects will redefine their role so that it includes an essential component of verification. They should not engage yet another consultant—a social scientist would be an obvious choice—to do the work for them. If verification is to be part of architectural creativity, it must be carried out by the architect himself. A continuing concern for the building-in-use and for the user should be shown by the creative architect."

—Peter Stringer, "The Myths of Architectural Creativity," *Architectural Design*, October 1975

In view of the vast preponderance of *existing* environments at any given moment compared to newly designed environments, it is interesting to note that the profession of environmental *management* has a potential for affecting the quality of human experience much greater than that of environmental *design*.

For more on this see: Serge Boutourline, "The Concept of Environmental Management," in Proshansky et al., eds., *Environmental Psychology* (New York: Holt, Rinehart and Winston, 1970); and F. I. Steele, "Problem Solving in the Spatial Environment," in H. Sanoff and S. Cohn, eds., *EDRA 1: Proceeedings of the 1st Annual Environmental Design Research Association Conference* (Chapel Hill, North Carolina, 1970).

See also: Robert Sommer, *Design Awareness* (San Francisco: Rinehart Press, 1972); C. Perin, *With Man in Mind* (Cambridge, Mass.: MIT Press, 1970); C. M. Deasy, *Design for Human Affairs* (Cambridge, Mass.: Schenkman, 1974); and Amos Rapoport, "The Design Professions and the Behavioral Sciences," *Architectural Association Quarterly*, Winter, 1968/69.

Having thus discussed the nature and process of design, we now come to the question of the designers and their relationships with society and the people they serve. First of all, who are the environmental designers?

We have suggested earlier that all our environmental interventions of whatever nature sooner or later involve some visual consequences. For this reason, in one sense we are all inadvertently environmental designers or managers, although in many cases, unfortunately, we do not always anticipate or notice the visual results, or have much interest in them.

But there are several groups of people who are professionally concerned with the visual environment. One of these groups includes those who are working with chiefly ephemeral or spatially limited effects: the sign painters and the electric sign designers; the graphic designers of posters, newspapers, magazine and television advertisements; the mural artists, painters and sculptors, shop and window display artists, stage designers, lighting experts, and typographers. And here we may also include the fabric and clothing designers, as well as film directors and editors.

In addition to these there is another group of people who are also concerned with the visual environment, but are working on somewhat larger scales and with more permanent effects. We can broadly identify them as the environmental design, planning, and management professions consisting of industrial designers, interior designers, building designers and architects, landscape architects, civic or urban designers, urban and regional planners, transportation planners, civil engineers, and environmental facility managers.

We have previously discussed the importance of the visual environment as one of the chief sources of our images of our social reality. Let us now consider the nature of the roles of those who would, as environmental designers, presume to determine these images.

"The American Architect," from *Architectural and Engineering News,* January 1966

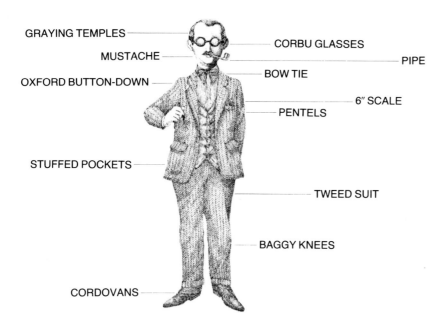

GRAYING TEMPLES

MUSTACHE

OXFORD BUTTON-DOWN

CORBU GLASSES

PIPE

BOW TIE

6″ SCALE

PENTELS

STUFFED POCKETS

TWEED SUIT

BAGGY KNEES

CORDOVANS

"Our images of this world and of ourselves are given to us by crowds of witnesses we have never met and never shall meet. Yet for each of us these images—provided by strangers and dead men—are the very basis of our life as a human being. None of us stands alone directly confronting a world of solid fact. No such world is available; the closest we come to it is when we are infants or when we become insane; then, in a terrifying scene of meaningless events and senseless confusion, we are often seized with the panic of near-total insecurity. But in our everyday life we experience not solid and immediate facts but stereotypes of meaning. We are aware of much more than what we have ourselves experienced, and our experience itself is always indirect and always guided. The first rule for understanding the human condition is that men live in a second-hand world.

"The consciousness of men does not determine their existence; nor does their existence determine their consciousness. Between the human consciousness and material existence stand communications and designs, patterns and values which influence decisively such consciousness as they have.

"The mass arts, the public arts, the design arts are major vehicles of this consciousness. Between these arts and the everyday life, between their symbols and the level of human sensibility, there is now continual and persistent interplay. So closely do they reflect one another that it is often impossible to distinguish the image from its source. Visions whispered long before the age of consent, images received in the relaxation of darkness, slogans reiterated in home and in classroom, determine the perspective in which we see and fail to see the worlds in which we live; meanings about which we have never thought explicitly determine our judgements of how well and how badly we are living in these worlds. So decisive to experience itself are the results of these communications that often men do not really believe what they 'see before their very eyes' until they have been 'informed' about it by the official announcement, the radio, the camera, the hand-out. Communications not only limit experience; often they expropriate the chances to have experience that can rightly be called 'our own.' For our standards of credibility, and of reality itself, as well as our judgements and discernments, are determined much less by any pristine experience we may have than by our exposure to the output of the cultural apparatus.

"For most of what we call solid fact, sound interpretation, suitable presentation, we are increasingly dependent upon the observation posts, the interpretation centers, the presentation depots of the cultural apparatus. In this apparatus, standing between men and events, the meanings and images, the values and slogans that define all the worlds men know are organized and compared, maintained and revised, lost and found, celebrated and debunked.

"By the cultural apparatus I mean all those organizations and milieux in which artistic, intellectual and scientific work goes on. I also mean all the means by which such work is made available to small circles, wider publics, and to great masses."

—C. Wright Mills, "The Man in the Middle," *Industrial Design*, November 1958

38

Interest in this question arises from an awareness of our increasing collective control of the environment and our decreasing individual control of our own lives. The growth of technology and the associated increase of professionalism have contributed to this; and just as in the earlier case of fire, it is a situation that humanity must learn to carefully manage for its own safety and well-being. One contribution to this end would be to identify alternative role models for those experts to whom we are abrogating our responsibilities. One such characterization by Lars Lerup may be paraphrased as follows:

Lars Lerup, "The Designer as Co-Learner," *Ekistics*, no. 216 (November 1973)

The designer as "operator," in which the designer does *to* passive, object-like clients what the clients cannot do, as in a surgeon-patient relationship.

The designer as "prescriber," in which the designer does *for* dependent clients what the clients cannot do, as in a parent-child relationship.

The designer as "co-learner," in which the designer does *with* actively participating clients, in a process of shared, mutual learning, what the clients may eventually do for themselves, as in a sibling or friendship relationship.

The issue here is the difference between confronting the public with some manifestation of a designer's viewpoint, willy-nilly, or of seeking a congruence between the viewpoints of the designer and the public users. By definition we assume that designers are possessed of some socially valuable insights, but by experience we know that sometimes the public may not be able to adapt to them, or may not care to accept them.

Thomas Markus, in Nigel Cross, ed., *Design Participation* (London: Academy Editions, 1972)

A second and roughly analogous modeling by Thomas Markus suggests a continuous spectrum of roles ranging through three main types. These may be characterized by:

The designer as "master," in an extension of formal professionalism, and depending on public or private patronage from the centers of power.

The designer as "illuminator," using participatory design processes to develop ranges of possibilities for public choice, thus involving the users to a greater degree in the decision-making.

The designer as "midwife," working directly for those end-users who are without power or authority, as a means of helping them discover solutions latent in their own values and patterns of life.

This view of possible roles of the designer reminds us that interventions in the environment eventually come down to a matter of the exercise of power, literally and figuratively; someone's money or muscle must be engaged to move the earth or shift the material and mold it nearer the heart's desire. As part of the "cultural apparatus," the designer, along with the artist and the scientist, is in the control room, but not at the controls. Without private means, the designer depends on others for the opportunity to operate, and thus must develop a mode of relating to others to direct that power.

The noted architect Kevin Roche has agonized over this problem in a discussion with J. W. Cook, as follows:

"KR: It's possible, truly possible, that architecture should go no further than dealing with the lowest possible desires of people who, in fact, have no education at all in the world of architecture. This is the modern hotel or motel which creates an environment immensely satisfying to an enormous number of people out of *trash*. And there is, in fact, a whole school of architecture headed in this very direction.

"There are still things which have true value which require attention and dedication and study, at least to the same extent as the effort which was put into them in the first place. You can't pick up a book by a creative writer and skim through it. Nabokov wrote a book which was just published. He spent six years writing it. It is virtually impossible to read, unless you spend almost six years reading in order to get it. Joyce has that same quality. Unless you attend to the thing, nothing at all comes out.

"In a general sense, architecture is a situation in which the viewer who approaches will get varying degrees of satisfaction, depending on the level of education or sophistication or awareness that he brings to it as viewer. It's easy to bring everybody along, if you start with neon signs, or colorful little things of plastic, or psychedelic effects, or whatever. It's easy to bring the masses along to a certain point, and then you go ahead and do the architecture. Having brought the people along, you then do something else. I feel you must go the whole way. You must, in fact, deal with every man. However, it hasn't been in the tradition of modern architecture to do so.

"JC: As a reaction to that, an architect like Morris Lapidus builds the New York Americana or Miami Beach hotels. He does what he thinks the man on the street wants but does not find in modern architecture; he makes every man feel like a movie star by putting him in a rather exciting, colorful, and funny environment of kitsch.

"KR: I agree that one should cover the whole spectrum of architectural possibilities, but the problem is how to do it, how to cover the whole spectrum of human needs without pandering to the tasteless level of people. You could make an environment that is at once appealing on all levels, but at the same time is not junk, not made out of junk, and has those qualities which survive all periods, and all cultures, and everything else.

"JC: You don't want to pander to a tasteless society, and yet you want to speak to everyone.

"KR: I think you want to speak to everyone, but in an understandable way which will appeal to him, and which he will enjoy without using the devices such as are used in the motel world. One has to find that vocabulary and, at the same time, carry the environment and architecture along at a much higher level.

"JC: Would you explain what you mean by the 'higher level' which must be included along with this human attractiveness?

"KR: Well, that's the thing that's almost impossible to say. I would really not even try to do it, because that's the seat of your pants that you're really working with. That's the whole instinctive . . . . I wouldn't even try to define what the limits were, or what it should embrace, or what its highest objectives were, or anything else, because I don't know. I don't know if I can put it into words. I think that one should have the consciousness, one should have the sense of responsibility, one should have the vision to see the dimension of the problem. One should accept all of this and do the best he can do in response to these realizations. And it has no pretensions of doing anything for anybody; it is just the best assemblage of answers which can be produced out of the given problems."

—from "Kevin Roche," in J. W. Cook and H. Klotz, *Conversations With Architects* (New York: Praeger, 1973)

Note that the "client" who authorizes or pays for the new environment, as the School Board, Building Committee, State Housing Authority, or Vice President in Charge of Production, is usually not the same "client" who lives or works or studies or plays or travels or convalesces in that new environment. If the experiences of these latter people in the new environment are our ultimate concern, we must then be able to deal with the differences in life styles, values, education, and environmental attitudes between ourselves, as designers, and the ultimate users; and even between us and the project commissioners. It is only recently that the environmental design professions have come to realize that this gap in perceptions is too big to be bridged by intuitive empathy, and "participatory planning" has entered the picture.

Peter Stringer, "A Rationale for Participation," in Nigel Cross, ed., *Design Participation* (London: Academy Editions, 1972)

Peter Stringer suggests that because of the greater "complexity" of the designers' constructs or personal views of the world, the burden is on them to make their views intelligible to the public in a full, two-way communication, and further that this can only be done by an expository process in a real situational test and in a context of public interest and commitment. Stringer concludes that the only way to accomplish this is to involve the lay public, as individuals, in an exercise of their own considerable insights at some level of the more technical planning of their environment. And this, he points out, implies some radical differences from present practice.

". . . probably the greatest 'complexifiers' of recent times in architecture are not new developments but rather recognitions of issues that were obvious to any sharp observer all along and can no longer be ignored by anyone. These are the social, psychological and even political impacts of the built or man-made environment. In the 18th century, say, society was an easier milieu to work in than it is today, and when an architect was called upon to design a summer palace for a nobleman there were many design decisions that never had to be made—they were simply understood. No one worried about the 'psychological impact' of the mansion on the nobleman because there was an existing 'noble' style that fit his entire social class. Site planning and regional planning were not problems either because the nobleman owned vast lands to choose from and had to make concessions to no one. But, as the Dutch architect Aldor van Eyke has pointed out, '. . . the Prince and the Priest are disestablished. Now, if not an architecture for all, then no architecture for anyone.'

"Society today is much more fluid and mobile with regard to social strata—facilities are used by rich and poor alike. Social class is still very much with us but it tends to be measured in more temporal and democratic terms such as money rather than lineage, or education rather than titles. What kind of architecture is appropriate for a city hall when the mayor is a 28-year-old radical? 'Styles' as such are less meaningful today because no one knows to whom they apply.

"Briefly, these larger questions fall into two categories. The first one is 'meaning.' What is the meaning of a large public performing arts building—built with public dollars—that is site-planned in such a way as to be virtually inaccessible to 'common' people? A building, say, that is not on convenient bus routes, is not near subway stations, and does not have convenient and inexpensive parking facilities? What is the meaning of a city hall plaza—a traditional place for public gatherings since ancient Greece—that does not permit the public gatherings of which it is clearly a symbol? It is obvious that architecture and planning 'say things'—they broadcast messages, often loudly and clearly. Architecture, like anything else that is man-made, embodies values and cultural priorities. Ar-

cheologists have for years been trying to reconstruct the values of ancient cultures from their artifacts. Only recently have we begun to examine this process in the present, before it becomes ancient history.

"The second category has less to do with philosophy and culture and more to do with the social sciences. It involves an attempt to answer, for the first time in the history of architecture, what the social and psychological impact of space is on people. Architecture projects today affect too many people to guess at these things in the way they did in the Beaux-Arts days. A perfect example of 'wrong guessing.' Is a large public housing project in the Midwest which was built and torn down within a ten-year period recently. It was torn down because the vandalism and crime were so extensive as to make the buildings uninhabitable. The question of what generated such an overwhelming self-destructive impulse is still unanswered."

—Karen Collier Hegener and David Clarke, eds., "The Nature and History of Architectural Education," *Architecture Schools in North America* (Princeton, N.J.: Peterson's Guides, 1976)

The central issue here is the means by which *personal* visions of what *could* be, become accepted by a *community* as visions of what *should* be; and thus implemented in a viable social context. Images of desirable alternatives are of great social value, and it is a necessary but not sufficient leadership function to provide them. The sufficient leadership role requires that social acceptance of these alternatives also be obtained.

In any event, and irrespective of whether you operate as a master-operator handing down your immaculate conceptions to a more-or-less comprehending and appreciative audience, as an illuminator-prescriber opening new doors of perception and guiding a more-or-less willing public to them, or as a colearner-midwife laboring in a more-or-less proletarian vineyard in a mutual process of discovery and self-development, there is still the prior matter of developing your ability and qualifying yourself to participate as a designer, one way or another. To this we now turn our attention.

For some accounts of these new approaches, see Chester L. Sprague, "American Indian Communities: Toward a Unity of Life and Environment," in *Technology Review,* July/August, 1972; Christopher Alexander et al., *The Oregon Experiment* (New York: Oxford University Press, 1975); and Hassan Fathy, *Architecture for the Poor* (Chicago: University of Chicago Press, 1973).

See also: "Participatory Planning and Design," *DMG-DRS Journal: Design Research and Methods,* vol. 9, no. 4 (October-December 1975); "Modes of Participation," *Ekistics,* no. 251 (October 1976); and Abraham Wandersman, "User Participation in Planning Environments: A Conceptual Framework," *Environment and Behavior,* vol. 11, no. 4 (December 1979).

Introduction

Program and Procedure

This program is concerned with the development of your competence in visual expression and communication, as applied to the physical environment and for social purposes. As such it involves the growth of your perceptual sensitivity to visual qualities and your conceptual understanding of visual structure. Since the teaching method is based on the use of studio exercises and problem-solving, you will also become acquainted with the practical issues of design processes and techniques, time budgeting and management, serendipitous awareness, and the matters of design constraints, performance criteria and evaluation, and personal responsibility. Although some principles of visual perception and organization are most effectively studied by means of abstract exercises, whenever possible assigned problems are applied to environmental design situations.

The intent is to advance you, through your performance of this work, from an assumed position of unawareness to a position of proficiency on the following scale:

Adapted from Michael Brill in *Progressive Architecture,* July 1971

Unawareness   Has no knowledge of subject; has never attempted design; novice.

Acquaintance   Knows it exists and what it is; is aware of approximate relationship to field.

Understanding   Knows jargon, how to use consultants; understands potentials and limitations.

Proficiency   Informed as to principles, processes, and state of the art; competent in design under supervision, as apprentice.

Expertise   Has expert knowledge of principles, processes, and state of the art; skilled in design without supervision, as journeyman.

Mastery   Has extraordinary knowledge and skill and demonstrated capacity to innovate.

To summarize the objectives of this program we can reformulate the issues in terms of three areas in which it proposes to foster your growth and thus help you progress from a condition of "unawareness" to a state of "proficiency."

Conceptual awareness (the "scientist's brain")
Since "the eye is blind to what the mind does not see," the conscious development of ability in visual design requires a rational, word-mediated attention to ideas, concepts, structures, and processes.

Perceptual sensitivity (the "painter's eye")
The perceptual readiness thus engendered is the prerequisite for your enhanced discrimination of sensory qualities, and for your effective use of these qualities in the process of communication and expression.

Simulation skills (the "artisan's hand")
The process of design is based on the use of a variety of tools and media in the extensive simulation of design hypotheses. Your ability to use time effectively in visually manifesting your ideas to yourself and others is crucial to your professional operation.

Of course none of the above attributes by themselves achieve any significance without the "poet's heart," a willingness to share feelings about what the world could or should be. A sense of social purpose based on your empathy with the human condition is required to set the goal and establish the criteria of acceptance.

This program is one of the many courses you will take as part of your training for a professional career in environmental design, planning, or management. If your commitment to such a career is still only tentative, the program may serve as an aptitude test in that it will introduce you to some aspects of the field and, equally important, to the kinds of skills and self-discipline required. In any case, you should note that the skills acquired and awarenesses developed in this work will heighten your sensitivity to the visual environment and deepen your insight into the expressive signification of the world in which you live, and will thus serve the personal interest of *any* person open to a richer experience of life.

Assuming you are committed to pursuing this program, the question of the moment is: "How can you maximize the return to yourself of your forthcoming investment in time, energy, and materials?" To answer this you should note first of all that you are involved with the matter of your own growth. You wish to become wiser, more skilled, more sensitive, and more aware. You want to leave this class a much different person than when you entered it. Growth, of course, means change: the more you change during the course of this program, the greater your growth. Your real objective here is self-transformation, and this requires an openness to experience—the curiosity to consider new ideas, the interest to see new relationships, the courage to feel new emotions, and the bravery to try new patterns of behavior. The amount you change depends on the degree of your participation, and on your willingness to risk that misunderstood and undervalued experience called "failure." No significant change will occur of itself; it will require your involvement and commitment on all levels of being. The *only* thing you have to lose is your standing as a "novice"!

"The common denominator of artistic expression has been the ordering of a vision into a consistent, complete form. The difference between a mere expression, however intense and revealing, and an artistic image of that expression lies in the structure of the form. This structure is specific. The colors, lines, and shapes corresponding to our sense impressions are organized into balance, a harmony or rhythm that is in an analogous correspondence with feelings, and these in turn are analogues of thoughts and ideas. An artistic image, therefore, is more than a pleasant tickle of the senses and more than a graph of emotions. It has meaning in depth, and at each level there is a corresponding level of human response to the world. In this way, an artistic form is a symbolic form grasped directly by the senses but reaching beyond them and connecting all the strata of our inner world of sense, feeling, and thought. The intensity of the sensory pattern strengthens the emotional and intellectual pattern; conversely, our intellect illuminates such a sensory pattern, investing it with symbolic power. This essential unity of primary sense experience and intellectual evaluation makes the artistic form unique in human experience and therefore in human culture. Our closest human experience is love, where again sensation, feeling, and idea compose a living unity.

"The essential unity of first-hand percept and intellectual concept makes artistic images different from scientific cognition or simple animal response to situations. To repeat, it is the unity of the sensory, emotional, and rational that can make the orderly forms of artistic images unique contributions to human culture. The meaning of the artistic experience is impoverished if any one of these areas of experience takes undue preponderance.

"Images deriving solely from a rational assessment of the external world, without passion of the eyes, are only topographical records. Images of emotional responses without real roots in the environment are isolated graphs of a person's inner workings: they do not yield symbolic form. And the most beautiful combinations of color and shape, the most exquisitely measured proportions of line, area, and volume, leave us where they find us if they have not grown out of rational and emotional participation in the total environment. Each of these visions is a fragment only."

—Gyorgy Kepes, from Introduction to *The Visual Arts Today* (Middletown, Conn.: Wesleyan University Press, 1960)

"One of the reasons why mature people are apt to learn less than young people is that they are willing to risk less. Learning is a risky business, and they do not like failure. In infancy, when the child is learning at a truly phenomenal rate—a rate he will never again achieve—he is also experiencing a shattering number of failures. Watch him. See the innumerable things he tries and fails. And see how little the failures discourage him. With each year that passes he will be less blithe about failure. By adolescence the willingness of young people to risk failure has diminished greatly. And all too often parents push them further along that road by instilling fear, by punishing failure or by making success seem too precious. By middle age most of us carry in our heads a tremendous catalogue of things we have no intention of trying again because we tried them once and failed—or tried them once and did less than our self-esteem demanded.

One of the virtues of formal schooling is that it requires the student to test himself in a great variety of activities that are not of his own choosing. But the adult can usually select the kinds of activity on which he allows himself to be tested, and he takes full advantage of that freedom of choice. He tends increasingly to confine himself to the things he does well and to avoid the things in which he has failed or has never tried.

We pay a heavy price for our fear of failure. It is a powerful obstacle to growth. It assures the progressive narrowing of the personality and prevents exploration and experimentation. There is no learning without some difficulty and fumbling. If you want to keep on learning, you must keep on risking failure—all your life. It's as simple as that. When Max Planck was awarded the Nobel Prize he said:

'Looking back . . . over the long and labyrinthine path which finally led to the discovery [of the quantum theory], I am vividly reminded of Goethe's saying that men will always be making mistakes as long as they are striving after something.' "

—John W. Gardner, from *Self-Renewal* (New York: Harper & Row, 1963)

Gardner also notes that " 'Nothing fails like success,' because you do not learn anything from it. The only thing we ever learn from is failure. Success only confirms our superstitions."

46

In all these problems we will take the work through operation 7 of the design process, in the preliminary design phase.

You are, at this moment in world history, a member of a small and fantastically privileged elite, with an unparalleled opportunity to develop your own potential. As a design student, thousands of books and images are available for your use; many dedicated faculty with interests akin to yours are ready to consult with you; and similar-minded students have been scheduled to participate with you in a cooperative form of mutual stimulation and collaborative enlightenment. But these resources and opportunities will be of use to you only to the degree that you are willing to abandon comfortable prejudices, normative stereotypes, facile assumptions, and familiar procedures; and actively challenge yourself in the uncomfortable process of self-discovery, agonizing reappraisal, and persistence to the point beyond exhaustion, thinking the unthinkable and gradually realizing that you are much stronger and more capable than you ever thought possible.

Now that we understand each other, let us get down to details of procedure, time, standards, evaluation, and materials.

This program is a studio course. You will be presented with a series of open-ended problems, each incorporating several aspects of professional concern and building on the content of the preceding problems. In general the class acitivity will take place in the following three stages:
(1) the assignment of the problem and posting of deadlines. Following your out-of-class reading of the assignment, procurement of materials, and collection of references, there may be some in-class slides, films, and a discussion with the instructor. Following this there will be
(2) a period of design work, during and outside of class time; in some cases divided into phases with interim class reviews at the end of each. During this time you will be following the steps of the design process and, with the help of your colleagues, the references, and possible consultants, you will be increasing your awareness of the issues and your understanding of the problem. This activity is terminated by
(3) the submission of your work at the assigned deadline, followed by a class discussion of the individual results and of the problem in general, followed in turn by a private written self-evaluation of your performance.

Note that your colleagues, in their diversity of background and experience, constitute a most valuable resource to you as critics, consultants, and advisers. In this collaborative and noncompetitive situation you will soon discover that you will learn as much, if not more, from them as from the instructor. You will also discover that if you do not work in the studio space (your home away from home), you will forfeit this advantage and needlessly impoverish your experience to the equivalent of a correspondence course.

Let us now preview a possible scenario of your implementation of the design process in the studio. Having previously procured the required materials and supplies (as specified at the beginning of each problem), and after the initial reading and discussion of the problem (which, you will find, will only partially explicate the problem and its constraints and criteria—their full identification in your own terms is of course up to you, and will probably not be complete even after the problem is handed in and discussed), you will eventually "put some ideas down on paper." That is, you will externalize some of your tentative thoughts in the form of a doodle, a word, a sentence, a sketch, a diagram, a model, or some tangible *thing* which will be the first public evidence of what has been going on in your mind.

At that point you may very quickly discover, with chagrin or horror, that what seemed so clear and satisfactory in the warm, cozy interior of your mental incubator, when now exposed to the harsh light of day, seems to be either (a) a pale mocking shadow of your genius (because you cannot adequately communicate your idea), or (b) (assuming that your skill at simulation is reasonably adequate) an embarrassingly deficient or pathetically unconvincing muddle.

? ? ! ! ? ?

(You have just applied the criteria in a test of the simulation of the hypothetical solution to the identified problem.)

BUT   DO   NOT   PANIC!

This result is predictable at this stage of the game. Note that you now have several options:

1. Transfer to a different field or career.

2. Downgrade your criteria.

3. Try another mode of simulation (models, instead of sketches, for example).

4. Recognize the fact that you have identified some new aspects of the problem; revise your criteria and constraints accordingly, and hypothesize another solution.

Options 1 and 2 do not concern us here, and we limit our attention to options 3 and 4. Option 3 may save the day, but what it really implies is an imperative to develop your skill at simulation. Option 4, let it now be noted is the *standard operating procedure* in design. In this recycling of the several operations, the hypothesized solutions gradually approach the satisfaction of increasingly refined criteria. The objective is always to reduce the time it takes to reach this condition or, alternately, to achieve the best possible solution in a given period of time—for example, the time you have budgeted to work on this problem.

From this we discover that success in design depends on two time-bound factors: *fluency* in formulating hypotheses and *ability* in simulation.

If you cannot externalize your thinking, or have trouble doing so, you may be suffering from the very common ailment of the "conceptual block." In this case you will find a book by James L. Adams called *Conceptual Blockbusting* (San Francisco: W. H. Freeman, 1974) most helpful. Adams identifies perceptual, cultural, environmental, organizational, emotional, intellectual, and expressive blocks, and presents a number of useful suggestions for circumventing them.

See also Arthur Koestler, *The Act of Creation* (New York: Macmillan, 1964), for an exhaustive discussion of the structure and process of creation and creativity; and Robert H. McKim, *Experiences in Creative Thinking* (Monterey, Calif.: Brooks/Cole, 1972), for a presentation of a variety of exercises designed to facilitate creative thinking.

"Regardless of the level of his measured intelligence, what seems to characterize the creative person—this is especially so for the artistically creative—is a relative absence of repression and suppression as mechanisms for the control of impulse and imagery. Repression operates against creativity regardless of how intelligent a person may be because it makes unavailable to the individual large aspects of his own experience, particularly the life of impulse and experience which gets assimilated to the symbols of aggression and sexuality. Dissociated items of experience cannot combine with one another; there are barriers to communication among different systems of experience both conscious and unconscious. Furthermore, because the unconscious operates more by symbols than by logic, the creative person is more open to the perception of complex equivalences in experience, facility in metaphor being one specific consequence of the creative person's greater openness to his own depths."

—Donald W. MacKinnon, "What Makes a Person Creative," *Saturday Review*, 10 February 1962

"Ideas aren't real estate; they grow collectively, and that knocks out the egotistical loneliness that generally infects art."

—painter Robert Rauschenberg, quoted in *Time*, 29 November 1976

What can we say about developing fluency in formulating hypotheses? Several strategies offer themselves for consideration:

1. Display your work and continue to discuss the issues with several of your classmates; review their ideas and contribute your own. This collaborative approach provides the opportunity for a mutually stimulating environment in which one mind strikes sparks off another, one idea suggests a second, and the second suggests a third, in a continuing (and usually entertaining) escalation. As this occurs, *do not evaluate* these ideas—let them pour out in free fun and fantasy. You are "kicking ideas around" and thus priming the pump of your imagination; all ideas are "good" at this stage, and premature evaluation inhibits the creative process.

2. Hold nothing back; do not censor these ideas. Unlock all the doors in your memory; apply all your experiences, first- or secondhand; transfer everything you have learned or dreamed of to the problem at hand. Everything applies in one way or another; in life everything connects. All your ideas are like needles in the haystack of your mind, and in these collaborative sessions your colleagues can act as magnets to help you extract them. Don't worry about "ownership" of these ideas. Under these circumstances of procreation, parentage is difficult to prove, and in any event you will discover that each person will be attracted to different versions of any idea, and will certainly give them individualistic treatment.

3. Recognize that once you have spent some time intensively engaged in a problem, your subconscious will continue to work on it after you have turned to other matters. For this reason you will often find that on resuming work on the problem after an interval of several hours your ideas will be much clearer. This has important implications in your management of your time, on which more later.

Studies of the process of creation suggest that after an initial "preparation" period of conscious activity in which the identity of the problem—its nature, scope, and constraints—comes into clearer focus, there then follows an unconscious period of "incubation." About this phase Anthony Storr writes:

". . . during this period, important unconscious or preconscious processes take place in the mind; some kind of preliminary 'scanning' and rearrangement, which is absolutely necessary if a new and satisfying pattern is to emerge. Many creative people, being, as we shall see, active executants, as well as passively open to their own and other people's new ideas, find this waiting period of incubation extremely tiresome. Those, especially, who have been brought up to think that idleness is a sin, and constant activity a virtue, find it hard to believe that there are times when more is accomplished by passivity than by activity. Bertrand Russell furnishes an example of what is meant with his habitual lucidity.

" 'Very gradually I have discovered ways of writing with a minimum of worry and anxiety. When I was young each fresh piece of serious work used to seem to me for a time—perhaps a long time—to be beyond my powers. I would fret myself into a nervous state from fear that it was never going to come right. I would make one unsatisfying attempt after another, and in the end have to discard them all. At last I found that such fumbling attempts were a waste of time. It appeared that after first contemplating a book on some subject, and after giving serious preliminary attention to it, I needed a period of subconscious incubation which could not be hurried and was if anything impeded by deliberate thinking. Sometimes I would find, after a time, that I had made a mistake, and that I could not write the book I had had in mind. But often I was more fortunate. Having, by a time of very intense concentration, planted the problem in my subconsciousness, it would germinate underground until, suddenly, the solution emerged with blinding clarity, so that it only remained to write down what had appeared as if in a revelation.' " [Bertrand Russell, "How I Write," in *Portraits from Memory and Other Essays* (London: Allen and Unwin, 1965)]

—Anthony Storr, *The Dynamics of Creation* (New York: Penguin, 1976)

See also: Arthur Koestler, *The Act of Creation* (New York: Macmillan, 1964); Desy Safan-Gerard, "How to Unblock," *Psychology Today,* January 1978; James L. Adams, *Conceptual Blockbusting* (San Francisco: W. H. Freeman, 1974); and Graham Wallas, *The Art of Thought* (London: Jonathan Cape, 1926).

"In every work of genius we recognize our own rejected thoughts: they come back to us with a certain alienated majesty."

—Ralph Waldo Emerson

In the case of ability in simulation, the strategies will be suggested or incorporated in each problem. Almost every problem will introduce you to a new technique or new medium, and gradually your skill in simulation and your ability to perform it rapidly will increase. The important thing at first is to put *something* down on paper—make *any* sort of mark. It will immediately suggest something else and you will at once feel impelled to modify or correct it. Do so at once and just keep going, for by now you must realize that in this iterative process your hand, eye, and brain interact with and *stimulate* each other. The quicker your hand can externalize some representation of an idea, the quicker your eye and brain can respond to it with a revised or new idea, and thus maximize the number of ideas generated in a given time. The ultimate condition is that you become a fountain, pouring out ideas in a free flow of fantasy which gradually consolidates as a number of viable alternative solutions.

Formerly at the Ecole des Beaux Arts in Paris the architecture students worked in the ateliers of different masters at various locations about the city, and were required to bring in their work for judgment on specified dates. Their large colored renderings were transported for this purpose in two-wheeled carts called *charrettes*. Human nature being what it is, inevitably some students would be seen hard at work in these carts attempting to finish their drawings while being trundled over the cobblestoned streets of Paris. Thus the romantic expression to be "en charrette" means working overtime to finish up. It also means you have badly mismanaged your time.

It is essential that you understand the necessity of externalizing your thinking in graphic form. Furthermore, having this material on hand will save you from having to *tell* your instructor about your intentions (instead of *showing* him or her your ideas), and thus spare you the possible embarrassment of being advised to transfer to the music department, where hearing is more important than seeing. Your instructor (and you) will be interested in the growth and development of your ideas; and in the repeated cycles of the design process you will *need* to refer to earlier stages of your thinking. Thus, irrespective of what you think of it at the time, you must save all your work; identifying it with your name and date (a *very* professional habit) and keeping it filed or posted where you and others can readily view it. In this game *there is no such thing as scratch work:* as a professional, every mark you make on a piece of paper is significant and has a value.

As for the matter of *time,* undoubtedly you have heard the old saying, "Art is long, life is short." This is only to suggest that you will *never* have enough time, and the necessity thus arises for you to develop effective means of using well the time that you do have. Time, like fire, can be a good friend if managed well, but a deadly enemy if neglected. Professional time-budgeting proceeds something like this:

1. Having established your priorities, estimate the total net time available for work on the project.

2. Identify the several stages of the project and estimate the percentage of time necessary for each.

3. Set subdeadlines for each stage, allowing some margin at each.

4. Monitor and keep track of your performance with respect to these subdeadlines.

5. Revise subdeadlines as the inevitable contingencies occur. (Murphy's Law states that "if anything can go wrong, it will—at the worst possible time.")

(See Problem 14 for a suggested time-schedule worksheet.)

You will also find that taking an objective and critical view of your own working habits and use of facilities will help you use your time advantageously; for example, procuring all required materials and equipment ahead of time before class, using the specified sketch paper for your design sketches and studies, displaying all this work on the wall and keeping it in a file so that your instructor will have something to *look at* when attempting to critique your work, as well as the time-saving common sense of keeping your working surfaces clear and clean, your paints well capped, and so on.

As for *standards,* you have noted from the description of the design process that the identification of acceptance criteria is one of the first key steps. We might also point out now that both an expansion of your awareness to additional criteria relevant to each problem and the upgrading of your standards of acceptability for each of them are also key parts of this program. In this connection it is worth noting that novices are generally pleased with their performances, but professionals are never satisfied. Many professionals view their past work as a succession of greater or lesser failures, and of all their work the job they like best is "the next one" in which they will have a fresh opportunity to apply the lessons they have learned from the "mistakes" of the past. Thus, if at any time you find yourself feeling satisfied with your work, you should take it as a warning that you are still complacent, and are neglecting to drive yourself to higher levels of performance and broader terms of reference. Narrow terms of reference and low standards can only be associated with mediocre and insignificant work. Broad awareness and demanding levels of performance are the prerequisites of significance.

The development of this awareness and the raising of these standards can only be achieved through your own consciousness of and concern for your performance. To require your instructor to tell you how well you are doing by means of "grades" is a fraud and an insult to your integrity, to say nothing of the chilling effect it has upon your creativity. The responsibility is always, and can only ever be, yours and not that of some pesky professor, whose main job is to help you, and certainly not to do your work for you.

But *evaluation* is a skill that must be exercised to be effective. Consequently at the time the problems are due, they should all be displayed together on a wall and discussed constructively, if not coolly, in an open class meeting in terms of what the problem requires—not "what the instructor wants"—and the individual degree of success in meeting these

"For the individual to find himself in an atmosphere where he is not being evaluated, not being measured by some external standard, is enormously freeing. Evaluation is always a threat, always creates a need for defensiveness, always means that some portion of experience must be denied to awareness. If this product is evaluated as good by external standards, then I must not admit my own dislike of it. If what I am doing is bad by external standards, then I must not be aware of the fact that it seems to be me, to be part of myself. But if judgments based on external standards are not being made, then I can be more open to my experience, can recognize my own likings and dislikings, the nature of the materials and of my reaction to them, more sharply and more sensitively. I can begin to recognize the locus of evaluation within myself. Hence I am moving toward creativity.

". . . The permissiveness which is being described is not softness or indulgence or encouragement. It is permission to be *free,* which also means that one is responsible. The individual is as free to be afraid of a new venture as to be eager for it; free to bear the consequences of his mistakes as well as of his achievements. It is this type of freedom responsibly to be oneself which fosters the development of a secure locus of evaluation within oneself, and hence tends to bring about the inner conditions of constructive creativity."

—Carl R. Rogers, "Towards a Theory of Creativity," ETC., vol.XI, no.4 (reprinted by permission of the International Society for General Semantics)

52

The "Raspberry Club" provides an opportunity for the development of another personal skill as well—that of effectively presenting your ideas while on your feet before a group of people. As a professional you will often be required to do this, and now is an excellent time to become aware of such practical matters as facing the audience and speaking clearly (and not mumbling or facing the wall), of being sure your body is not blocking a view of your material for some of the audience, and of using the pointer to calmly identify the material to which you are referring (and not as a drumstick beating out an accompaniment to your nervousness).

requirements. You will soon discover that these meetings of the "Raspberry Club" provide some of the richest learning experiences of the entire process.

Following the class discussion you will be asked to evaluate privately your own performance (not your intentions—as Samuel Johnson remarked, Hell is paved with good intentions) and describe your experiences in explicit written form in a permanent notebook. For this "True Confession" it is suggested that you consider each of the several aspects of the problem: (1) conceptual awareness of all the issues, (2) perceptual sensitivity to the visual attributes and their organization, and (3) craft skills in simulating and presenting your work. For each of these aspects, you should rate yourself on the following scale:

Breakthrough: when you have transcended yourself and achieved an unexpected insight, or surprised yourself by accomplishing more than you ever imagined you could.

Average: an ordinary, perfunctory performance of no particular value, or of marginal growth-significance (keeping in mind that growth is a function of *your* courage and interest to explore new areas and *your* thoroughness and responsibility in following up the implications of your discoveries).

Deficient: an inferior, low-level, or shabby performance; but of interest to you in that it contains some important clues about your priorities, motivation, and attitudes.

Writing out these True Confessions will help to clarify and objectify your recent experiences to a most significant degree. Rather than lazily sweeping some fuzzy memories, good and not-so-good, under the rug of hazy forgetfulness, instead confront your adventures in the revealing light of candid self-examination, and focus your responses with explicit verbal formulations. This introspective exercise in self-disclosure is an important means of overcoming one's tendencies toward the selective repression of experience, and thus facilitates the growth of creativity. Keeping such a diary or daybook is an old-fashioned idea today, but is one that has much to recommend it in a personal growth situation such as this. (And think of what a treasured family legacy it will become for your grandchildren!)

In this evaluation you should keep in mind that we are involved here with an educational activity and that your work on the wall is only a symptom, or the tangible evidence, of the more important experience you have undergone. We use your work only as a sort of (admittedly imperfect) measuring device to gauge the change that has taken place within you. The point of all this work, you should remember, is your transformation.

But you should note that your "products" do have a perhaps unsuspected value for you. Carefully protected (covered with tracing paper and stored in a portfolio or, better, copied onto color slides) they will be most useful when you apply for admission to advanced design programs or other schools, or for a job. A good collection (or "brochure") of your work, well presented (in itself an important design problem) is indispensable for these purposes.

Furthermore, because of the inadequacy of these graphic products as indicators of your cognitive development, you should test yourself (or better, be tested by your instructor) on the quiz material found in the Appendix. A superior performance here will be convincing evidence that you have mastered the concepts that underlie your work and ensure its significance.

Finally, we must remind you that this program itself is only an introduction, and that in all this material we really can only scratch the surface. For this reason, each problem is followed by a discussion of relevant questions and suggestions for further studies, for those interested in a do-it-yourself advanced course. In many cases the investigation of some of these issues could well become a lifetime career.

Now we take up the matter of *materials,* noting the fact that to make an omelet one must break some eggs. The following equipment and supplies are required for this program; note that it is not necessary to acquire all of them at once, and that those items starred (*) may also be required for one or more of your other courses.

Properly a part of this list of materials are the references cited throughout the text. *They* are tools for your mind, and are no less important than those you will use with your hands. Frequent reference to them will enable you to see further by, in effect, standing on the shoulders of others, and thus save you the trouble of rediscovering the New World, or reinventing the wheel. A "survey of the literature" must become an automatic part of your response in the first operation of the design process: the identification of the context and constraints.

White illustration board requirements, as cut from 30″ x 40″ sheets

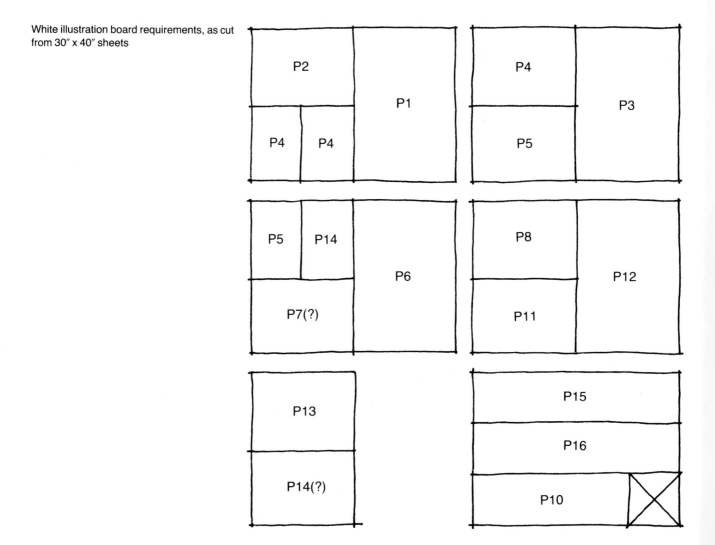

Covered drawing board: minimum 24″ x 30″ *

T-square: 30″ with transparent edge*

Triangles: 45°-8″; 60°-10″ *

Architect's scale: 12″, triangular with engraved scale*

Ames (Post) lettering guide*

Metal erasing shield*

Drafting tape: roll* (*not* cellulose tape)

Architect's sketch paper: rolls, buff and/or white, 15″ and 20″ wide*

College dictionary* (*not* a pocket-sized paperback!)

Paint brushes: ¼″ round and ⅜″ or ½″ flat (soft)

Tin can (for water)

White plastic egg tray or plate (for palette)

Black and white tempera paint

Padlock (for securing your equipment and supplies in your desk or locker)

Expanding wallet-type envelope or artist's portfolio to take 20″ x 30″ sheets

Standard file folder (for design notes and sketches)

Metal straightedge: 24″

Bound notebook (for self-evaluations and True Confessions)

Heavy-duty pocket knife, with pocket hone (Schrade No. 175 recommended)

White illustration board: no. 300 (medium weight) cold pressed (sizes and amounts specified in each problem: total requirements summarized in adjacent figure)

Colored paper: as specified in each problem

Rubber cement and dispenser

Casein glue: white "Elmer's"

Pencils: hard, medium, soft

Felt pens: fine and broad tips, various colors

Pair of dice

Acrylic paint set (Liquitex Modular No. 7112 recommended)

Munsell 11-chart student color set (may be available in class, and shared with others) available from Munsell Color, 2441 No. Calvert Street, Baltimore, MD 21218

The optical mechanism of the camera provides a two-dimensional *record* of light-events in time and space.

Photograph by Kenji Thiel

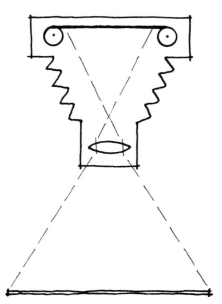

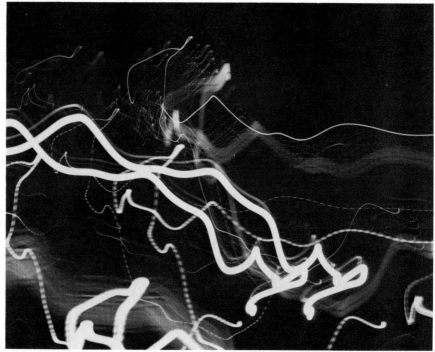

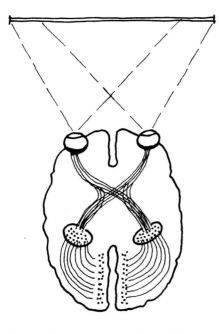

The mobile perceptual system of the eye and brain interprets available light information to derive denotational, connotational, and prescriptive *meanings* in the context of time, place, and occasion.

For an example of the wide range of meanings which may be ascribed to an available pattern of light-energy, consider the following description (of a domestic interior) from a classic children's book:

"The floor was well-worn red brick, and on the wide hearth burnt a fire of logs, between two attractive chimney-corners tucked away in the wall, well out of any suspicion of draught. A couple of high-backed settles, facing each other on either side of the fire, gave further sitting accommodation for the socially disposed. In the middle of the room stood a long table of plain boards placed on trestles, with benches down each side. At one end of it, where an arm-chair stood pushed back, were spread the remains of the Badger's plain but ample supper. Rows of spotless plates winked from the shelves of the dresser at the far end of the room, and from the rafters overhead hung hams, bundles of dried herbs, nets of onions, and baskets of eggs. It seemed a place where heroes could fitly feast after victory, where weary harvesters could line up in scores along the table and keep their Harvest Home with mirth and song, or were two or three friends of simple tastes could sit about as they pleased and eat and smoke and talk in comfort and contentment. The ruddy brick floor smiled up at the smoky ceiling: the oaken settles, shiny with long wear, exchanged cheerful glances with each other; plates on the dresser grinned at pots on the shelf, and the merry firelight flickered and played over everything without distinction."

—Kenneth Grahame, *The Wind in the Willows* (New York: Charles Scribner's Sons, 1933)

Form Perception

Some evening while you are downtown (where the lights are bright), bring your camera and take a variety of time-exposures as you stroll about. You will get some interesting "abstract" photos, but hardly anything that looks like what you saw while you were there. Why?

You and your camera were in the same environment and were both exposed to the same scene. The second-by-second patterns of radiant energy available to your eyes and to the camera lens were essentially similar, yet you saw objects in space while the camera registered only streaks and blurs of light. The reason is, of course, that although the time-patterns of light reaching the retina of your eyes and the surface of the film were analogous, the camera does not have a system to process this sensory material and make something out of it.

In this problem we will examine some of the conditions under which the brain does (or does not) "make something" out of an environmental scene.

"The fact that the eye has a lens that forms an image on the retina leads at once to an analogy to a photographic camera, and it may be true that knowledge about the eye led to the addition of a lens to the 'camera obscura' to improve its image. The analogy, however, is very misleading in that it suggests that the mind sees the image so formed.

"A somewhat better, although still misleading, analogy is to a television camera. In this the scene is scanned constantly, point for point, at high frequency. Thus its image is transient and constantly being renewed. In a way this resembles the rapid 'saccadic' movements of the eye that make it constantly traverse boundaries and, to some extent, the frequent blinking of the eyelids. Modifications of the image in the circuitry in television, particularly the so-called 'crispening' circuits, may also have close parallels in vision, but little is gained by pursuing the analogy. . . .

"The analogies with photography and television break down because it is not the image formed by the eye lens that we see. The image of a room, or any other situation, is in the mind. Any details in that image, except the very broadest, have been built up by successive glances directly *at* these details; both the details and the broad image are retained by the mind for as long as they are wanted and then as quickly erased. The optical image is constantly changing and moving as the eye jerks rapidly from one point to another; the mental image is stationary for stationary objects regardless of the eye motion, or, for that matter, the motion of the head or of the person."

—Ralph M. Evans, *The Perception of Color* (New York: Wiley, 1974)

See the following books by James J. Gibson: *The Ecological Approach to Visual Perception* (Boston: Houghton Mifflin, 1979), and *The Perception of the Visual World* (Boston: Houghton Mifflin, 1950). See also Carolyn M. Bloomer, *Principles of Visual Perception* (New York: Van Nostrand Reinhold, 1976); J. S. Bruner, "On Perceptual Readiness," *Psychological Review* 64 (1957): 123-52; R. L. Gregory, *The Intelligent Eye* (New York: McGraw-Hill, 1970); and R. L. Gregory, *Eye and Brain: The Psychology of Seeing* (New York: McGraw-Hill, 1970).

Materials

20″ x 30″ white illustration board, as specified in the list of materials

Casein glue, knife, metal straightedge

Drafting equipment, scale, pencils

White construction paper

Black and white tempera paint, brushes, etc.

One yard (3′ x 3′) of black-and-white patterned cloth

Procedure

Phase A

Construct three 4″ cubes of white illustration board. A "cube" is taken here to mean a three-dimensional opaque solid form bounded by six identical square surfaces. The "tolerance," or allowable variation from the 4″ dimension, is ±1/16″. In other words, your cubes should go through an opening 4 1/16″ square but should not go through an opening 3 15/16″ square. (A pair of such go/no-go gauges made of plywood or masonite should be available for this test. Note that each cube must be tested in three orientations with each gauge.)

Your subproblem here will be to devise ways of accurately cutting the panels, jointing the edges, and assembling them into cubes. It may be expedient to make some "trial and error" experiments first, and certainly you can collaborate with your classmates on this.

Gauges made of ⅛″ tempered Masonite or ¼″ plywood.

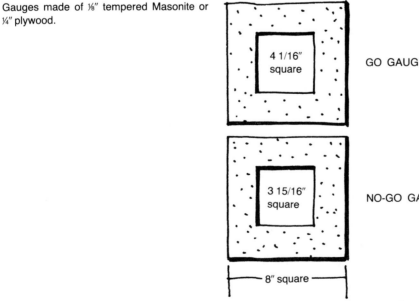

4 1/16″ square   GO GAUGE

3 15/16″ square   NO-GO GAUGE

8″ square

Phase B

Using only paint, (a) treat one cube so that visually it either disappears as a form, *or* becomes unrecognizable as a cube; and (b) treat another cube so that it appears to be a "three dimensional opaque solid form bounded by identical square surfaces," when in each case the cube is placed in a random manner against your irregularly draped piece of cloth as a background.

In both cases the physical form of the cube is to be preserved, and in feeling them a blind person should perceive no difference. But to a normally sighted person one cube should be practically invisible, or unrecognizable as a cube, when seen in the given context; and the second cube should appear to be the epitome of cubicity under the same conditions.

At this point (with reference to the flow chart of the design process described in Introduction B, Design and Designers) the context and constraints have been *identified,* and the goals and criteria *specified.* Your task now is to *hypothesize* the first of many tentative solutions to (either part of) the problem.

You should quickly *simulate* your idea by painting it, freehand, on white paper taped over three sides of one of your cubes; and *test* this idea in position against your cloth backdrop.

But how can you evaluate your design? In Phase A there was an objective test: assuming that the cubes held together in normal handling, each one either would "go" in three orientations with the appropriate gauges, or it would not, and that was the end of the matter. However, here in Phase B there are no "objective" gauges, and although quite possibly you will subjectively feel that there is some merit in your design hypothesis, you (should!) have a nagging suspicion that it may not be the best idea of which you are capable.

Thus a different evaluation procedure is necessary. The method is to hypothesize an alternative solution: not just a minor variation of your first one, but a basically different concept; and simulate it just as in the first case. Then *compare* the two alternatives simultaneously, side by side in the context of the cloth. Undoubtedly, one will appear to be better than the other, and, from a consideration of the reason why this is so, some further ideas will occur to you.

By now you certainly get the picture, and begin to realize that design is an *active* process, involving continuous simulation. By your use of this process of hypothesis, simulation, testing, and simultaneous comparison of adjacent alternatives, your designs will quickly evolve in effectiveness. As you evaluate the alternatives, you will become increasingly confident that you are not overlooking any good bets.

By following your time schedule, you will be able to spend the maximum amount of time on design development, and still have adequate time to rank your hypotheses and prepare your final presentation, painted on all six sides of the cubes. Then, for the meeting of the Raspberry Club convened to review the class performance on this problem, we will employ a similar process:

1. With a table placed next to a wall, three, four, or five persons should pin and drape their cloth on the wall and over the table in irregular folds, so as to provide a series of adjacent backdrops for the display of the cubes.

2. Each person should place one cube representing his or her solution of the form-concealment problem in a "random" manner against the appropriate backdrop.

3. A concurrent, side-by-side comparison of these several solutions is then made, with the intent of ranking the several designs in order of effectiveness.

4. This sequence of steps is repeated for a similar consideration of the second set of cubes which were prepared so as to display their form.

This procedure provides a reasonable means for the relative evaluation of different design hypotheses, and can be generally applied in all other problem areas where "absolute" measures (such as "go/no-go" gauges) do not exist, or where subjective criteria are involved. It should be used for all the problems in this course—in both the public assessment of the "final" presentations, and prior to that in your personal assessments of your simulations. It will be clear to you now that this side-by-side comparison is a means by which you can evolve a series of better and better solutions converging toward an optimum resolution of the problem. Note that it requires the simultaneous, adjacent presence of several tangible alternatives. This brings us to the three magic words in visual design:

COMPARE ADJACENT ALTERNATIVES

Discussion

What does this exercise tell us about form perception?

First let us consider the following: tourists arriving in London for the first time and wishing to send postcards home may have some difficulty in finding a place to mail them. Eventually they will discover that the British mailboxes are large vertical cylinders painted a bright red and embossed with the royal initials. After making this discovery, they will have no trouble in "seeing" a mailbox the next time they need one. But note that mailboxes were present in the visual environment before our tourists made this discovery. They did not *perceive* them to be mailboxes until some additional knowledge became available to them. Perception, defined as "the ascription of meaning to one's environment through the interpretation of sensory data," can now be understood (given both a functioning sensory system, and adequate illumination) to depend on:

1. empirical experience or prior knowledge serving to support your interpretive hypothesis,

2. the situational context and your perceptual "set,"

3. your personal needs or interests, and

4. the visual context, and the patterning of the elements in the visual field.

Thus in London if you see someone drop a letter in a large red vertical cylinder embossed with the royal initials, your hypothesis that the object is a mailbox will be reinforced; such highway signs as "Deer Crossing" or "Rocks on Highway" are warnings provided to alert you, or change your "set," so that you will be more likely to see these hazards; if your stomach is empty or your bladder is full you will be more likely to notice means for relief in either department; and if the British mailboxes were not painted to contrast with the usual colors of the British streets, they would be much harder to see.

In the case of our exercise we were all familiar with the concept "cube" and had an image of what a cube is. We knew that all our cubes were physically identical (± 1/16″), we were looking for cubes, and we expected to see cubes; yet in many cases one set of cubes was "hard to see."

To explain this you must understand, first of all, that the only "material" of visual perception that enters our eyes is radiation in the electromagnetic spectrum between 400 and 700 millimicrons in wavelength. This energy reaches our eyes directly from light sources, and/or indirectly as reflections from illuminated surfaces in the environment. In all cases this light-energy is modulated, or *patterned,* in both its spatial and temporal dimensions by the interaction of the specific light sources in reflection, refraction, and diffraction with the atmosphere and the environmental surfaces. If no radiant energy reached our eyes, or if the energy reaching our eyes were unpatterned and uniformly distributed in space and time, we would see "no-thing," or no event. But any modulated pattern of light-energy that does reach our eyes, because of its environmentally caused differentiation, carries latent information about that environment. Visual perception is thus the process of decoding the latent environmental information contained in the space-time pattern of light energy reaching our eyes. We can also say that visual *design* is the purposeful modulation of the light-energy reaching our eyes, as accomplished by our interventions in the environment.

To perceive, then, we must interpret the fluctuating pattern of light-energy that constitutes our field of view. We attempt to make sense of, or find meaning in, this sensory raw material by creating the simplest organization of the elementary units of this pattern that is in accordance with our situation and set, our current needs and interests, and our past experiences. Sometimes the patterns may be interpreted in several different ways, as illustrated by the so-called "ambiguous figures" which, as we study them, tend to fluctuate between alternative explanations.

In other cases the information is contradictory and no reasonable interpretation is possible, as illustrated by the so-called "impossible" forms.

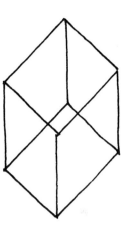

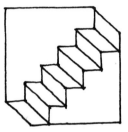

Ambiguous or reversing figures. (Which corner, edge, or surface is nearest to you? When?)

Impossible figures. (Could you build a three-dimensional model of them?)

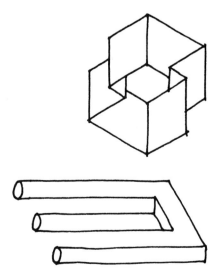

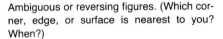

64

The principles underlying this creative assemblage of the elementary pattern units have been described by the Gestalt psychologists in the "laws" of perceptual organization. We will study them later, in Problems 8 and 16.

In some instances our interpretation is correct, as far as it goes, but "there is more 'there' than meets the mind." This occurs when the elementary units of the patterned field have such a strong visual relationship to one another that we are unable to organize them into an alternate arrangement. Such a suppression of perceptual alternatives, of course, is called camouflage, and is an important technique in animal survival and military disguise. By reviewing some applications we may illustrate this principle.

In general there are six types of camouflage. The first, called **somatolysis,** or "body dissolution," describes the situation where the size, shape, and color-patterning of the surface of the object to be concealed are similar to that of its usual background environment, and have no reference to the form, edges, or contours of the object itself.

When the object must appear in a variety of environments, and under different lighting conditions, another approach is indicated. This is called **disruptive coloration,** or "dazzle painting," in which strongly contrasting colors are applied in bold, irregular patterns across the several different parts of the object in contradiction of the actual form.

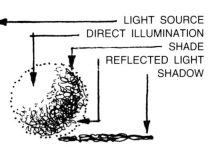

— LIGHT SOURCE
— DIRECT ILLUMINATION
— SHADE
— REFLECTED LIGHT
— SHADOW

A third method is called **countershading.** Here the form-revealing interaction of an object with the light source is negated by the use of a light color where a shaded surface would normally occur and a dark color where a lighter surface would usually appear.

A white tennis ball in the sun illustrates the form-revealing modulation of light by a characteristic distribution of illuminated, shaded, and shadowed surfaces. Countershading tends to neutralize the first two effects, and the suppression of shadows eliminates the latter clue to form.

A fourth type of disguise takes place in several ways: by means of the **suppression of** form-revealing **cast shadows** through the crouching or flattening of an animal on the ground; by an orientation to the light source such as to minimize an object's cast shadow; or by the use of flaps or screens to break up the shadow.

For further information see: H. B. Cott, *Adaptive Coloration in Animals* (London: Methuen, 1957); A. Portmann, *Animal Camouflage* (Ann Arbor: University of Michigan Press, 1959); R. L. Gregory and E. H. Gombrich, eds., *Illusion in Nature and Art* (New York: Scribner's, 1975); M. and P. Fogden, *Animals and Their Colors* (New York: Crown Publishers, 1974).

The remaining types of camouflage involve either the use of *masks* or the *imitation* of the form of other objects, neither of which interests us here.

In any event it is important to realize that our mobile perceptual system, involving both the eyes and the brain (in point of fact, the retina of the eye is actually a part of the brain), deals with *all* the visual data or clues present in the visual field in a given situation. Like a detective trying out a number of hypotheses to account for all the data, it comes up with that probabilistic "explanation" which we call a perception.

The dependence of perception on context can be readily illustrated by a number of demonstrations. The point of these visual illusions is to emphasize that there are no absolute visual attributes: size, position, number, shape, direction, texture, color, and surface quality are all *relative* and are partial functions of the entire visual field.

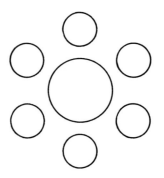

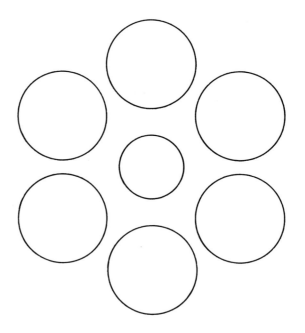

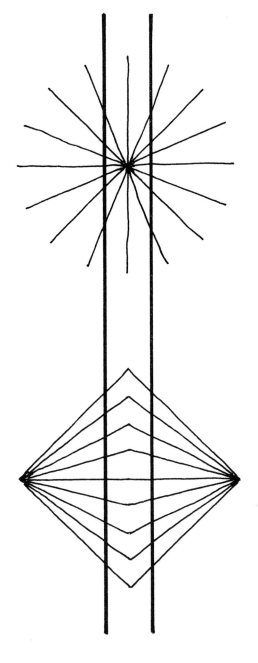

Visual illusions of size and shape. (Are the inner circles the same size? Are the vertical lines straight and parallel?)

For further information on visual illusions, see Matthew Luckiesh, *Visual Illusions* (New York: Dover, 1965); Richard Gregory, "Visual Illusions," *Scientific American,* November 1968; and Barbara Gillam, "Geometric Illusions," *Scientific American,* January 1980.

In the preceding problem we mentioned the elementary units which pattern the visual field. Now we will investigate the nature of the visual field, the patterning of the elements of this field, and the visual attributes of these elements. In addition we will consider a general model of communication and the requirements of freehand lettering as a means of communication.

James J. Gibson, *The Perception of the Visual World* (Boston: Houghton Mifflin, 1950)

Let us start by establishing the difference between the visual world and the visual field. For this we refer to James Gibson, who suggests:

"Try making this observation for yourself. First look around the room and note that you see a perfectly stable scene of floor and walls, with an array of familiar objects at definite locations and distances. Every part of it is fixed relative to every other part. If you look out the window, there beyond is an extended environment of ground and buildings or, if you are lucky, 'scenery.' This is what we shall call the *visual world*. It is the familiar, ordinary scene of daily life, in which solid objects look solid, square objects look square, horizontal surfaces look horizontal, and the book across the room looks as big as the book lying in front of you. This is the kind of experience we are trying to account for.

"Next look at the room not as a room but, insofar as you can, as if it consisted of areas or patches of colored surface, divided up by contours. To do so, you must fixate your eyes on some prominent point and then pay attention not to that point, as is natural, but to the whole range of what you can see, keeping your eyes still fixed. The attitude you should take is that of the perspective draftsman. It may help if you close one eye. If you persist, the scene comes to approximate the appearance of a picture. You may observe that it has characteristics somewhat different from the former scene. This is what will here be called the *visual field*. It is less familiar than the visual world and it cannot be observed except with some kind of special effort. The fact that it differs from the familiar visual world is the source of a great deal of confusion and misunderstanding about vision. It is the experience on which the doctrine of visual *sensations* is based. It is strictly an introspective or analytic

Basic Pattern Areas

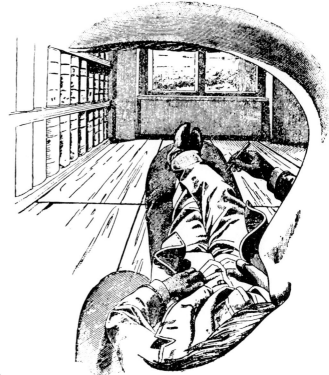

phenomenon. One gets it only by trying to see the visual world in perspective and to see its colors as a painter does.

"Both the visual world and the visual field are products of the familiar but still mysterious process known as seeing. Both depend upon light stimulation and upon a properly functioning eye. But the differences between them are so great as to suggest two kinds of seeing. Let us try to list and describe these differences. Most of them can readily be observed without special apparatus, and the reader should therefore check them for himself as we go along.

The Bounded Visual Field

"In the first place, the visual field has boundaries, whereas the visual world has none. If you keep your eyes fixed but put your attention on the periphery of the field (a trick that may require practice) you can observe that things are visible only to a limited angle out to the right and left and to an even more limited angle upwards and downwards. These boundaries, it is true, are not sharp like the margins of a picture and they are hard to notice, since all vision is unclear in such eccentric regions, but they are nevertheless present. The field is roughly oval in shape. When measured, it extends about 180 degrees laterally and 150 degrees up and down. If you close one eye you will notice that about a third of the field on that side disappears and also that the boundary is now the outline of your nose. Many an otherwise observant individual does not realize that his nose is represented in his visual field. Even if shadowy, however, it has always been there and its discovery only illustrates the unfamiliarity of this kind of seeing as compared with the familiar reality of ordinary perception.

"What Ernst Mach, analyzing his sensations, called the phenomenal ego is illustrated in [the adjacent figure]. It is a literal representation of his visual field, with his right eye closed, as he reclined in a nineteenth century chaise longue. His nose delimits the field on the right and his moustache appears below. His body and the room are drawn in detail, although he could not see them in detail without moving his eye. The margins of the field are shown as definite and clear whereas of course their actual appearance was very vague. The point of fixation cannot be shown in the drawing; actually it is the center of the field and this should be the only part shown as wholly clear.

"The visual world, on the other hand, is certainly not delimited by an oval-shaped boundary. Floors, walls, and terrain are visibly continuous. As Koffka has pointed out . . ., one is ordinarily aware of a world which extends backward behind the head as well as forward in front of the eyes. The world, in other words, surrounds us for the full 360°, in contrast to the visual field which is confined to about 180°. Whether the world which includes this space behind us is a strictly visual world or not is a question of definition rather than a matter of ordinary observation. It cannot be answered by inspection for the reason that in the effort to examine the experienced world one finds oneself inspecting the visual field instead. The visual world, as we shall discover, will not bear up under much introspection and analysis without changing its character. It is at least clear that the visual world does not have boundaries. It has a panoramic character which the field does not possess."

The binocular bounded visual field may be represented in the circular format of a so-called "fish-eye" photograph, or hemispherical projection, in which the intersection of the horizontal and vertical axes at the center denotes the observer's point of fixation, and the intersection of these axes with the circumference denote points 90° off the visual axis or observer's line of sight. Here the *zenith* is that point directly above the observer; the *nadir* is that point directly below him or her; and the left and right points are those to his or her extreme left and right side respectively. Distances from the center of the circle on any radius denote the angle of any point in the visual field from the observer's fixated line of sight and vary from 0° at the center to 90° at the circumference.

To Construct an (Equidistant) Hemispherical Projection

Given point P, a stationary point at eye level; line PF, the horizontal line of sight; and point 0, any point in the forward field of view;
to find 0′, the hemispherical projection of point O, in a circle of any convenient radius H; with horizontal axis L′R′, vertical axis Z′N′, and center P′:
1. Establish plane PSOF through point O and line PF. This intersects vertical plane LR-ZN in line PS.
2. Find β, angle APS in right triangle PAS, using true lengths of AP and AS.

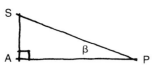

3. Find α, angle FPO in right triangle PFO, lying in plane PSOF; using true lengths of PF and FO. Note that FO = PS.

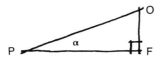

4. Draw radius H from center P′ at angle β.
5. Lay out distance r from P′ on H, where r = (α/90) H. This locates 0′.

Note that when α = 90°, r = H, and that when α = 0°, r = 0. Note also that lines and edges parallel to PF will lie along a radius in the hemispherical projection.

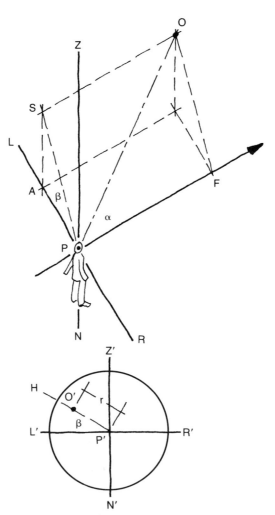

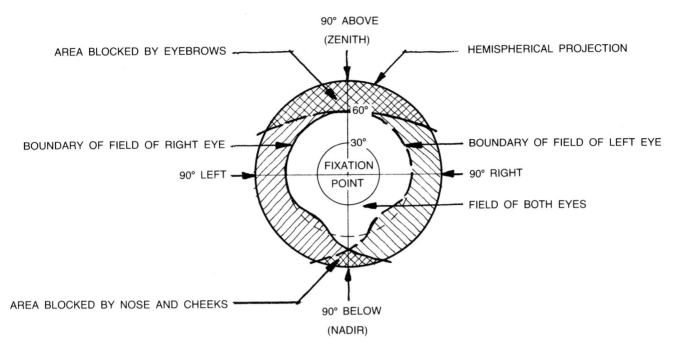

90° ABOVE
(ZENITH)

AREA BLOCKED BY EYEBROWS

HEMISPHERICAL PROJECTION

60°

BOUNDARY OF FIELD OF RIGHT EYE

30°

FIXATION POINT

BOUNDARY OF FIELD OF LEFT EYE

90° LEFT

90° RIGHT

FIELD OF BOTH EYES

AREA BLOCKED BY NOSE AND CHEEKS

90° BELOW
(NADIR)

Using this representational format we can now graphically compare the visual fields of a "normal," wide-angle, and fish-eye camera lens, as well as a conventional perspective drawing and a cylindrical projection.

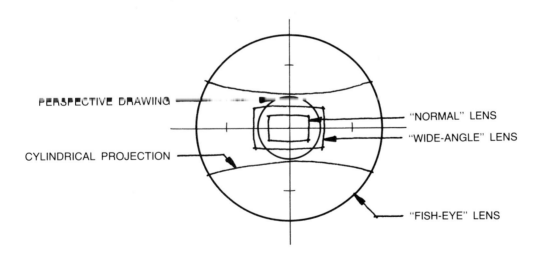

PERSPECTIVE DRAWING

"NORMAL" LENS

"WIDE-ANGLE" LENS

CYLINDRICAL PROJECTION

"FISH-EYE" LENS

Having discussed the extent of the bounded visual field we may now consider a second characteristic—the gradient of clarity in that field. Referring again to Gibson:

"A second characteristic of the visual field is that it is sharp, clear and fully detailed at the center, but progressively vaguer and less detailed toward its boundaries. For instance, the contours and patterns of the array of surfaces in your field can be observed to become gradually less determinate as you attend to those out toward the periphery. So difficult are the latter to see that the impulse to turn the eyes and fixate them may seem almost irresistible.* If you move your eyes down this page of print, for example, and fixate at random one letter of a single word, you will probably find that you can perceive that word and the words adjacent to it on the right and left and above and below, but no more. The visual field, therefore, possesses a central-to-peripheral gradient of clarity. The visual world does not. It does not even have a center, which agrees with the fact that it does not have boundaries. The world is ordinarily perceived by *scanning*, that is, by moving the eyes rapidly from point to point, and the objects and surfaces which compose it are always clear and fully detailed. If the objection be advanced that they are in fact only clear and detailed *when fixated*, the answer is that the objector gets this fact from an inspection of his visual field, not his visual world."

*"The center of clear perception corresponds, of course, to the fovea of the eye—that area of the retina best equipped anatomically for discrimination of fine detail and on which is projected an image of the object toward which the eye is pointed."

To summarize:

the **visual world** is unbounded and uniformly clear;

the **visual field** is bounded (extending approximately 180° horizontally, and 150° vertically), and has a center-to-periphery gradient of clarity;

the **hemispherical projection** (or fish-eye photograph) as an approximate representation of the visual field, includes a slightly larger vertical subtense (180°) and a uniformly clear field.

Let us now turn our attention to the "areas of patches of colored surface, divided up by contours" which Gibson describes as the sensory content of the visual field. We can diagram these areas in a hemispherical projection with each different portion indicating the projection of a different environmental surface, such as vegetation, floor, wall, table top, book, sky, etc., or whatever is in the visual field. The visual field consists of a number (N) of these areas or elements, and we can now give them the name of *"basic pattern areas,"* or BPAs.

Note that if there were *no* patterning of the visual field (N = 1), it would be completely uniform with "nothing" to be seen. This condition of a completely homogeneous visual field is called the *ganzfeld*. Can you think of some real-life examples?

Environmental surfaces as represented in a fish-eye photograph, and the major BPAs of this environmental scene as diagrammed in a hemispherical projection.

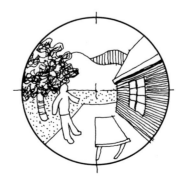
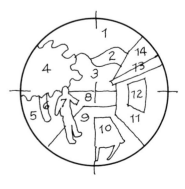

In what way are these basic pattern areas different?

As presented in a two-dimensional hemispherical projection, they can be described as having different shapes and sizes, as being in different positions, as having different colors and textures, as being vertical or horizontal, and as being glossy or matte. Thus we identify the primary *static* visual attributes of the basic pattern areas in the two-dimensional context of a bounded visual field in terms of:

In the four-dimensional visual *world* we must also consider duration, motion, and brightness. For a further discussion of these "attributes of the modes of appearance" see Ralph M. Evans, *An Introduction to Color* (New York: Wiley, 1948).

Number (of BPAs), both cardinal (depending on the "degree of patterning": 1, 20, 250, . . .) and ordinal (1st, 16th, 39th, . . .)

Position in the field; for example, upper left, far right, . . .

Size relative to the field; for example, large, small, . . .

Shape as determined by the contours; for example, round, oblong, square, . . .

Direction relative to the field; for example, vertical, diagonal, . . .

Texture as a visual surface pattern; for example, striped, dotted, smooth, . . .

Surface quality; for example, specular, glossy, matte, lustrous, iridescent, . . .

Color as a property of the surface; for example, red, light blue, dark green, . . .

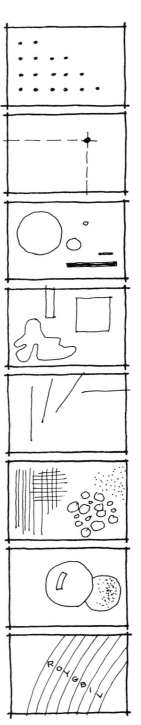

The following problem will now provide you with an opportunity to clarify for yourself the concept of basic pattern areas and of their attributes as characteristic of the visual field, and challenge you with an opportunity to clearly communicate your understanding of these issues in a graphic presentation.

Materials

15″ x 20″ white illustration board

Rubber cement

Drafting gear, pencils, pens

Architect's sketch paper

Several examples of color illustrations or advertisements about 8″ x 10″, cut from magazines, with ten to twenty basic pattern areas varied in all attributes.

Procedure

Turn your magazine clipping sideways or upside down, so you will tend to see it as a two-dimensional visual pattern rather than as an illustration of some three-dimensional scene or object. Identify all the basic pattern areas (BPAs) by carefully and completely outlining their contours on an overlaid piece of tracing paper. Number each BPA consecutively, with a different number for each BPA.

Next, prepare an inventory of all the static visual attributes of each of these BPAs. Remember: what you are dealing with now are only the different patches that pattern the surface of the piece of paper in front of you—nothing more than that. Your problem at this point is to describe as clearly as you can the attributes (number, size, position, shape, direction, color, texture, and surface finish) of each of these patches in the context of that piece of paper.

If you divide the diagonal of your clipping overlay into ten equal parts (how?) and draw a horizontal/vertical grid through all these points, the area of your clipping will thus be divided into one hundred equal parts. Each of these "cells" of this grid will then be 1 percent of the total area, and it will be very easy to estimate the relative size of each BPA using this grid.

To minimize the merely clerical work in this problem, it is recommended

"There lived in England in the Fourteenth Century a monk named Occam, to whose philosophical mind occurred one of those bright ideas which make history: he formulated for the first time the basic principle that truth is not complicated beyond necessity; in other words, that no solution to a problem can be right if a simpler and more direct solution can be found. This principle has been known, for obvious reasons, as 'Occam's razor' and by it centuries of scientific investigation have been shorn of avoidable complexities. The art of design also requires an Occam's razor, ruthlessly wielded. . . ."—Walter Dorwin Teague, *Design This Day* (New York: Harcourt, Brace and Company, 1940)

that you select a clipping with a maximum of about twenty BPAs. This will be easier if you have available a number of illustrations to consider as alternatives. You should neglect any BPA of less than 0.5 percent of the total area, and should aggregate *adjacent* areas of nearly similar color. Where two adjacent BPAs blend together without a clear ("hard-edge") boundary, you will have to arbitrarily establish a bounding contour.

Present the original clipping, the BPA identification, and your descriptive attribute-inventory in a simple, two-dimensional layout on the illustration board, in horizontal or vertical format. In designing this presentation your objective is to achieve a clear, orderly, logical, and comprehensive arrangement, for the most effective communication of the concept to a naive viewer, unaware of BPAs.

You may want to take advantage of the convention in our culture of reading from left to right and from top downwards. Also bear in mind that any graphic element that is not absolutely necessary will needlessly complicate the presentation and act as "noise" in the system. The simpler, less complicated alternative is usually to be preferred. A good rule is "When in doubt, leave it out." In addition, remember that personal graphic mannerisms communicate only information which is irrelevant to the present purpose.

Here is a diagram of the general communication model adapted from Geoffrey Broadbent, *Design in Architecture* (New York: Wiley, 1973), based on C. E. Shannon and W. Weaver, *The Mathematical Theory of Communication* (Urbana: University of Illinois Press, 1949).

"The information source (e.g. a human brain) wishes to pass a message to the information destination (e.g. another human brain) so as to modify the latter's behaviour.

"This information consists of ideas, thoughts, concepts (*signifieds*) about people, objects or things (*referents*), which have to be *codified* into words, images, symbols (*signifiers*) selected from those available in the *language*. Sometimes no precise signifier exists, i.e. one which denotes the referent directly; the message has to be codified in terms of analogies, metaphors etc. selected by the information source for their connotations. This may introduce distortions (*semantic noise*) into the coding process.

"The encoded message is then *transmitted* by some appropriate medium—speech, writing, drawing etc. according to the nature of the communications channel. The transmitter converts the message into a *signal*.

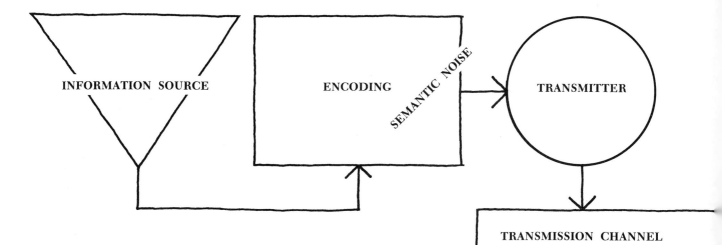

"The channel may take any form which is capable of conveying information: radio, TV, a book, a letter, a drawing etc. Strictly speaking it is the medium used in conveying the signal from transmitter to receiver; a pair of wires, coaxial cable, band of radio frequencies, beam of light, marks on surface of paper etc. Whatever channel is used, the signal may be perturbed by mechanical noise—a term which betrays the origins of information theory in telecommunications, where it refers to the clicks, bumps and hisses of a telephone channel. But it can be applied to any disturbance in any channel; smudged lettering, tea-stains on a drawing etc.

"The receiver performs a reverse function to the transmitter; it decodes the signal and reconstructs the original message from it.

"If the original signifiers carried largely denotational meanings, communication will be accurate—provided that the signal was not perturbed too much by mechanical noise as it passed through the channel. But if it contains signifiers with connotational meanings—analogies, metaphors and so on, then it is likely that the decoding will result in meanings which are rather different from those the source intended. The decoder will draw on his own experience of connotational meanings and this will introduce *perceptual* noise.

"The destination's behaviour *will* change as a result of receiving the message—if only to the extent of rejecting it. But if the change is other than that desired by the message source, the latter will have failed to communicate."

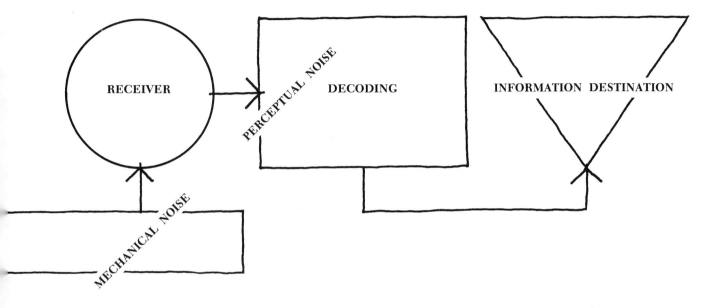

Note that in the absence of supplementary information, or information inherent in the context, it is usually necessary to introduce some "redundancy" in the message to offset the effect of "noise." R. L. Meier, in *A Communication Theory of Urban Growth* (Cambridge, Mass.: MIT/Harvard University Press, 1962), explains:

"Redundancy, which implies an overdetermination of meaning, has value in overcoming the effects of disturbance, noise, forgetfulness, typographical errors and the like. On the other hand, it uses up the time of *sender* and *receiver* alike. Too much redundancy in a channel causes disinterest in a *receiver*, while too little causes confusion and an inability to specify what it was that was communicated. The proper amount is arrived at through trial and error. Speech is typically more redundant than prose, but through the influence of radio, loudspeakers, and new forms of fiction, the properties of the two sides of language are beginning to converge. Pictures contain much greater redundancy, a great deal of which can be removed by making cartoon-like drawings. It is often convenient to assign payoffs to the meaningful, or nonredundant, fraction of a message. Experience shows that in most circumstances the returns obtained from redundancy and outright repetition are vanishingly small for any given individual. However, when a single message is directed to many different persons, as in the mass media, the uncertainty about the vocabulary of the *receiver*, and the environmental interferences affecting his receiving make the use of considerable amounts of redundancy efficient for the *sender*. Thus we may assert that though the payoff resides in the meaningful fraction, the *insurance* that the meaning will be received as intended resides in the redundant fraction. If there is growth in cultural interaction, there must be expansion of the quantity of meaningful communication on a per capita basis, and this almost certainly involves a reduced need for insurance."

For an extensive discussion of the role of contexts in human culture and communication, see Edward T. Hall, *Beyond Culture* (Garden City, N.Y.: Doubleday, 1976).

All the lettering in this presentation is to be done freehand by you directly on the illustration board using only the specified letter style and conventions. You may use any medium for this lettering—pencil, crayon, felt pen, ink, etc.—and you should experiment with all of them to discover which is best for this case.

THIS IS AN EXAMPLE OF HOW LETTERING SHOULD BE USED VERTICALLY.

THIS IS AN EXAMPLE OF WHAT IS TO BE AVOIDED.

Here now are our specifications for freehand lettering:

1. Use *only* the letterforms shown herewith. These alphanumeric characters are modeled on those which have been found to have the best legibility and readability. See E. J. McCormick, *Human Factors in Engineering and Design,* 4th ed. (New York: McGraw-Hill, 1976), or Rolf F. Rehe, *Typography: How to Make It Legible* (Carmel, Ind.: Design Research International, 1974).

2. Draw *light* upper and lower guidelines for each line of lettering.

3. Take care to make all vertical elements of the letterforms truly vertical: draw *light* vertical guidelines.

4. Provide vertical spacing between lines of lettering (this is called "leading" in typography, and is pronounced "ledding."

5. Try to achieve an apparent uniform spacing of letters in words.

6. Be sure that there is more space between words than there is between letters in words.

7. Arrange the lettering in horizontal lines to read from left to right and the lines to read from top to bottom. If for some reason it is necessary to arrange the lettering vertically, the convention is to turn the paper or board 90° clockwise and letter the *lines* in this format (see example).

8. Do not try to go too fast! Take time to form each letter properly and master this before you build up speed. Speed will come later—about three years later. Until then make sure your lettering is *good.*

Freehand lettering is one area in which beginning design students often experience conceptual difficulties. These problems are in addition to those related to the mastery of the necessary craft skills, and arise from certain confusions over the proper use of creativity and the question of self-expression.

In our work here we use lettering as a means of communicating information connected with the assigned problem, and not as a means for the self-expression of the designer's personality. The use of personalized letterforms and idiosyncratic lettering styles is thus irrelevant to the issues we are concerned with, and can only add "noise" to the communication process. For our present purposes, lettered communication requires the use of basic, standardized letter forms and conventionalized formats, and the designer's creativity is best employed with optimizing the use of these forms in these formats.

It has been suggested that the greatest art is to conceal art: to achieve a result so natural and inevitable in character that there is no evidence of artifice, or of the designer. Such design anonymity represents, perhaps, the ultimate possible design achievement: on a par with nature itself. But the young designer's ego is sometimes like the baby monkey's tail—always getting in the way and interfering with operations. Eventually, of course, the monkey manages to gain control of its tail and the tail is no longer a problem. How about you?

A B C D E F G

H I J K L M N O

P Q R S T U V

W X Y Z 1 2 3

4 5 6 7 8 9 0

In designing this presentation you will need to invent and simulate a large number of hypotheses and through a comparative evaluation of these alternatives arrive at an optimum solution. Two of the elements (the original clipping and the BPA tracing) are fixed in size and shape, but the third element of your composition on the board (your inventory of BPA attributes) is not, and it may be varied in size, shape, and direction. The best procedure here is to prepare three or four alternate versions, each one full size and on a separate piece of tracing paper.

Each of these alternates may then be tried out in a number of positional arrangements on the board along with the original clipping and the BPA overlay (in fact, by moving these separate items around on the board you can quickly simulate hundreds of alternatives). When you hit on a composition that seems to offer some possibilities, superimpose a sheet of white tracing paper (15″ x 20″) over the arrangement on the board, and carefully reproduce on it all the essential visual characteristics of that layout. These "comprehensives" should be complete representations (*not* abstract outline drawings) and should be carefully prepared *freehand* on a single sheet of paper to communicate the appearance of the future, final, finished presentation. Note that your usual pencil may not be the best tool for this job.

Tack or tape each of these alternative layouts up on the wall near your table (you should put up at least three at first, and ultimately not less than six). By comparing them as you prepare others, you will progress and serendipitously discover more and better ideas. Remember the three magic words:

COMPARE ADJACENT ALTERNATIVES!

Note also that mechanical copies of your clipping (such as Xerox, etc.) are both unusable and inadvisable: unusable because they are not adequate representations, and inadvisable because your use of them precludes your own development of an essential graphic skill.

Note that these alternatives which you put up on the wall are of the nature of "dress rehearsals" of your final production, and should provide a comprehensive representation of your final product. They should look like black-and-white photographs of your final design, which means that labeled outline diagrams are explicitly excluded. Thus you must reproduce the position, size, shape, texture, direction, number, and dark-and-light attributes of all the elements of your layout. Note that pencil alone may not be adequate for this purpose.

The preceding phase describes the process of studying your design, or developing your ideas through successive sequences of hypothesis, simulation, and evaluation. When you have satisfied yourself that you have explored *all* the possibilities open to you (keeping in mind the difference between the novice and the professional), you are then to execute your final *two*-dimensional design (using no lift-ups, overlays, or fold-outs) directly on the board. The original magazine clipping, as well as the tracing-paper BPA-identification, are to be rubber-cemented to the board; and all lettering is to be done freehand directly on the board surface. Please hand in your last comprehensive simulation, *just as it was before you started on your final presentation,* along with this final design, so we may compare them to evaluate the effectiveness of your simulation techniques.

Keep in mind that your simulations are the means by which you develop your design. There is no point in wasting what could have been useful design time in "improving" a simulation *after* you have made your final design decision and completed your presentation.

Discussion

How effective is your graphic layout in communicating the concepts that are at issue here?

1. Would a logical order of scanning be the following?

(a) original clipping

(b) BPA identification tracing

(c) BPA attribute inventory

Does your layout implement this order by following our culturally determined reading conventions? If you used a title on your presentation, is it located in a position that is effective in terms of these criteria?

2. Is there a close, logical relationship between the original clipping and your BPA identification tracing? Have you communicated this relationship by positioning them close together, in the same orientation, and in horizontal or vertical alignment? (Does any departure from these conditions aid communication, or does it add "noise"?)

3. Have you positioned the three elements (original clipping, BPA identification, BPA inventory) on the board with some regard to the "white space" as a "positive" element in itself, or have you used this white space as a sort of "packing material," in equal amounts around each of the elements so as to keep them from rattling around in the illustration board "box"?

4. Have you used any graphic material (borders, margins, boxes, arrows, horizontal and vertical division lines, decorations) in your presentation without making a visual comparison, side by side, with an alternate design *without* such material, to check to see if it is visual "noise," impeding communication?

5. Have you realized that in all probability the "surface quality" attributes of each BPA on your original clipping are identical, since the surface in question is only that of the piece of paper?

6. Is your "re-coding" of the several attributes of each BPA a clear and adequate graphic and/or verbal characterization? (Note that merely using a sample from a duplicate illustration only avoids the essential effort you must make to reformulate these attributes.)

7. Have you followed all the specifications for freehand lettering? Does your graphic craft reflect a professional level of responsibility?

Rubber cement is specified for all work with paper in this program because of its quick drying, transparent, flexible, stainless, waterproof, nonwrinkling, and noncurling properties. There are a few points you should know about using it. For most applications of a nonpermanent nature, brush on an even coat of cement over the larger surface, extending the area of application slightly beyond the boundary to be covered so as to ensure complete coverage, including the edges; then immediately join the other surface. Slight positional adjustments are possible. Then cover the surface with a clean sheet of paper and rub gently from the center outwards. Excess cement beyond the boundary may be *gently* rubbed off, when the cement is dry. This attachment will hold for a week or so and is adequate for most class work.

For a somewhat more permanent job, apply a uniform coat to *both* surfaces and let them both dry. When these surfaces so prepared are placed in contact, they cannot be shifted or separated. To permit the accurate positioning of the work, it is therefore necessary to use a "slip sheet." When the cement coatings are dry, use a clean sheet of tracing paper to cover all but a small edge of the lower surface. The upper surface may now be accurately positioned with reference to the lower one, and fixed in place at the exposed area. The slip sheet is then withdrawn bit by bit and the two surfaces are gradually brought into contact. Again cover and rub gently from the center outwards, and remove excess cement.

If your cement becomes too thick, it may be thinned with rubber cement solvent or thinner, obtainable at art supply stores. A consistency like that of a thin cream is usually most suitable.

Texture Archetypes: Introduction

When we look around us in our environment, we can now see the visual field as being composed of a number of subareas. These "basic pattern areas," or BPAs, are differentiated from each other in a variety of ways, one of which is the attribute of texture. Texture, as defined here, is the visually perceived, more-or-less regular patterning of an environmental surface, localized within the contour of a basic pattern area and helping to distinguish it as such.

This patterning may be due to the differential pigmentation or coloring of a surface, as in the case of a smooth black-and-white tiled floor; or may occur as the result of the physical roughness of a surface and the consequent variations in light, shade, and shadow when seen under directional lighting, as in the example of a rough stucco wall in the sunlight. These two modes may of course coexist in the same surface.

All surfaces in the environment have some texture, but whether we can see the texture of a given surface depends on such factors as the kind, amount, and direction of the illumination; the condition of our eyesight; the size of the basic texture elements patterning the surface; the contrast in the differential pigmentation of the basic texture elements; the reflectance of the surface; and our viewing distance from it.

Let us consider the last factor for a moment. When we stand rather close to a brick wall, the different **forms** of the individual bricks can be distinguished. But when we move farther back this discrimination gives way to a sense of the **pattern** of the bricks composing the wall. Increasing our distance still farther leaves us with only a sense of the wall's **texture;** and at the farthest remove, only an impression of **tone** remains. Thus we see that there is a hierarchy in the appearance of a textured surface, which, all else being equal, is a function of viewing distance, and follows the order of:

form / pattern / texture / tone

In the case of an environmental surface inclined to our line of sight, all these elements of the hierarchy may coexist in a continuous gradient.

Such texture gradients in environmental surfaces constitute one of the thirteen categories of "cues" involved in the perception of space and form. (Another is element size, which underlies the important and subtle higher-order attribute of the environmental scene known as "scale.") Texture in addition strongly modifies the appearance of colored surfaces.

Note that the individual bricks themselves may also be toned, textured, and patterned, and thus we realize that any such hierarchy is repeated on smaller and larger scales.

James J. Gibson, *The Perception of the Visual World* (Boston: Houghton Mifflin, 1950), classifies these cues into two types: *perspectives,* corresponding with the gradients of adjacent stimuli on the retina; and *sensory shifts,* corresponding with abrupt changes in such stimulation. Gibson identifies them as follows:

1. texture perspective

2. size perspective

3. linear perspective

4. binocular perspective

5. motion perspective

6. aerial perspective

7. blur perspective

8. relative upward location in the visual field

9. shift of texture-density

10. shift in amount of double imagery

11. shift in rate of motion

12. continuity of outline

13. transitions between light and shade

Edward T. Hall, *The Hidden Dimension* (Garden City, N.Y.: Doubleday, 1966), gives a useful discussion of these cues; and Gyorgy Kepes, *The Language of Vision* (Chicago: Paul Theobald, 1948), discusses the use of some of them in two-dimensional spatial representation.

The following collateral problem, scheduled to run concurrently with the regular studio problems, provides you with an opportunity to investigate the basic-pattern-area attribute of texture in some detail, and to appreciate the variety of aleatory textures in the surfaces of the natural environment. In addition, you will have an opportunity to develop a good measure of competence in the documentary and creative use of photography and other light-sensitive media. Subsequently, in Problem 17, you will use some of the material produced in this work as a means for the study of the effect of texture on environmental space and scale.

"Inability to use a camera will in the future undoubtedly be regarded as analogous in point of illiteracy as inability in the use of the pen . . . ."—Laszlo Moholy-Nagy, "Problems of the Modern Film," in *Cahiers d'Art,* vol. 7, nos. 6-7 (Paris, 1932)

Materials

A photographic darkroom equipped to print and process photo-enlargements

8″ x 10″ projection (enlargement) paper

20″ x 30″ white illustration board

Still camera and black-and-white film (alternative A only)

Procedure

The accompanying illustration of archetypical basic texture-element patterns presents a conceptual structuring of the fine-scale regular patterning of environmental surfaces which we call texture. The hypothesis is that all possible texture patterns can be realized from various combinations of these six archetypes.

Your assignment will be either:

(a) to locate natural examples of each of these six archetypes, photograph them, make technically perfect enlargements of these photographs, and present the results; or

(b) to develop experimentally a prime example of each of these six archetypes as a photogram, and to present them in the same way as the photographs.

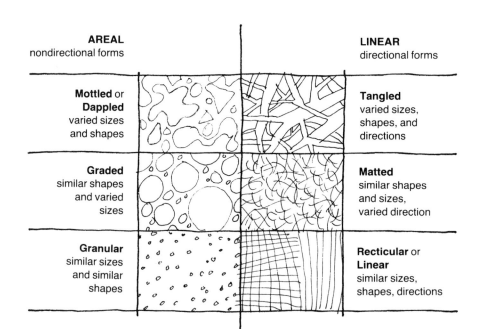

AREAL
nondirectional forms

LINEAR
directional forms

Mottled or **Dappled**
varied sizes and shapes

Tangled
varied sizes, shapes, and directions

Graded
similar shapes and varied sizes

Matted
similar shapes and sizes, varied direction

Granular
similar sizes and similar shapes

Recticular or **Linear**
similar sizes, shapes, directions

Alternative A (Photographs)

In essence your problem is to discover and record photographically a rich and varied collection of the permanent or transient aleatory textures that characterize so much of the natural visual environment, and which are emblematic of the processes of nature. At the same time each of these photographs is to be restricted to single examples of the given archetypes.

Phase 1 starts now and continues to the end of Problem 16. Using black-and-white film and whatever camera is available to you, discover and photograph examples of two- and three-dimensional texture patterns which occur in the environment as the result of an accidental, nondesigned process. In photographing try either to find a large example of the texture or to approach it close enough (within the limits of your lens) so that your negative will register only or mostly the texture that interests you. This will reduce the amount of "cropping" you will have to do later.

Phase 2. First contact *proofs* to be available for critique of content and technique. Please submit them in an envelope on which you have lettered your name.

Contact proofs are working prints made from your negatives and the same size as them; they are used for inspection and discussion in lieu of the delicate and fragile negatives. (Negatives should be held only at their edges, and kept in the individual glassine envelopes made to store them, where they will not accumulate dust or scratches. Oil from your fingers, dust, and scratches easily and quickly ruin negatives.)

You may develop and print proofs of your negatives yourself, or have this done commercially. In the latter case your proofs may be small enlarge ments rather than contact proofs.

Phase 3. First 8″ x 10″ *enlargements* to be available for critique of content and technique. From a selection of the dozens of photographs you have taken and are continuing to take, *you* are to make technically perfect 8″ x 10″ glossy enlargements on single-weight paper of *several examples of each of the six archetypes.*

The entire area of each enlargement should represent only one archetypical texture pattern. To achieve this you may have to enlarge only part of the negative, eliminating or "cropping" that part which is irrelevant to the present purpose. (Do not cut the negative!)

Please present these prints in an envelope with your name on it. Do not write on the back of your enlargements, as this will emboss the paper and ruin the surface of your print.

Phase 4. Final presentation (due after Problem 16). See Problem 3b, Texture Archetypes: Conclusion.

A "technically perfect" print is in sharp focus; incorporates the full tonal range of all the gray tones in the scale, from a rich velvet black to a clear pure white; shows clear detail in both deep shadows and bright highlights; and has no dust, lint, hair, fingerprints, or stain blemishes. For technical information on cameras and darkroom techniques you may want to consult *The Camera, Light and Film*, and *The Print*, all from the *Life Library of Photography* (New York: Time-Life Books, 1972); or Charles Swedlund, *Photography* (New York: Holt, Rinehart and Winston, 1974).

Alternative B (Photograms)

The *photogram* is also known as "cameraless photography." It involves the manipulation of light sources and light-modulating materials in the darkroom, on or over the surface of light-sensitive photographic enlarging paper which is subsequently developed and fixed. We will use 8″ x 10″ enlarging paper, and the light sources may be an enlarger, large or small flashlights, or other illuminants. The modulating material may be opaque, transparent, refractive, or reflective.

As Laszlo Moholy-Nagy suggests, there are a number of possible techniques beyond the very elementary procedure of making mere "shadow" photograms produced by laying opaque objects on the light-sensitive paper. Your task is to experiment with these *other* methods and serendipitously discover techniques which have a potential for your purposes. In other words, you are challenged here to demonstrate your imagination and inventiveness in free exploration of a medium, along with your alertness to the results, and your ability to exploit and adapt them to your purposes.

Phase 1 starts now and continues nearly to the end of Problem 16. Using a wide variety of materials which obscure, transmit, reflect, and refract light, experiment with ways to generate texture patterns uniformly distributed over the surface of 8″ x 10″ sheets of enlarging paper. Your first experiments should be most free and aimed at the discovery of the potentials and limitations of the medium. In the course of this exploration, however, you should be looking for suggestions of those pattern types that relate to this problem. Eventually, after you are convinced you have discovered all there is to the photogram, you should return to those procedures that seemed to have some promise relative to the required texture patterns, and produce many border-to-border examples of each.

Phase 2. First results due for a critique of content and technique. Please present at least two examples of each of the six archetypical categories in an envelope with your name on it.

Phase 3. Additional examples of each of the six archetypical categories are due for critique; as before, in an envelope identified with your name.

Phase 4 is the same as for the photographic option.

Schedules for interim Phases 2 and 3 will be posted in class, and your work will be reviewed and discussed at those due dates. This problem concludes with Phase 4 (after Problem 16) and a further discussion of issues and implications is given then. Please be sure to retain your unused prints (for either alternative) to use in connection with Problem 17.

Laszlo Moholy-Nagy, the "Johnny Appleseed" of design, has commented on the photogram as follows:

"In order to learn about the properties of the light sensitive emulsion, which is the basic element of photography, it is best to start with the making of cameraless photographs . . . .

"Photopaper or film exposed to light will record the varied intensity of light sources in black and white and gray values. Practically, this is nothing more than a photonegative, produced by laying objects on the emulsion-covered surface. Opaque objects contacting this surface block out all light leaving that part of the sheet unexposed, i.e., white. Shadows of these objects caused by lighting during the exposure result in varying gray-values depending upon the density of the shadows. Areas flooded with light, that is, fully exposed, become black.

"The photogram exploits the unique characteristics of the photographic process—the ability to record with delicate fidelity a great range of tonal values. The almost endless range of gradations, subtlest differences in the gray values, belongs to the fundamental properties of photographic expression. The organized use of that gradation creates photographic quality. The photogram can be called the key to photography because every good photograph must possess the same fine gradations between the white and black extremes as the photogram.

"The photogram conjures up as many interpretations as it has viewers and with new discoveries its original range can be greatly enlarged. For example, printed transparent cellophane sheets, blank films, engraved, scratched glass plates covered with ink drawings can be used as 'negatives.' In an enlarging apparatus combined with the usual technique of the photogram these materials may give startling results. The photogram may also be used as a new method of recording light values when materials such as oil, paint or ink are squeezed between glass plates. This procedure flattens out the oil drops or the still wet, painted lines and fashions them into astonishing shapes which vary with the pressure applied . . . .

"The photogram understood as a diagrammatic record of the motion of light translated into black and white and gray values can lead to a grasp of new types of spatial relationships and spatial rendering. The receding and advancing values of the gradations, which are projec- tions of the 'light tracks,' can be used for space—that is, space-time articulation . . . .

"This work need not only be for the sophisticated. Both the photographic amateur and the layman, acquiring through the photogram a deeper understanding of light and space values, will be inspired to explore the potentialities of the camera since the photogram teaches that the same characteristics of gradations and contrasts have to be applied to camera work too. Good photography with the camera must enable us to capture the patterned interplay of light and shadow exactly as in cameraless photography. Thus photography becomes the translation of a world saturated with light and color into black, white and gray gradations."

—Laszlo Moholy-Nagy, *Vision in Motion* (Chicago: Paul Theobald, 1947)

Laszlo Moholy-Nagy (1895-1946), one of the inspired teachers of our century, taught at the Bauhaus in Germany, and later at the New Bauhaus and the School of Design (subsequently Institute of Design) in Chicago. Extraordinarily innovative in many areas of design and art, he combined a keen interest in all aspects of technology with a passionate concern for the individual, and a belief in the social value of art.

Photograph by Serge Chermayeff

Form Genesis

Let us now consider some additional aspects of the patterning of the visual field. As mentioned before, the function of our perceptual systems is to provide us with a probabilistic explanation of our surroundings. In this process our perceptual systems are sensitive to *all* the stimuli patterning the sensory fields, continuously monitoring these signals and interpreting their contextual significance.

A key step in this perceptual process is the division of the sensory field into a "figure" and a "ground." In the visual field, some basic pattern areas appear to belong together as parts of some "thing" (the "figure"), while the rest of the field is relegated to the ("back") "ground." Visual demonstrations of this elementary tentative organization are given in the adjacent examples. In many cases we speak of the figure-ground dichotomy in terms of "positive" and "negative" areas or spaces or forms. By paying attention to the bounding contours which are common to both these forms, with a change in our perceptual set we can discover the "negative" spaces between objects as objects in their own right. This fluctuation of figure and ground indicates the tentative exploratory nature of this phase of the perceptual process. When we attempt to penetrate a camouflage, we try to regroup the basic pattern areas in terms of alternate figures on new grounds.

The "laws" governing these associations of basic pattern areas will be presented in Problems 8 and 15.

Above: the letter F
Below: a view of downtown Seattle, as represented in an enlarged halftone (from a newspaper advertisement)

"In every clear concept of the nature of vision and in every healthy approach to the spatial world, this dynamic unity of figure and background has been clearly understood. Lao Tse showed such grasp when he said: 'A vessel is useful only through its emptiness. It is the space opened in a wall that serves as a window. Thus it is the nonexistent in things which makes them serviceable.' Eastern visual culture has a deep understanding of the role of the empty space in the image. Chinese and Japanese painters have the admirable courage to leave empty large paths of their picture-surface so that the surface is divided into unequal intervals which, through their spacing, force the eye of the spectator to movements of varying velocity in following up relationships, and thus create the unity by the greatest possible variation of surface. Chinese and Japanese calligraphy also has a sound respect for the white interval. Characters are written in imaginary squares, the blank areas of which are given as much consideration as the graphic units, the strokes. Written or printed communication is living or dead depending upon the organization of its blank spaces. A single character gains clarity and meaning by orderly relationship of the space background which surrounds it. The greater the variety and distinction among respective background units, the clearer becomes the comprehension of a character as an individual expression or sign."

—Gyorgy Kepes, *The Language of Vision* (Chicago: Paul Theobald, 1948)

Follower of Hsia Kuei (c. 1250), *Windswept Lakeshore,* ink on silk, 15½" x 13½". The Metropolitan Museum of Art, purchase, bequest of Theodore M. Davis, by exchange, 1973

This perceptual process serves our other senses, too. The existence of an auditory discrimination of figure and ground is demonstrated by our ability to listen to one person in a room full of conversing people, and to shift our attention to other talkers at will. Another common example is found in music where one may follow a given instrument, or a particular theme, as the "figure" against the "ground" of the other instruments or the accompaniment.

In a similar way we also recognize the bipolarity of elementary cognition in that a reference, for example, to light, strong, high, justice, far, or old necessarily implies a corresponding reference to dark, weak, low, injustice, near, or new. From this we may understand that any entity, perceptual or conceptual, achieves an independent existence only as it is differentiated from other things, and as it coexists in a dynamic unity with its opposite.

An awareness of this *unity of opposites* leads us to an appreciation of "the weight of the empty space" and "the sound of the silent interval" as vital elements of composition in space and time. In the following exercise you will have an opportunity to feel these weights and hear these sounds. And, while you are becoming familiar with this process of the perceptual forming of the sensory pattern, you will be introduced to some considerations underlying the process by which natural physical patterns are generated, and the virtual forces and tensions inherent in their spatial configurations.

The pervasive importance of the interval in Japanese culture is suggested by Gunter Nitschke in the accompanying table (from "The Japanese Sense of Place," *Architectural Design,* March 1966). Note that the character

is read as "Ma," "Aida," "Gen," or "Kan," depending on the context.

Realm of 1 dimension 梁　間 Hari-　Ma		*Beam-span* Representing a linear space measurement, not related to anything.

Between heaven and earth
Representing simultaneous awareness of the two poles and all that lies between, of a larger space unit.

天　と　地　の　間
Ten-　To-　Chi-　No-　Aida

Realm of 2 dimensions
六　疊　の　間
Roku-　Jo-　No-　Ma

A 6-tatami room
A recognizable area. The average Japanese immediately associates a certain number of *tatami* with a certain kind of room, since, in their traditional architecture, measures of length, area and volume are coordinated and therefore certain room sizes are used for specific purposes. Thus a 4½-*tatami* room means a private room, a 6-*tatami* room means a living room, an 8-*tatami* room means a guest room with a *tokonoma* (alcove).

Realm of 3 dimensions
空　間
Ku-　Kan

Space, literally 'empty space'
In China *Ku* means 'hole in the ground,' but the Japanese later altered it to mean 'hole in the universe' ie, heaven. It is also used for 'empty' in the normal sense of the word, and for 'void' in the Buddhist metaphysical sense. The combination of *Ku* and *Ma*, in Japanese *Ku-kan*, was recently coined to represent Western three-dimensional space. But the connotations of the *Ma* part of it influenced and changed the meaning of the whole. So now the confusion is so great that 90 percent of the writing about space by Japanese architects is not understood by even their peers.

Realm of 4 dimensions
一　時　間
Ichi-　Ji-　Kan

One Hour
Representing a linear measure of time, not related to anything.

Between one and two o'clock
Representing simultaneous awareness of two poles of a unit of time as well as all that lies between, thus isolating a finite time from infinite time.

一　時　と　二　時　の　間
Ichi-　Ji-　To-　Ni-　Ji-　No-　Aida

So far *Ma* has constituted a measure of length or area of volume or even time, used in an objective sense. In the following examples the human element is introduced: aesthetic taste and subjective imagination, a fifth dimension.

Realm of 5 dimensions
間　が　悪　い
Ma-　Ga-　Warui

Literally 'the "Ma" is bad' = I am embarrassed
The feeling expressed is that one cannot remain any longer in a certain place because both one's own *Ma* and that of the place would be bad. Thus *Ma* here represents the quality of a place as perceived by an individual.

話　の　間　が　旨　い
Hanashi-　No-　Ma-　Ga-　Umai

Literally 'the "Ma" of his speech is excellent' = it is an excellent speech
The manner and timing of the speech are good. (The Japanese are highly sensitive to the length and character of pauses in speech and music.) So *Ma* here indicates the quality of an event—speech, dance, music—as perceived by an individual.

人　間
Nin-　Gen

Literally 'among men' (man in the philosophical sense)
This expresses that man is not truly 'man' as an individual, but only as part of 'man,' the unit within a unity. If he withdraws from the field of communal action, this great dynamic place, and goes, say, into the mountains, a different word is used depicting him as already a ghost.

96

Materials

4 10″ x 15″ white illustration boards

1 15″ x 20″ white illustration board

30 2″ x 3″ pieces of black construction paper

Black tempera paint, brushes, etc.

Procedure

Phase A

Using as few or as many of the 2″ x 3″ pieces of black construction paper as you wish, make a number of different arrangements in black and white on several of your 10″ x 15″ boards. You may overlap the pieces, and the pieces may "bleed," or overlap the edges of the board. Your purpose here is to discover a relationship of the black and white forms in which the black shapes and the white shapes will readily alternate as figures against the opposite as ground. By manipulating the 2″ x 3″ movable pieces, you will be able to quickly simulate a great number of hypotheses. If you work on several alternatives at the same time, using two or more boards, you can readily compare and rank your acceptable hypotheses.

When you have worked up something to your satisfaction, lightly in pencil trace *freehand* around the outline of the form(s) you have produced. Work carefully so as not to disturb the position of the pieces of black construction paper. When this is done, remove the black paper rectangles and if necessary go over the lines *freehand* to make them a bit more definite. Then, using black tempera paint, carefully paint in the areas which were white a solid black, doing this work *freehand* and without using any masking tape. By thus reversing the areas, you have turned the formerly "positive" areas into "negative" forms and vice versa. In this way you discover that your temporary focus on what "is" obviously also requires that which "is not" in a dynamic unity of opposites.

See the comments of Dorr Bothwell and Marleys Frey in *Notan: The Dark-Light Principle of Design* (New York: Reinhold, 1968), and Gyorgy Kepes on "Value Relationships" in *The Language of Vision* (Chicago: Paul Theobald, 1948).

Phase B

Place one of your 10″ x 15″ boards on the table (or floor) and one by one drop the 2″ x 3″ pieces of black construction paper onto it from a height of about 24″ and from a position directly above its center. Let the pieces flutter from your hand one by one in *exactly* the same manner, and make no attempt to control their fall or to arrange their position on the board. Not all will fall within the 10″ x 15″ area, and those that do in whole or in part will form a quite accidental pattern therein. Repeat this process several times and study the effect of different hand positions and of the initial position of the 2″ x 3″ pieces of paper on the resulting pattern. Here again work on several alternatives simultaneously, so you can compare results.

In all cases pause after three to ten pieces (in addition to parts of others) have fallen wholly within the boundary of the board and study the difference in the character or feeling of the abstract compositions on the boards. Quite obviously there are objective differences in the shape, size, position, and direction of the positive and negative forms on the several boards. But perhaps not quite as immediately obvious is the fact that as a result of your unconscious perceptual efforts to impute some meaning to each abstract pattern, the boards will take on the appearance of three-dimensional space, and you will see virtual movements (up, down, left, right, in, out, expanding, contracting, rotating) on them. Your awareness of this is a key part of your visual sensitization. Try to describe what you see in terms of spatial forces and movements in each successive pattern, and compare and share your impressions with your colleagues.

Then, taking three 10″ x 15″ boards one after another, and using whichever hand position and orientation seems to work best, again drop the thirty pieces, one by one, on each board, until between three and ten pieces are wholly within each area. Carefully compare these three boards in terms of the dynamic tensions and forces and "virtual movement" of the resulting patterns, and select the one which to you seems to be the most powerful, or active.

Now, working carefully so as not to disturb their positions, trace lightly in pencil around the outlines of the forms; remove the pieces of construction paper; and paint in what were the white areas with black tempera paint.

Has this reversal changed the dynamic qualities of the field?

"Positions, directions and differences in size, shape, brightness, color and texture are measured and assimilated by the eye. The eye lends the character of its neuro-muscular experience to its source. Since each shape, color, value, texture, direction and position produces a different quality of experience, there must arise an inherent contradiction from their being on the same flat surface. This contradiction can be resolved only as they have the appearance of movement in the picture-plane. These virtual movements of optical qualities will mould and form the picture space, thus acting as spatial forces. Only incidentally does the spatial quality derive from the fact that optical signs resemble objects known empirically. One experiences space when looking at an articulated two-dimensional surface mainly because one unconsciously attempts to organize and perceive the different sensations induced by the optical qualities and measures as a whole, and in so doing is forced, by the various qualities in their relationships to each other and to the picture-surface, to impute spatial meaning to these relationships."

—Gyorgy Kepes, *The Language of Vision* (Chicago: Paul Theobald, 1948)

The same three elements may be arranged in many different ways in a given visual field to produce radically different spatial and kinetic "feelings." These subjective differences depend only on the positional relationships of the elements with respect to one another, and to the field. Can you find words descriptive of these feelings, in each of these cases?

Phase C

In the preceding phase of this exercise your final form was the result of a process of growth—the accumulation of fallen rectangles of paper. So also are all forms, natural and artificial, at any moment in time the consequence of the processes that preceded them. Sometimes the processes are too slow or too fast for us to perceive, as in the case of a stone or a city or a flash of lightning, but in all circumstances the history of a form's transformations is represented in the form itself, and can convey to us an impression of this process.

A consideration of this visual biography enables us to discriminate between natural and artificial form. C. H. Waddington suggests:

". . . there is some general character which pervades the whole realm of organic form. If one found oneself walking along the strand of some unknown sea, littered with the debris of broken shells, isolated bones, and odd lumps of coral of some unfamiliar fauna, mingled with the jetsam from the wrecks of strange vessels, one feels that one would hardly make any mistakes in distinguishing the natural from the man-made objects. Unless the churning of the waves had too much corroded them, the odd screws, valves, radio terminals, and miscellaneous fitments, even if fabricated out of bone or some other calcareous shell-like material, would bear the unmistakable impress of a human artificer and fail to make a good claim to a natural origin.

"What is this character, which the naturally organic possesses and the artificial usually lacks? It has something, certainly, to do with growth. Organic forms develop. The flow of time is an essential component of their full nature, and the spatial objects we can hold in our hands and examine, with eyes or microscope, during a short few minutes is only a single still out of a continuous sequence of forms which continuously unfolds, sometimes quickly, sometimes more slowly, throughout the life of the organism of which it is a part. All scientific consideration of organic form must start from this point. Science is essentially concerned with causal relations; and causal relations cannot be expressed unless there is change. It is therefore in the changes of form—during individual development, during evolution, or under the influence of function—that the biologist is mainly interested."

Waddington thus characterizes organic form as "something which is produced by the interaction of numerous forces which are balanced against one another in a near-equilibrium that has the character not of a precisely definable pattern but rather of a slightly fluid one, a rhythm . . . ." Whereas "man-made mechanical forms, such as screws, cogs, propellers, are usually designed to serve one single function, or at most two or three, and their unity is correspondingly blatant and single-minded . . . ." He also notes that "it is only in those human artifacts whose form, perfected over centuries, is designed to be an appropriate extension of the human or animal body or to meet the exigencies of some ever-variable medium such as the sea—in the handle of a scythe, the saddle of a horse, or the hull of a boat—that we meet an approximation to the character of the natural forms of life."

Waddington comments further:

"The requirements of general living, for all but the simplest animals, cannot be reduced to performance of any one series of actions. The shape of a limb-bone has to be adapted to walking, running, jumping, sitting, leaping sideways or backwards, and this multiplicity of actions requires it to have a more subtle and less immediately perspicuous unity . . . .

"Organic form is, then, the resultant of the interaction of many different forces. The wholeness of the form indicates that this resultant is always in some sense an equilibrium. The internal tensions are balanced against one another into a stable configuration—or rather, nearly balanced, since the configuration is destined slowly to change as development proceeds. . . .

" . . . another type of form which needs to be distinguished from the organic, although the distinction is not always easy . . . is a typical pebble. That is to say, a mass which has been moulded, like an organic one, by a very large number of forces, but in this case by forces which are external and uncoordinated. It repre-

sents not the equilibration or balancing of many conflicting tendencies, but the chance outcome of a series of random and unrelated events; in fact, Whitehead's mere confusion of detail. But there is a complication here. If the number of detailed events is large enough, and if they are all of approximately the same magnitude, a certain statistical regularity will emerge, and there will be a tendency for the production of some reasonably definite shape, which may perhaps simulate an organic shape produced by an internal equilibrium. Thus the artistic developments of the pebble form may be very similar to those derived from a knee-cap or knuckle bone. . . .

"Primitive man was surrounded by organic forms. So nowadays is the agriculturalist or anyone who lives in the country. It might be expected that the specific biological character would impress itself by mere familiarity on artists who lived in close contact with nature, and would be particularly apparent in their works. But it is only to a slight extent that this is true. The most primitive paintings of the European Stone Age and

the African Bushmen indeed often express the qualities we have been describing, but most folk art lacks them. Man, it seems, when he begins to create, is usually more single-purposed than living Nature. The inner logic of his constructions is simpler; or he is concerned more with an externally imposed logic, of representation or symbolism. There is, in a human work of sculpture, no actual multitude of internal growth-forces which are balanced so as to issue in a near-equilibrium of a rhythmic character. We should therefore not expect that works of art will often arrive at the same type of form as we commonly find in the structures of living matter. Much more can we anticipate an influence of man's intellectualising, pattern-making habit of simplification, diluted perhaps by an intrusion of unresolved detail. Only the extremely simple, or the extremely sophisticated, are likely to stray into the realm of form which is the proper outcome of the blind but complex forces of life."

—C. H. Waddington, "The Character of Biological Form," in L. L. Whyte, ed., *Aspects of Form* (London: Lund Humphries, 1951)

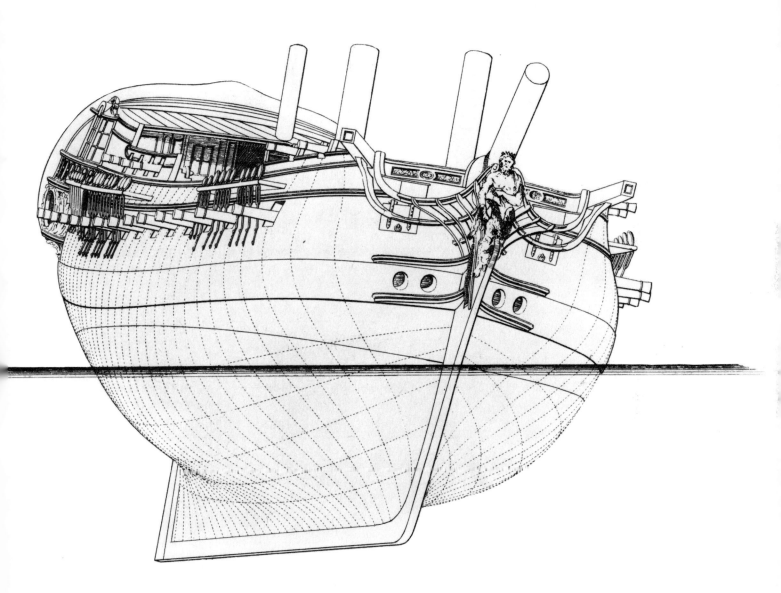

Forty-gun frigate, from Fredrik Henrik af
Chapman, *Architectura Navalis Mercatoria*
(reprint ed., VEB Hinstorff Verlag: Rostock,
1970)

In this final phase of the exercise you will have an opportunity to become a form-process biographer by developing a means to record a dynamic process. In essence you are to repeat Phase B, but this time the means of aleatory form generation will not be 2″ x 3″ pieces of black construction paper, and the method of operation will not necessarily be a free-fall aerodynamic process. What it will be is up to you, and should be selected from a series of several *dozen* different and imaginative experimental investigations. Please use only black and white media, and this time work in terms of a final presentation on a 15″ x 20″ piece of board, subsequently trimmed to 10″ x 15″ to provide comparability with the results of Phases A and B.

The only restriction in the execution of this problem is that *chance* must be the *only* factor determining the form-pattern on your board. You will, of course, set up a situation which results in the generation of forms, but *you must do absolutely nothing whatever to guide, control, direct, or design what happens on the surface.* You are to set the stage, but are not to write the play. Here you serve only as a midwife, or an accessory before the fact.

Discussion

If the class work on the three phases of this problem is displayed in this suggested format, you will be able to make some additional discoveries:

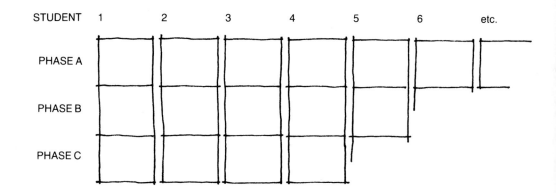

Can you detect a difference in the physiognomy, or "personality," of the different examples of the Phase A work? Are there similar differences in the Phase B (or C) work?

Can you describe the differences between the work for Phase A and for Phase B and C?

If you were placed in solitary confinement, and were allowed only one example of all this work for your cell wall, which would you choose? Why? What are the implications of this?

Our involvement with the physical mechanics of form generation has provided us with an opportunity to compare idiosyncratic procedures and personal criteria, on the one hand, with aleatory methods and external constraints on the other. In the first case (Phase A) your efforts ended with the production of a form, or a pattern; and in the second (Phases B and C) the result of your work was the documentation of a process. In one case there is a final, finished *product,* while in the other there is a representative sample of a continuing *process.*

We find an eternal fascination in watching similar effects in the metamorphosis of the sunset, the surf breaking on the shore, the flames in a fireplace, and the wind in the field of grain: all evidence of organic processes whose rhythmic variations cause our spirits to resonate in harmony with a larger unity. Artists, both East and West, have long sought to manifest the essence of this rhythmic vitality in their work. The First Canon of Chinese painting, *ch'i yün shêng tung,* expresses the idea that *ch'i* (the Breath of Heaven, the Spirit) "stirs all of nature to life and sustains the eternal processes of movement and change; and that if a work has *ch'i* it inevitably reflects a vitality of spirit that is the essence of life itself." In Japan this precept found expression in the *haboku* ("splash-ink") style of painting, in which a swift and spontaneous manner of execution accorded with the Zen principle of *satori,* or sudden enlightenment. In Europe appreciations of the fortuitous accident go back through a number of painters to Leonardo da Vinci and his famous advice for "quickening the spirit of invention," and beyond him to Pliny, the Roman encyclopedist, who celebrated the role of chance in the inventions of art. In our own century the painter Wassily Kandinsky reaffirmed in his work the liberating role of improvisation, and Jean (Hans) Arp welcomed the authenticity of the transient in compositions in many media "arranged according to the laws of chance." Kepes points out that both "great scientists and great artists, in some of their lucky moments, were able to make use of the spontaneity of chance events in unlocking imprisioned imaginative power. Some of the greatest masters of East and West, in their old age, came to recognize that there are greater masters within than disciplined knowledge and consciously willed goals. Only by standing back humbly and letting these real masters take over sometimes can, on a new higher level, man and nature meet."

Mai-Mai Sze, *The Tao of Painting* (New York: Pantheon Books, 1956). See also: Shio Sakanishi, trans., *The Spirit of the Brush* (London: John Murray, 1939); and Laurence Binyon, *The Flight of the Dragon* (London: John Murray, 1911).

See James Thrall Soby, ed., *Arp* (New York: Museum of Modern Art, 1958); and E. H. Gombrich's "The Image in the Clouds" in his *Art and Illusion* (New York: Pantheon Books, 1960). See also the comments of Gyorgy Kepes on the process of making, in *The Language of Vision* (Chicago: Paul Theobald, 1948); and what J. F. O'Brien has to show in *Design by Accident* (New York: Dover, 1968).

As for the technical and social implications of the visible history of form transformations, you will find D'Arcy Thompson's *On Growth and Form* (Cambridge: Cambridge University Press, 1942) and Gyorgy Kepes' *The New Landscape in Art and Science* (Chicago: Paul Theobald, 1956) both fascinating. For a latter-day version of D'Arcy Thompson's great work, see Rene Thom's *Structural Stability and Morphogenesis* (Reading, Mass.: W. A. Benjamin, 1975), which "attempts a degree of mathematical corroboration" of that classic; and E. C. Zeeman, "Catastrophe Theory," *Scientific American,* April 1976 (as an introduction to that book).

"The seat of this poetic inner world was the unconscious. To penetrate that well-protected region the artist had to invent a variety of devices. Accidental and chance events were introduced to trigger deeper poetic responses. Joan Miro, for instance, spilled paint on paper and let it run. The shapes that emerged became pathways to his own inner mythology of private shapes. Those chance events pregnant with unconscious meanings were, thus, set between two conscious acts that gave them shape. One was the initial decision to evoke chance processes, the other the terminal decision to stop them. Entering through these gates, the artist left the world of named, formed, and classified things and reached down to the unnamed, unformed events of his inner world. He hoped to escape from the anonymous beast of Twentieth Century life, the arrogant self-confidence of one-sided rationalism; the inner world seemed to offer moments of freedom and dignity. But this oasis of poetry could not be reached by using dishonest guides. The circus of self-display froze spontaneity, chained freedom, and killed dignity. But, in spite of some abortive attempts, the genuine core of artists' intentions touched upon the most crucial aspects of our contemporary need. They pointed to something missing, something about which we all dream: the freedom that comes from the spontaneity of chance events that we so much appreciate in the forms of nature. These qualities, discovered in the imaginative process and expressed in visible, tangible artistic forms, could become valuable guides for reshaping our ever more complex inner and outer world. They could evoke experiences with qualities both of life and of order and, thus, serve as the inner compasses needed in mapping out new territories."

—Gyorgy Kepes, "Kinetic Light as a Creative Medium," *Technology Review,* December 1967

Our investigation of the psychological genesis of form in the creative process of perception acquainted you with some of the "positive" aspects of "negative" time and space. Your further interest in these matters will be stimulated by reference to Lao Tsu's *The Way of Life,* as translated by Witter Bynner (New York: Capricorn Books, 1962), and to Amos I. T. Chang's application of these precepts to architecture in his *Intangible Content in Architectonic Form* (Princeton, N.J.: Princeton University Press, 1956).

"Wherever we look, we find configurations that are either to be understood as patterns of order, of closure, of a tendency toward a centre, cohesion and balance, or as patterns of mobility, freedom, change or opening. We recognize them in every visible pattern; we become aware of their existence as patterns of our motivations, feelings, states of mind. We respond to their expression in nature's configurations and in human utterances, gestures and acts. Cosmos and chaos, as the ancients called them, the Apolonian spirit of measure and the Dionysian principle of chaotic life; organization and randomness; stasis and kinesis; consciousness and unconsciousness; inhibition and excitation; association and disassociation, integration and disintegration, convention and revolt: all these are different aspects of the same polarity of configuration. In the field of art history, its manifestations are classified as Classicism and Romanticism and its characteristics are described as architectural and pictorial, respectively. The processes of the outer world and of the human brain are cast in this Janus-faced matrix."

—Gyorgy Kepes, *The New Landscape in Art and Science* (Chicago: Paul Theobald, 1956)

You may also find the associated notion of the "unity of opposites" a productive line of investigation. For example, make a collection of what you feel are "good" graphic designs (from magazine advertisements, posters, page layouts, etc.) and then analyze them in terms of the simultaneous presence of opposites in the visual attributes of their basic pattern areas: large/small, rough/smooth, high/low, far/near, chromatic/achromatic, horizontal/vertical. Look also at form quality, in terms of contrasts between the simple, regular, symmetrical, closed, and passive forms (the classical, or Apollonian) and those which are complex, irregular, asymmetrical, open, and active (the romantic, or Dionysian).

Then, to develop further your sensitivity to form, collect a large variety of small, three-dimensional objects, both natural and artificial (twigs, bark, stones, prisms, eggshells, machine parts, simple geometric solids in a variety of materials, etc.), and likewise a good selection of two-dimensional surfaces (papers, foils, cloth, veneers, etc.) with varied textures and surface qualities. Prepare a carefully selected assemblage of two of these objects on one of the surfaces, such that the association exploits the complementary visual qualities of each item to produce a rich "unity of opposites" in the combination. If several of your colleagues participate, you will have a number of such compositions to compare. By discussing the associations, connotations, and integrity of each combination, you may acquire increasing insight and sensitivity.

This problem introduced you to the visual dynamics of "spatial forces" and the "virtual movements" of basic-pattern-area elements—both positive and negative—on a graphic surface. You can explore these issues further by experimenting with ways to place one 2″ x 3″ black rectangle on each of two 8½″ x 11″ sheets of white paper. You should try to discover where to place each rectangle so as to:

(a) achieve a static feeling in one case, and a dynamic feeling in the other;

(b) produce a sense of rising on one, and a feeling of falling on the other;

(c) result in a hovering feeling on one, and a rotating movement on the other;

(d) and so on, inventing your own objectives for virtual movement.

Then, using two or three 2″ x 3″ black rectangles on each 8½″ x 11″ white sheet,

(e) create an expanded versus a contracting feeling;

(f) and so on: invent your own goals for different opposing tendencies.

And, finally, consider Christopher Alexander's contrast of the natural with the man-made, which brings us back again to design:

"A natural object is formed directly by the forces which act upon it and arise within it. A man-made object is also formed by certain forces, but there are many other latent forces which have no opportunity to influence the form directly, with the result that the system in which the object plays a part may be unstable. The form can be made stable with respect to all these forces only by artificial means. The most usual artificial method is that known as 'design,' in which an individual designer tries to generate the form intuitively. But 'design' is only a particular way of doing this; there are other ways . . . ."

These other ways Alexander characterizes as the numerical, the analogue, and the relational. He comments that although the first two are in most common use, they are almost entirely unsuited to environmental design since they are too simple. For his discussion of this and of the relational method, see his "From a Set of Forces to a Form" in Gyorgy Kepes, ed., *The Man-Made Object* (New York: Braziller, 1966).

"Rikiu was watching his son Shoan as he swept and watered the garden path. 'Not clean enough!' said Rikiu, when Shoan had finished his task, and bade him try again. After a weary hour the son turned to Rikiu: 'Father, there is nothing more to be done. The steps have been washed for the third time, the stone lanterns and the trees are well-sprinkled with water, moss and lichens are shining with a fresh verdue: not a twig, not a leaf have I left on the ground.' 'Young fool,' chided the tea master, 'that is not the way a garden path should be swept.' Saying this, Rikiu stepped into the garden, shook a tree and scattered over the garden gold and crimson leaves, scraps of the brocade of autumn!"

—Kakuzo Okakura, *The Book of Tea* (New York: Duffield, 1925)

"A fact that never loses fascination for me is that there is not only a universe, but that there also are elements which are capable of observing this universe. That life with its intricate order and complex control mechanisms could ever evolve is due to the fact that this universe is a highly ordered affair and not a sequence of completely random events. Life can only exist in a cosmos—in the Greek sense of an ordered universe—and not in a chaos. It is quite clear that for anything to be anything, it has to remain unchanged for a while, it has to be an 'invariant.' It is not necessary that this refers to a shape, or a volume or a particular configuration; it may also refer to a chain of events that follow each other. In a complete chaos everything can happen. In a world with some order, not everything happens that could happen. From a purely logical point of view, there is nothing which would prevent this package of cigarettes I just took out of my pocket from pumping itself up into an elephant who slowly becomes airborne and flies out of this tent while singing the Marseillaise in a high pitched soprano. However, I venture to say that this does not happen; or—to be a bit more cautious—that the probability for this chain of events is 'vanishingly small.' The nice thing about our universe is that there are invariants as, for instance, this package of cigarettes which I can put back in my pocket again, or its predictable trajectory if I would toss it in a particular direction. Thus, order presents itself in the form of constraints on a system that is not free to do what it would do if it were not subjected to these constraints. It is, therefore, not an accident that we denote these regularities of our universe as the 'Laws of Nature'; and it is only due to their invariance that we are able to name them. Since 'naming' is clearly a form of representation, it emerges that in order for something to be representable it must have some order. In a chaos, nothing can be named. Hence, whatever is representable in my environment must have some intrinsic order. Reversing this statement: my environment is defined by the kind and the amount of order I can discover.

"Permit me to elaborate on this point, because if I succeed in showing that it is the kind of constraints that are determining the particular kind of emerging order, I shall have an easy task in showing that the corresponding process in the internal representation of the environmental order is neural inhibition. Let me first demonstrate by a simple example, what I mean by the emergence of order by adding constraints to an initially chaotic—or random—system. Consider for the moment a gambling situation in which a 'fair' die is repeatedly tossed. As you all know, the outcome of a particular toss is completely independent of the outcome of a previous toss. In other

Aleatory Form

In the preceding problem we investigated several aspects of the perception and generation of form, and produced some forms using aleatory processes. In the present problem we will continue our study of form, and again involve ourselves with the generation of form by chance, but this time all the factors that enter into the process will be made explicit.

Here you will have an opportunity to develop and specify a strictly logical series of operations, and to present it as an algorithm in the form of a flow chart. You will also consider the meanings and implications of such terms as constraint, determinancy, process, chance, order, chaos, and entropy, with reference to human values, ethics, urban form . . . and Mozart. Your drafting and lettering skills will be exercised along with your mind, and you will be asked to formulate a clear, unambiguous, specific, and comprehensive set of written specifications, as by a designer for a builder.

words, if face 4 has just come up and one picks up the die to toss it again, one is again completely uncertain about the next outcome, it can be 1, 2, 3, 4, 5, or 6, with equal probabilities. Let's consider for the moment an extraordinarily simple 'universe' that is represented by this die. There are just six states in this universe S_1, S_2, S_3, S_4, S_5, and S_6, namely the six faces of the die. The 'behavior' of this universe is described if we are able to state the probabilities for this universe to go from any one of its six possible states into any other one of these six possible states. A representation of this situation is most easily done in the form of a quadratic matrix as shown in Table I, which lists on the left hand side all the present possible states, on top all possible subsequent states, and inserts at the places where rows and columns cross the appropriate probability for the transitions of the corresponding states.

"In the particular case of our 'fair' die, this matrix will be filled everywhere with equal probabilities of 1/6, because—as we have seen before—all outcomes are equi-probable and independent of past outcomes. I now propose to get a bit more zing into this boring game by slightly manipulating this die. Let's drill a hole into the die, and fill it with a viscous goo into which we insert a heavy piece of metal. Of course, we do not forget to seal up the hole so that this die

looks like any other harmless die. However, its performance will be quite different from before. If we now allow the die to rest after each toss, the piece of metal will slowly sink and will load the die so it tends to fall on the same face. With this manipulating our previously unpredictable simple 'universe' has become more predictable, because, if, say face 4 has come up, we will be right in most cases if we predict that face 4 will come up. This situation can similarly be expressed in form of a transition probability matrix which may look as in Table II if we do not let the die rest too long between tosses.

"In comparing the two Tables I and II one easily sees that the distribution of probabilities has shifted from a uniform distribution for a 'free' system to a probability distribution where certain transitions are more probable than others. In other words, the system is no longer free to go into any possible states with equal chance, but has to yield certain constraints within its structure. This, I believe, will become quite apparent if we let our die sit and wait between tosses until the piece of metal has settled on the ground. Under these circumstances, the die will come up in subsequent tosses with overwhelming probability on one and the same side and all other state transitions will be 'vanishingly small.'

Present State	Subsequent State					
	S_1	S_2	S_3	S_4	S_5	S_6
S_1	1/6	1/6	1/6	1/6	1/6	1/6
S_2	1/6	1/6	1/6	1/6	1/6	1/6
S_3	1/6	1/6	1/6	1/6	1/6	1/6
S_4	1/6	1/6	1/6	1/6	1/6	1/6
S_5	1/6	1/6	1/6	1/6	1/6	1/6
S_6	1/6	1/6	1/6	1/6	1/6	1/6

TABLE I. Transition probability matrix for a completely undetermined (free) system (unloaded die)

Present State	Subsequent State					
	S_1	S_2	S_3	S_4	S_5	S_6
S_1	1/4	1/6	1/6	1/6	1/6	1/12
S_2	1/6	1/4	1/6	1/6	1/12	1/6
S_3	1/6	1/6	1/4	1/12	1/6	1/6
S_4	1/6	1/6	1/12	1/4	1/6	1/6
S_5	1/6	1/12	1/6	1/6	1/4	1/6
S_6	1/12	1/6	1/6	1/6	1/6	1/4

TABLE II. Transition probability matrix for a partially determined (constraint) system (loaded die)

Present	Subsequent State					
State	S_1	S_2	S_3	S_4	S_5	S_6
S_1	1	0	0	0	0	0
S_2	0	1	0	0	0	0
S_3	0	0	1	0	0	0
S_4	0	0	0	1	0	0
S_5	0	0	0	0	1	0
S_6	0	0	0	0	0	1

TABLE III. Transition probability matrix for a completely determined system (Law of Nature)

"The corresponding matrix is shown in Table III, which now contains probabilities being either zero or unity depending upon the state transitions being impossible or being certain.

"In this case the constraints in our simple universe are so strong that it is impossible for the system to do anything else but to 'obey the laws of nature' which are intrinsic in the structure of this system.

"I realize that I may have used an oversimplified example to demonstrate the difficult concepts of determinacy and in-

FIGURE 1. Snow crystals. Photo courtesy of the National Oceanic and Atmospheric Administration

determinacy. Nevertheless I hope that the methods of describing these situations have become palatable. My excuse for elaborating on these ideas, perhaps unduly, is that in my next step I would like to show that small constraints on an otherwise random system represent themselves in the form of remarkably developed structures. This I shall do with the aid of three examples. Two of these are taken from Nature with the constraints fixed; the third example is an artificial system in which the experimenter is in a position to manipulate the transition probabilities.

"Figure 1 shows a collection of twelve patterns all displaying a beautiful hexagonal symmetry. Of course, you recognize these stars immediately as snow crystals. Why is this recognition carried out so quickly on such a relatively large set of different objects? The reason is that the growth mechanism of these snow crystals is subjected to a major constraint, and it is this constraint which is 'sized up' immediately. The growth mechanism of snow crystal is determined by the triangular shape of the water molecule, having two small hydrogen atoms attached to the big oxygen atom in angles which are close to either 30° or 60°. This, on the other hand, accounts for a certain 'freedom' in attaching themselves to each other, which in turn allows for the large variability within this constraint which we recognize as a unifying principle in the construction of these shapes.

We have a name for this constraint; we call it 'snow-crystal.' However, this microscopic constraint would not become apparent to us if it were not applied over and over again. Since such a snow flake contains approximately a billion billion H_2O molecules, this constraint has been in operation in exactly the same number of times.

"My second example from Nature refers to a case where she anxiously has to guard against even the slightest variations occurring. I am referring to the 'genes,' those macromolecules which govern the stability of the hereditary traits from generation to generation. It is their particular molecular configuration which determines the building program of the organism in its macroscopic appearance. But a program is nothing else but a set of commands: do this; do that . . . which in other words means: don't do this; don't do that . . . . Again we have words for the various sets of these invariable constraints as, for instance, 'elephant,' 'mouse,' 'hippopotamus,' etc. We may even recognize the fine-structure of these constraints by referring to certain family traits: 'Oh, he is a typical Jones.'

"In these two examples you may argue that the constraints I am talking about are rather strong, because they are produced by the strong electrostatic forces which bind the atoms together to form the various molecules. Hence one

should not be too surprised if this results in a variety of remarkable structures. However, one should not forget that all these molecular configurations are subjected to a strong random thermal agitation which tends to destroy all order and symmetry. Let me show now in a final example the emergence of structure in a system where we have the transition probabilites from state to state, so to say, at our fingertips, because it is only necessary to turn a knob which will automatically regulate these probabilities.

"In Figure 2a you see the first 23 steps of a luminous spot produced by an electron beam on a television screen: The motion of this spot upwards or downwards, and from left to right, or from right to left, is 'determined' by a fast electronic 'coin tosser' which makes about twenty thousand random decisions in one second. Clearly there are only four states, namely a unit step into any one of the four directions. The transition probability matrix for these states looks exactly like that in Table I, with, of course, only 4 x 4 entries, all filled with a probability of 1/4. We now apply to our electronic coin tosser the constraint that it should become slightly 'loaded' in the sense that it should (a) give slightly higher probabilities to switching the spot into another direction by reducing its probability to continue its movement in either the horizontal or the vertical direction, and (b) give slightly higher probabilities for

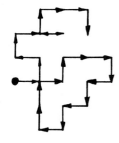

FIGURE 2a

FIGURE 2b

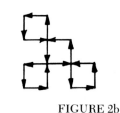

FIGURE 2c

FIGURE 2d

switching the spot in a clockwise direction. In Figure 2b you see the result of the first 200 steps of this spot after the uniform probability distribution has been shifted only a few percent in the desired direction. Since this pattern shows only 16 steps, it is clear that the spot must have run several times through this configuration. In other words, such a pattern shows a certain amount of stability produced by the constraints inherent in the motion of this spot. Another feature may be noteworthy, and that is that adjacent squares are being circumnavigated in opposite directions as indicated by the arrows pointing in the direction of motion.

"A highly sophisticated configuration is shown in Figure 2c which presents the results of the first 200,000 steps of the motion of four spots each of which has the same constraints as our spot before, with the additional constraint that they all interact weakly with each other in the sense that they 'repel' each other when they come too close (the transition probability for turning away from each other is slightly increased when near), and that they 'attract' each other when they go too far (the transition probability for turning toward each other is increased when apart). Clockwise circumnavigated squares are painted black. Since there are only 256 steps visible in this pattern, it is clear that some of the steps must have been repeated several thousand times. Hence, this pattern has reasonable stability.

"A student of this structure, who does not know how it is created, will come to the conclusion that this 'molecule' is built of two kinds of 'atoms,' one black (+) and one white (−), with shapes as suggested in Figure 2d, which obey a law of nature that forces them to bind into higher structures such that opposite signs attract. We may smile at the naiveté of this natural scientist who discovers these 'laws,' because we know that this whole pattern is generated by only four spots zooming around like mad in an almost random fashion. However, we should not forget that the accent lies on the *almost*. That is the crux of my thesis: Small constraints are sufficient to produce considerably ordered structures. Hence, the discoveries of our natural scientist are not so naive after all; he only put his knowledge into a different language. The two descriptions are equivalent . . . .

". . . we have just attempted to show that order, not chaos, is that which can be communicated; and order is the result of constraints."

—Heinz Von Foerster, excerpted from "Logical Structure of Environment and Its Internal Representation," in R. E. Eckerstrom, ed., *International Design Conference 1962* (Zeeland, Michigan: Herman Miller, 1963)

Materials

1 15″ x 20″ white illustration board in horizontal format

1 10″ x 15″ white illustration board in vertical format

Rubber cement

Pair of dice

Drafting gear

Colored construction paper: of two different colors which you particularly dislike, in sufficient amount to provide about twenty 2″ x 2″ right triangles in each color.

Procedure

Grid the 15″ x 20″ board in 2″ squares lightly in pencil with a 1″ margin at the bottom. You are then to invent a system whereby for *each* of the seventy resulting squares on the board, *each* decision in the following sequence is *separately* determined only by rolling the dice:

1. Which square is at issue?

2. Is a triangle to be cemented in it? (Note that only one triangle may go in a square.)

3. If so, which color triangle shall be used?

4. If so, which of the four possible orientations shall the triangle take in the square? (Note that the hypotenuse of the triangle is to coincide with one of the diagonals of the square.)

For practical reasons you should put a time limitation on the operation of your system, since it may require an unreasonably long time to consider all seventy squares. But in any case a minimum of twenty-five triangles should end up cemented on the board.

Your system should be described as an algorithm in the form of a flow chart, drawn on the 10″ x 15″ board. An algorithm is a set of instructions for a sequence of operations which leads to the solution of all problems of a particular type. (The name comes from al-Khowarizma, who was a ninth century Uzbek mathematician.) We use the word here in the sense of a recipe, or formula, in which the procedures for the use of certain ingredients are specified as a means to produce a given *type* of result.

See D. E. Knuth, "Algorithms," *Scientific American,* April 1977; H. R. Lewis and G. H. Papadimitiou, "The Efficiency of Algorithms," *Scientific American,* January 1978; and Thomas F. Heath, "The Algorithmic Nature of the Design Process," in Gary T. Moore, ed., *Emerging Methods in Environmental Design and Planning* (Cambridge, Mass.: MIT Press, 1970).

A flow chart (also called a "logical tree" or a "directed graph") is a graphic means for specifying a sequence of operations, expressed in terms of simple instructions and questions, ordered in a logical hierarchy from the most general to the most specific, and related in a network of contingent decisions. You have already become familiar with one example of a flow chart: the description of the design process. A more complex example is presented in the accompanying figure.

This facetious algorithm for maximizing your intake of free beer illustrates some flow-chart conventions. Please note them and follow them faithfully!

Operations are shown in rectangles, with only *one* command per box.

Decisions are shown in diamonds, in terms of a single question answerable by either a YES or NO.

Arrows indicate the one-way sequence of flow, and the lines are not to cross each other.

The **circle** shows the termination of the whole process.

You will probably have to make a number of trial layouts of your flow chart, using tracing paper, to achieve a clear and simple overall arrangement. The quality of your drafting and lettering, as always, is important.

Your flow chart should be prefaced (on the same board) with a concise and complete set of lettered specifications for the grid, triangles, dice, and cement. These definitions of *materials and equipment*, together with the flow chart itself, which defines the complete *operating process*, constitute a comprehensive specification of the form-generating system. If this sheet were to be mailed to a stranger (in the antipodes, let us say), that person should be able to follow the procedure *without making a single procedural decision on his or her own*, and without having to write or telephone you for any further instructions, or clarifications.

After you have developed a system and carefully checked your algorithmic description of it, we will give your flow chart (as laid out on the 10″ x 15″ board) to someone else (as "builder") who will use it to produce a pattern on his or her board with his or her colors. This will provide a test of the clearness, coherence, and workability of your algorithm, as communicated in the form of your flow chart. If any problems arise with your "contract" plans and specifications, the "builder" will return them to you (as the abashed "designer") for corrections and/or revisions. Make sure this will not happen! When you are finished with the algorithm you received, letter DESIGNER on the bottom of the board, followed by the name of the author of the algorithm; and BUILDER, followed by your name.

This flow chart was designed by British architectural students (source unknown).

How about getting your roommate or a sibling to test it for you? If they can follow the procedure easily without encountering any ambiguities, you are probably in good shape.

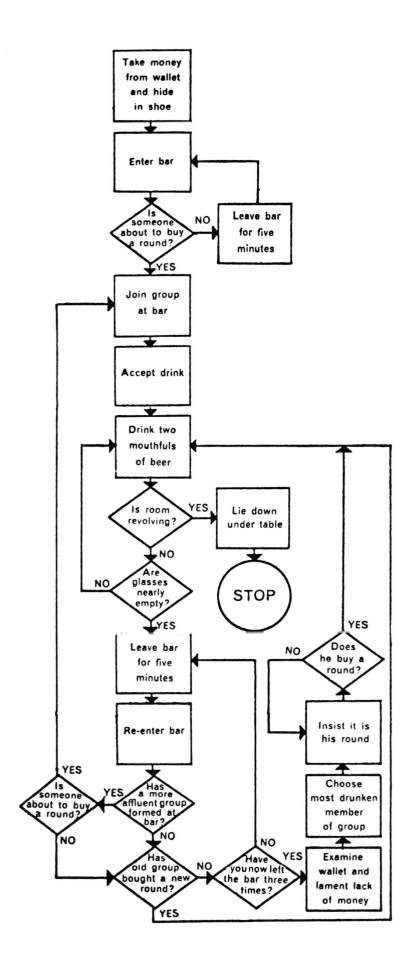

114

Discussion

How do you feel now about the two colors you picked for this problem? Quite possibly after using them under these conditions, these two colors you particularly disliked may not seem as repugnant to you. Or perhaps not. But what brings one to have such feelings about colors—is it inherent in the colors themselves? Do you think others share your feelings about the colors you chose? If not, does this have implications about your professional attitudes to color?

Consider the work of the painter Ellsworth Kelly shown in the adjacent reproduction. This is based on a grid of forty-one rows and eighty-two columns, which was filled by drawing forty-one numbered slips of paper from a box in the following process: no slips were drawn for the first column; one slip was drawn for the second, and the number of the square indicated on this slip was then painted in. Then two slips were drawn for the third column and the two squares thus indicated painted in; and so on, up to the center, where the process was reversed.

For further examples of Kelly's work, see E. C. Goossen, *Ellsworth Kelly* (New York: Museum of Modern Art, 1973).

At this point can you invent any variations on this problem that you might like to explore on your own? What about using a pattern arrangement other than a grid, or form elements other than a triangle; and additional attributes such as texture and/or surface variations? What about working in *three* dimensions, as with blocks of wood, uniform in cross-section (a nominal 1″ x 2″) but of six different graded lengths, to be assembled as a bas-relief panel or full sculpture according to the laws of chance as determined by the roll of dice?

How could you explicitly involve the time factor in such a process of form generation? What about working with photograms, and making incremental changes in the position of the shadow-objects on the light-sensitive paper, over successive exposures; or, alternately incrementally varying the position or directon of the light source?

But what do all these studies illuminate? Is there a larger significance in this investigation of the time-based generation of form by the action of chance within systematic constraints? Both Waddington (quoted in the previous problem) and Von Foerster (quoted in the present problem) have commented on the role of chance and constraint in the genesis of organic form. Long ago the Greek philosopher Democritus said, "All that exists in the universe is the fruit of chance and necessity." Recently Jacques Monod, a molecular biologist awarded the Noble prize for his work in genetics, has returned to this theme with the existentialist argument that the human mind has no choice but to accept the fact—and the ethical implications that follow—that the cosmos is based on chance alone.

Ellsworth Kelly (1923-), *Seine* (1951), oil on wood, 16½″ x 45 ¼″. Courtesy of the artist

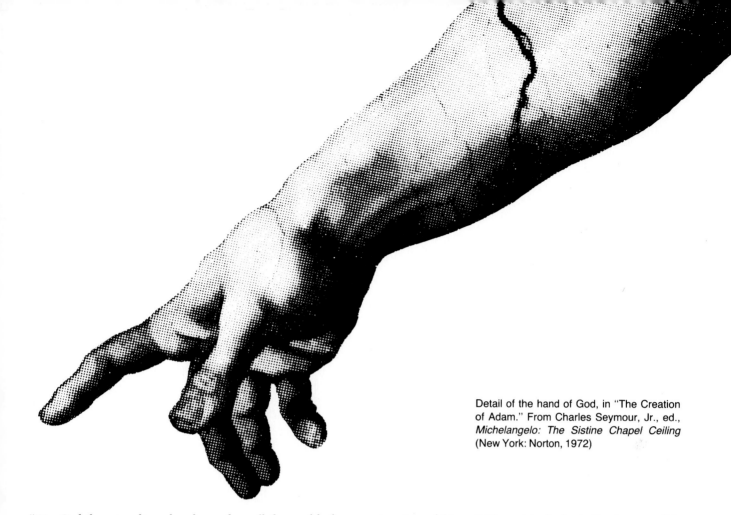

Detail of the hand of God, in "The Creation of Adam." From Charles Seymour, Jr., ed., *Michelangelo: The Sistine Chapel Ceiling* (New York: Norton, 1972)

"Was God throwing dice when he made the universe?

" 'Yes indeed!' says Jacques Monod. 'Yes indeed!'

"Mr. Monod, who is to become the head of the Pasteur Institute next month, has undertaken a task perhaps more ambitious than the genetic studies for which he shared a Nobel Prize in medicine in 1965. That task, as he said in an interview the other day, is to sweep the slate clean of virtually all previous philosophies of life.

"He has begun the job in a book titled 'Le Hazard et La Nécessité,' or 'Chance and Necessity,' which to general astonishment has become the smash hit of the publishing season here, with 155,000 copies already in print and translations on the way.

"Recent discoveries about basic organic matter demonstrate, Mr. Monod holds, that all forms of life are the product of pure chance—through unpredictable mutation—and of necessity, or Darwinian selection. These discoveries make it impossible, he says, to accept any system, religious or materialist, that assumes a master plan of creation.

" 'Armed with all the powers, enjoying all the wealth they owe to science,' Mr. Monod writes, 'our societies are still trying to practice and to teach systems of values already destroyed at the roots by that very science.

" 'Man knows at last that he is alone in the indifferent immensity of the universe, whence he has emerged by chance. His duty, like his fate, is written nowhere. It is for him to choose between the kingdom and the darkness.'

"Mr. Monod shared his Nobel Prize with two other French scientists for discoveries concerning the way genes control enzyme and virus synthesis to produce the forms and functions of all living things.

"Mr. Monod talked about more recent work in the crowded, old-fashioned study of his apartment in the Seventh Arrondissement, the most traditional section of Paris. A slender man, his brushed-back hair barely graying despite his 61 years, he spoke mostly in a fluent and only slightly accented English. His mother was an American.

" 'What I have tried to show,' he said, 'is that the scientific attitude implies what I call the postulate of objectivity—that is to say, the fundamental postulate that there is no plan, that there is no intention in the universe.

" 'Now this is basically incompatible with virtually all the religious or metaphysical systems whatever, all of which try to show that there is some sort of harmony between man and the universe and that man is a product—predictable if not indispensable—of the evolution of the universe.

" 'Of course, naive faiths, fundamentalist beliefs in the Bible do just that. They put man in the center of the universe and believe that for some reason there is a necessity everywhere under God's command.

" 'In more elaborate modern versions of Christianity you find speculations like those of Teilhard de Chardin, which give an evolutionist interpretation of the universe in which man is a sort of achievement which had been predicted from the beginning. It is again an interpretation which denies the principle of objectivity.'

"He referred to the late French Jesuit and paleontologist, Pierre Teilhard de Chardin.

" 'In Marxism,' Mr. Monod said, 'it is a little bit more subtle to find this same attitude. But it is right there, though, in the belief of the laws of history, which are bound to lead to the sort of nirvana which is the classless society.'

"Mr. Monod, himself a former Marxist, places Marx and especially Engels among the animists, whose earliest forerunner was primitive man with his conviction that every object had vitality, or a soul.

" 'It would be wrong to smile,' he writes. 'Animism established a profound alliance between nature and man, beyond which there seems to extend only a frightful solitude. The history of ideas since the 17th century shows the efforts spent by the greatest minds to avoid the rupture, to forge anew the ring of the "ancient alliance." '

" 'One of the great problems of philosophy,' he went on, 'is the relationship between the realm of knowledge and the realm of values. Knowledge is what is, values are what ought to be. I would say that all traditional philosophies, up to and including Marxism, have tried to derive the "ought" from the "is."

" 'Now my point of view is that this is impossible, this is a farce. You cannot derive any sort of "ought" from the "is." If it is true that there is no intention in the universe and if it is true that man as any other animal species is a pure accident in evolution, it might just as well not have appeared.

" 'If this is so, then we cannot derive any "ought" from the "is," and our system of values is free for us to choose. In fact, we must choose a system of values. We cannot live without it: We cannot live personally, we cannot deal with society.'

"The need for such a system of values—what he has described as a humanist socialism—is desperate, Mr. Monod said.

" 'There is absolutely no doubt that the risk of the race committing suicide is very great,' he declared.

" 'In my opinion,' he said, 'the future of mankind is going to be decided within the next two generations, and there are two absolute requisites: We must aim at a stable-state society and the destruction of nuclear stockpiles.'

"A stable-state society, he explained, would be one with a very limited growth in population and even, perhaps, in technology. To achieve it, he said, will call for 'some form of world authority.'

" 'Otherwise,' he continued, 'I don't see how we can survive much later than 2050.'

"Mr. Monod acknowledged that the outlook could lead to profound pessimism, as expressed by such disparate writers as Arthur Koestler and Claude Levi-Strauss, and expressed distress that his own book had been interpreted by some as contributing to despair.

" 'We have no right to have no hope,' he said with a small smile, 'because if we have no hope, there is no hope. The basic ethics for the modern man conscious of what humanity is running into is to firmly stick to the will of doing something about it and therefore the belief that something can be done about it.'

"Mr. Monod said he drew his own system of values from the existentialist ethics of his friend the late Albert Camus—'an ethics based on a free choice.' He said the key to his book lay in the quotation from Camus on the dedication page. Describing the mythical struggle of Sisyphus to push the stone to the mountaintop, only to have it roll to the bottom in a mystery no longer to be ascribed to the punishment of the gods, Camus writes:

" 'This universe, from now on without a master, seems to him neither sterile nor futile. The struggle toward the summits itself is enough to fill the heart of man.' "

—John C. Hess, *New York Times*, 15 March 1971

"Necessity" refers to the "laws," or regularities, we find in the structure of nature. Chief among these is the second law of thermodynamics, involving the concept of entropy. As a measure of "disorder," entropy is important to such sciences as physics, chemistry, and biochemistry, but is also a significant concept in evolution, information theory, and art. Here are some comments by Leonard Cancler on "The Effect of the Application of Entropy on Your Life" (*Northwest Professional Engineer,* Summer/Fall, 1968):

"Entropy, among other things, is a measure of the equalization of temperature throughout a system. If the temperature is constant throughout a system, the entropy is greatest in it, and none of the heat is available for work.

"In classical thermodynamics, entropy was expressed in terms of the heat and the temperature of the system. With the advent of the kinetic theory of matter, an entirely new approach to thermodynamics was developed. Temperature and heat are now pictured in terms of the kinetic energy of the molecules comprising this system and entropy becomes a measure of the probability that the speed of the molecules and other variables of the system are distributed in a certain way. Entropy of the system is greatest when its temperature is constant throughout because this distribution of temperature is the most probable. Increase of entropy was thus interpreted as a passage of a system from less probable to more probable states.

"There is a similar process when we shuffle a deck of cards. If we start with an orderly arrangement, say the cards of each suit following each other according to their values, the shuffle will tend to make the arrangement disorderly. But if we start with a disorderly arrangement, it is very unlikely that through the shuffle the cards will become an orderly one. This is true because there are many more disorderly arrangements, and so the disorderly state of a deck of cards is more probable.

"Thus the 'amount of order' is connected with the probabilistic concept and through them with entropy (the less order, the more entropy). But it is also connected with the 'amount of information.' For example, far less information is required to describe an orderly arrangement of cards than a disorderly one. If I say, 'Starting with aces, deuces, etc. to king, hearts, diamonds, clubs, spades,' I have determined the position of every card in the deck; but to describe an arbitrarily random arrangement, I would have to specify every one of the fifty-two cards.

"It is through these notions of probability, order and disorder that entropy is related to information. The formal equivalence of mathematical expressions indicates that both concepts describe similarly structural events.

"Both entropy and information can be defined in terms of the same kinds of variables, namely, probabilities of events. Now entropy plays an important part in chemistry and biochemistry. For example, the knowledge of entropy of two states of a system indicates whether the system can pass from one state to the other spontaneously, whether a certain chemical reaction can take place without outside interference. An interesting thing about chemical reactions in the living organisms is that many of them do not ordinarily take place without interference. Such are, for example, the synthesis of complicated proteins from amino acids by animals (in these reactions the ordinary processes of oxidation of sugars and decomposition of proteins are reversed). Therefore, there must be interference. No evidence of any phenomenon violating known physical laws has ever been observed in any living organism. True, uphill reactions seen to contradict the law of thermodynamics which demands the continuous increase in entropy, but there is nothing in the law that says that it cannot be circumvented locally. In other words, what living things seem to do is create little 'islands of order' in themselves at the expense of increased disorder elsewhere. This is the meaning of Schroedinger's famous rule that 'life feeds on negative entropy.'

"Life, therefore, depends essentially upon an ordering process and upon fighting off the trend toward chaos which is always present in the non-living world. But to increase the order of anything means to make it describable with less information (less effort). Is not this process the very essence of knowledge, or science itself? Or of any behavior where complex skills are involved? When a chess genius plays a dozen games from memory or when a musician masters the complexity of a musical creation or when a scientist weaves a mass of seemingly unrelated data into a meaningful theory, they are all contributing to the process of decreasing 'entropy' of a portion of the world by making it more comprehensible with less effort.

"Organisms, geneticists tell us, evolve by suffering random genetic varieties which in the process of many generations are selected for their survival value. If these variations were independent of each other, nothing would ever come of evolution. God alone knows how many mutations it took to enable our ancestors to speak and to make them want to speak. Mutations, however, are not accumulated independently. Rather mutations may arrest, and be held in abeyance so that in the process of accumulation, gaps arise which later fill in by the process successive mutation.

"Thus evolution itself is an ordering process. Gross changes of structure and of behavior are made possible because structure and behavior patterns are always being organized into assemblies. A measure of a structure or of the amount of organization is required. The more disordered a portion of the world is, the more information is required to describe it completely. The process of obtaining knowledge is quantitatively equated to the process of ordering portions of the world. Usually the more complex an organism is, the more ordered it is, and the less entropy it contains . . . ."

For an extended discussion of the relationship of entropy to the perception of order and disorder, see Rudolf Arnheim, *Entropy and Art* (Berkeley: University of California Press, 1971).

"A city, as I see it, is *process*. Not *a* process leading to some result, but a constant series of motions, actions and events. It is *process in itself*. This distinction is important. The city is in constant flux, always going but never arriving. It is process, everchanging and limitless. This process, the city, is a combination of forces. The question is, then, what forms do these forces have. We wish to find their forms. And beyond that we wish to find the structure of their relationships. Our problem is to represent the forces which create the city. The total form of the city is the structure of these forces in process; *the total form is a structured process*."

—J. Reichek, "On the Design of Cities," *Journal of the American Institute of Planners*, vol. 27, no. 2 (May 1961)

Lewis Mumford, *The Culture of Cities* (New York: Harcourt, Brace, and World, 1938). For a whole book of dice games simulating the process of human settlement from the prehistoric to the present, see Forrest Wilson, *City Planning* (New York: Van Nostrand Reinhold, 1975). See also Martin Gardner, "The arts as combinatorial mathematics, or how to compose like Mozart with dice," in the "Mathematical Games" section of *Scientific American,* December 1974; and "White, and brown music, fractal curves, and one-over-f fluctuations" in the same section of the April 1978 issue of *Scientific American.* The latter serves as a good introduction to Benoit B. Mandelbrot's rather recondite book on *Fractiles: Form, Chance, and Dimension* (San Francisco; W. H. Freeman, 1977). For an alternate discussion of the rules underlying the development of some natural forms, see Peter Stevens, *Patterns in Nature* (Boston: Little, Brown, 1974), and Theodore Schwenk, *Sensitive Chaos* (New York: Schocken, 1976).

Our dice-rolling exercise is technically known as a stochastic process, in which a sequence of probabilistic operations produce a series of unpredictable individual events but a predictable overall character. Natural examples of stochastic processes are patterns of falling rain and leaves; the motion of groups of insects, birds, and fish; and the random movements of smoke particles in the air.

Let us now consider the city as another example of a form generated by such process. In this case there are both natural and human constraints: the natural constraints include such givens as topography, geology, vegetation, and climate, while the human constraints include social conventions in land platting and street patterns, fire and building codes, the technology of materials and construction systems, the economic climate, and cultural factors determining land use and zoning. Within these constraints occur the randomized actions of many different individuals and groups over long periods of time in constructing, operating, and destroying the subelements—the buildings and structures—which manifest the "process form" we call the city. This is why Lewis Mumford can write that "the city is a fact in nature, like a cave, a run of mackerel, or an antheap."

Aerial photograph of part of Berkeley, California. Courtesy of Towill, Inc.

Do Americans have a special affinity for "process"? Consider John Kouwenhoven, who lists the following items:

1. The Manhattan skyline
2. The gridiron town plan
3. The skyscraper
4. The Model-T Ford
5. Jazz
6. The Constitution
7. Mark Twain's writing
8. Whitman's *Leaves of Grass*
9. Comic strips
10. Soap operas
11. Assembly line production
12. Chewing gum

and then comments:

"Here we have a round dozen artifacts which are, it seems to me, recognizably American, not likely to have been produced elsewhere. Granted that some of us take more pleasure in some of them than in others—that many people prefer soap opera to *Leaves of Grass* while others think Mark Twain's storytelling is less offensive than chewing gum—all twelve items are, I believe, widely held to be indigenous to our culture. The fact that many people in other lands like them too, and that some of them are nearly as acceptable overseas as they are here at home, does not in any way detract from their obviously American character. It merely serves to remind us that to be American does not mean to be inhuman—a fact which, in certain moods of self-criticism, we are inclined to forget.

"What, then, is the 'American' quality which these dozen items share? And what can that quality tell us about the character of our culture, about the nature of our civilization? . . .

"Here, I think, we are approaching the central quality which all the diverse items on our list have in common. That quality I would define as a concern with process rather than product—or, to reuse Mark Twain's words—a concern with the manner of handling experience or materials themselves. Emerson, a century ago, was fascinated by the way 'becoming somewhat else is the perpetual game of nature.' The universe, he said, 'exists only in transit,' and man is great 'not in his goals but in his transitions.'

"This preoccupation with process is, of course, basic to modern science. 'Matter' itself is no longer to be thought of as something fixed, but fluid and ever-changing. The modern sciences, as Veblen observed forty years ago, cluster about the 'notion of process,' the notion of 'a sequence, or complex, of consecutive change.' Similarly, modern economic theory has abandoned the 'static equilibrium' analysis of the neo-classic economists, and in philosophy John Dewey's instrumentalism abandoned the classic philosophical interest in final causes for a scientific interest in the 'mechanism of occurrences'—that is, process . . . .

"Change, or the process of consecutive occurrences, is, we tend to feel, a bewildering and confusing and lonely thing. All of us, in some moods, feel the 'preference for the stable over the precarious and uncompleted' which, as John Dewey recognized, tempts philosophers to posit their absolutes. We talk fondly of the need for roots—as if man were a vegetable, not an animal with legs whose distinction it is that he can move and 'get on with it.' We would do well to make ourselves more familiar with the idea that the process of development is universal, that it is 'the form and order of nature' . . . .

"As an 'organic system' man cannot, of course, expect to achieve stability or permanent harmony, though he can create (and in the great arts of the past, has created) the illusion of them. What he can achieve is a continuing development in response to his environment. The factor which gives vitality to all the component processes in the individual and in society is 'not permanence but development.'

"To say this is not to deny the past. It is simply to recognize that for a variety of reasons people living in America have, on the whole, been better able to relish process than those who have lived under the imposing shadow of the arts and institutions which Western man created in his tragic search for permanence and perfection—for a 'closed system.' They find it easy to understand what that very American philosopher William James meant when he told his sister that his house in Chocorua, New Hampshire, was 'the most delightful house you ever saw; it has fourteen doors, all opening outwards.' They are used to living in grid-patterned cities and towns whose streets, as Jean-Paul Sartre observed, are not, like those of European cities, 'closed at both ends.' As Sartre says in his essay on New York, the long straight streets and avenues of a gridiron city do not permit the buildings to 'cluster like sheep' and protect one against the sense of space. 'They are not sober little walks closed in between houses, but national highways. The moment you set foot on one of them, you understand that it has to go on to Boston or Chicago.'

"So, too, the past of those who live in the United States, like their future, is open-ended. It does not, like the past of most other people, extend downward into the soil out of which their immediate community or neighborhood has grown. It extends laterally backward across the plains, the mountains, or the sea to somewhere else, just as their future may at any moment lead them down the open road, the endless-vistaed street.

"Our history is the process of motion into and out of cities; of westering and the counter-process of return; of motion up and down the social ladder—a long, complex, and sometimes terrifying rapid sequence of consecutive change. And it is this sequence, and the attitudes and habits and forms which it has bred, to which the term 'American' really refers.

"'America' is not a synonym for the United States. It is not an artifact. It is not a fixed and immutable ideal toward which citizens of this nation strive. It has not order or proportion, but neither is it chaos except as that is chaotic whose components no single mind can comprehend or control. America is process. And in so far as Americans have been 'American'—as distinguished from being (as most of us, in at least some of our activities, have been) mere carriers of transplanted cultural traditions—the concern with process has been reflected in the work of their heads and hearts and minds."

—John Kouwenhoven, "What's 'American' about America," in *The Beer Can by the Highway* (Garden City, N.Y.: Doubleday, 1961)

Someone not knowing the provenance of your recent work on the 15″ x 20″ board might apply the word "chaotic" to the patterns he or she sees there, but you yourself would probably not be inclined to the same usage, because you are aware of the generating process. A dictionary defines "chaos" as "utter disorder and confusion," and there are many who would use this term in describing some of our contemporary cities. It may be, however, that this use of this term tells us more about the user than that to which the user refers. One who calls the city chaotic is probably indicating that either he or she is not aware of this process or does not like the result. The confusion is not in the *form,* but in the mind of the viewer. When we first arrive at a strange city, we are likely to be confused, but as we become more familiar with it over time the confusion lessens. During this interval the city has not changed—we have changed.

It is true, of course, that urban configurations differ in the degree of difficulty they present the users, who need to comprehend the pattern so that they may orient themselves in it to operate effectively. This is one of the many considerations that have at various times concerned city planners and urban designers; others include the requirements of defense, the modeling of cosmological images, the expression of temporal and spiritual power and wealth, the maximization of commercial advantage, the implementation of social principles, and the manifestation of aesthetic theories.

But, as Bernard Rudofsky reminds us, the environments resulting from the single-minded professional exercise of these concerns are historically fewer in number than those resulting from a more "organic" process of incremental construction by anonymous artisans, over generations of communal activity, and often are less livable.

A seminal study on this subject is Kevin Lynch, *The Image of the City* (Cambridge, Mass.: MIT Press and Harvard University Press, 1960). For examples of cities planned in accordance with these several objectives, see Paul D. Spreiregen, *The Architecture of Towns and Cities* (New York: McGraw-Hill, 1965).

See Bernard Rudofsky, *Architecture without Architects* (Garden City, N.Y.: Doubleday, 1964); *The Prodigious Builders* (New York: Harcourt Brace Jovanovich, 1977); and *Streets for People* (Garden City, N.Y.: Doubleday, 1969).

Also pertinent here are Christopher Alexander, "The City is not a Tree," *Design,* no. 206 (February 1966), and *The City as a Mechanism for Sustaining Human Contact* (Berkeley: Center for Planning and Development Research, University of California, 1966). See also Colin Rowe and Fred Koetter, *Collage City* (Cambridge, Mass.: MIT Press, 1978).

"We who have been initiated into the mystic rites of design look at our cities and cry 'chaos.' Of course we except those portions of the city which we have designed. And about those, others cry 'murder.' We claim that our cities have no order—no structure. I say that this is not so. Our cities do have an order. That which is without order cannot be thought of or objectively seen. Where there is no order, perception and cognition are not possible. When we cry 'no order' we are in fact saying that we don't know what the order is. Or if we know the order—which we almost never do and never admit to the fact that we don't—what we are then saying is that it doesn't please us. That we simply don't like it. In response to that kind of statement, I can say that *I* liked it. And where does that leave us? Whose father can beat whose father? The order of cities—any city, even Los Angeles—is open to rational understanding by the minds of men. I would suggest that the architect, urban designer and planner are seeking the lost paradise, the unity and order to simplicity, comprehensible at a glance, easily identifiable, and thus an easy way to one's own identity; having not the ambiguity of life, but the specificity of death."

—J. Reichek, "Questions Concerning Urban Design Principles," *Journal of American Institute of Architects*, December 1962

"The theorists point out that there are sound sociological, technical and practical explanations for the look of today's world, like it or not. We are asked to examine the mess again. They claim that we can deal with the chaotic environment in constructive and even creative ways by admitting its conflicts, analyzing its components and recognizing the purposes they serve and the contributions they make to our way of life.

"Is chaos really so chaotic, they ask? Does it not contain valuable elements of vitality and variety, complexity and contrast? Can we not learn from the organically evolving environment? What about planning by adaptive processes? Is there an esthetic of the Pop landscape? From this point on, you may have your choice of embracing chaos on any step of the scale from an instructive demonstration of contemporary realities to great art form, depending on the length of your hair.

"Chaos may even contain an order of its own, we are told. It is an order of 'inclusion' and 'the difficult whole' rather than an order of 'exclusion,' or 'rejection,' which has been the teaching and operation of modern architecture to date. It offers a pluralistic esthetic of 'both and' rather than the selective 'either or' decisions enforced by orthodox architectural theory. This is a far more complex approach to the environment than we have been taught to take.

"Rejection or exclusion has been a basic tenet of the modern movement. Its pioneers preached against the chaos of the contemporary environment with the same breath in which they called for a new architecture. If they could not eliminate the setting, they turned their backs on it. They were fighting for release from an accretion of smothering, pseudo-arty Victorian clutter and to them slob city and the landscape of the superhighway were just updated versions of the old enemy. It has now become terribly clear that they rejected too much. There are lessons of sterility wherever their reductive principles have been scrupulously carried out. That prescription for order didn't work. The present search for order calls for acceptance of the irreconcilables of our complex existences, new values and a new vision."

—Ada Louise Huxtable, "The Case for Chaos," in *Will They Ever Finish Bruckner Boulevard?* (New York: Macmillan, 1971)

See also Robert Venturi, Denise Scott Brown, and Steven Izenour, *Learning From Las Vegas* (Cambridge, Mass.: MIT Press, 1972).

122

Fumihiko Maki, *Investigations in Collective Form* (St. Louis, Mo.: Washington University School of Architecture, 1964), or Fumihiko Maki and Masato Ohtaka, "Some Thoughts on Collective Form," in Gyorgy Kepes, ed., *Structure in Art and Science* (New York: George Braziller, 1965).

Reyner Banham, *Megastructure: Urban Futures of the Recent Past* (New York: Harper & Row, 1977). See also N. Habraken, *Supports: An Alternative to Mass Housing* (New York: Praeger, 1972); and *Variations: The Systematic Design of Supports* (Cambridge, Mass.: Laboratory of Architecture and Planning at MIT, 1976).

For illustrations see, respectively, Camillo Sitte, *The Art of Building Cities* (New York: Reinhold, 1945); Constantine E. Michaelides, *Hydra: A Greek Island Town* (Chicago: University of Chicago Press, 1967); and Hassan Fathy, *Architecture for the Poor* (Chicago: University of Chicago Press, 1973).

Kevin Lynch discusses the resulting urban patterns in terms of size, density, grain, outline, and pattern, in "The Form of Cities," *Scientific American,* April 1954.

Some critics have suggested that our professional difficulties in coping with the collective aspects of the larger urban environment have been due to our historical preoccupation with the single splendid building, as a perfect, gemlike object. Fumihiko Maki provides a perspective by proposing the existence of three differing design approaches: the traditional *compositional form,* concerned with a formal statement expressed in terms of a single building or group of buildings (the Parthenon, the gothic cathedrals, Rockefeller Center, Seagram House, Chandigarh Government Center, and Brasilia); the contemporary *megastructure,* involving a large-scale technological concentration of integrated structure and mechanical services in which all the functions of a part of a city are housed (for examples see Reyner Banham's recent documentation); and *group form,* evolving over long periods of time from the efforts of many anonymous builders, and involving the consistent use of a limited range of materials to produce building units with a modest range of individual variation, and usually associated in repetitive patterns sensitively adapted to use, topography, and climate. Traditional examples of group form are the medieval European cities, towns in the Greek islands, and North African villages.

Contemporary urban developments of course usually include combinations of and variations on all these themes, representing the actions of many individuals and anonymous groups at different points in time and over various periods, and producing the "process form" we call the city. Our present problem is a metaphoric analogue of this "process form."

View of the town of Casares, in Andalusia,
Spain. From Bernard Rudofsky, *The Prodi-
gious Builders* (New York: Harcourt Brace
Jovanovich, 1977)

a b c d e f g h i j k l m r

Curvilinear Form

In this problem we continue our study of form with an investigation of the special category of the curved line. We will focus on the contour bounding the "negative" space between two letters or numerals of our Roman alphabet. This will enable us to consider some of the visual, technical, and historical aspects of the alphabet, as well as the perceptual significance of the contour line, and the use of curved lines in a number of practical design applications. Since our procedure will require your freehand enlargement of a small irregular form while preserving its original proportions, you will have an opportunity to exercise the coordination of your hand and eye in the accurate delineation of a subtle shape, as well as to reflect on some aspects of proportion itself, and on the uses of distortion.

First, let us take a look at our alphabet. Through constant use it has no doubt become almost transparent or invisible to you. But now reconsider these twenty-six very special graphic forms:

o p q r s t u v w x y z

"At your public library they've got these arranged in ways that can make you cry, giggle, love, hate, wonder, ponder and understand.

"It's astonishing what those twenty-six little marks can do.

"In Shakespeare's hands they became *Hamlet*.

"Mark Twain wound them into *Huckleberry Finn*. James Joyce twisted them into *Ulysses*. Gibbon pounded them into *The Decline and Fall of the Roman Empire*. Milton shaped them into *Paradise Lost*. Einstein added some numbers and signs (to save space and time) and they formed *The General Theory of Relativity*.

"Your name is in them.

"And here we are using them now.

". . .You can live without reading, of course, But it's so *limiting*.

"How else can you go to Ancient Rome? or Gethsemane? or Gettysburg?

"Or meet such people as Aristotle, F. Scott Fitzgerald, St. Paul, Byron, Napoleon, Ghengis Khan, Tolstoi, Thurber, Whitman, Emily Dickinson and Margaret Mead?

"To say nothing of Gulliver, Scarlett O'Hara, Jane Eyre, Gatsby, Oliver Twist, Heathcliffe, Captain Ahab, Raskolinkov and Tom Swift?

"With books you can climb to the top of Everest, drop to the bottom of the Atlantic. You step upon the Galapagos, sail alone around the world, visit the Amazon, the Antarctic, Tibet, the Nile.

"You can learn how to do anything from cooking a carrot to repairing a television set.

"With books you can explore the past, guess at the future and make sense of today."

From an advertisement prepared for the National Library Week program as a contribution by a major advertising agency, and used with permission of the American Library Association

126

Writing is probably the single most important invention in our panoply of technology. As the best means to transcend the impermanence of the spoken word and make contact with other minds, over space and time, it is perhaps the one social invention most closely connected with our unique cultural and biological evolution as a species. The development of graphic notations—from symbols representing objects (pictographs) or ideas (ideographs) to signs denoting sounds of the spoken language (phonograms)—makes a fascinating study. At this point, however, we will limit our investigation to some of the expressive qualities of the bounding edges of our Western letter forms as examples of abstract contours or outlines that separate figure from ground, or one basic pattern area (BPA) from another. The curvilinear forms we are concerned with here are characterized by smooth, regular curves with gradual changes in the radius of curvature, as in the case of the ellipse, parabola, the hyperbola of the conic sections, the involutes, and the several spirals. The study of the inherent character of these lines will help you to evaluate more objectively your performance in producing similar curved lines.

For example, see Robert Claiborne, *The Birth of Writing* (New York: Time-Life Books, 1974), and Etiemble, *The Written Word* (New York: Orion Press, 1961).

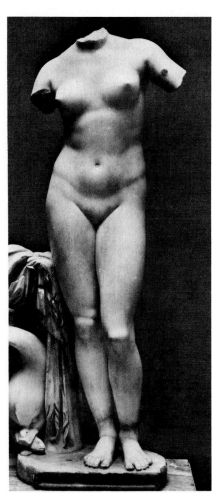

"Gestures often describe the shape of objects by their outlines, and it is for this reason that representation by outline seems to be the simplest psychologically and most natural technique for making an image by hand. The filling of the surface with paint or the modeling or carving of an object involves movements that may lead to the desired shape but are not in themselves an imitation of that shape. They serve visual representation more indirectly than recorded gesture.

"Line, the prime element of the child's work, must be considered a tremendous abstraction by the realist. 'There are no lines in nature,' he points out. Lines are indeed highly abstract if we view drawings merely in comparison to 'photographic' reality. However, if we understand representation to be the creation of a structural equivalent rather than a mechanical duplication, and if we remember that line is produced by a motor act in a pictorial medium, we find that the one-dimensional trace is the eminently concrete and direct rendering of perceived shape."

—Rudolf Arnheim, *Art and Visual Perception* (Berkeley: University of California Press, 1954)

Venus of Cyrene, National Museum, Rome

Drawings from Philip Thiel, *Freehand Drawing* (Seattle: University of Washington Press, 1965)

"Outline is used abstractly in the earliest human record of graphic communication. In perception, the figure contained by its own boundary line is part of a larger visual field, is colored, rounded, soft or hard, and exists in deep space. In early cave drawings, the outline is all—there are no interior details to complete the figure, no background to orient it in space. A three-dimensional object has been converted to a two-dimensional pattern. Many different experiences of an animal have been combined and reconciled; a composite experience is communicated. The creative faculties of early man have constructed what was clearly regarded as the animal's permanent, most characteristic aspect. We are given a symbol . . . .

". . . We approach abstract thinking as we sharpen our perception and learn by observation to distill invariant aspects of nature from shifting, complicated visual events. We distinguish the moon, animals, trees as figures—sensed forms—against the background of what they are not. Physiologically, we receive our strongest visual impression at the contour line, the boundary line between figure and background. Thus, our visual images of objects are defined by the contours.

"Defining objects by shape was only one aspect of the role of line, just as separating a thing from its metamorphoses is only one aspect of perception. Once invented, the graphic line could assume a kind of independent life. The movement of the graphic tool across a surface could convey experience of movement and change, abstracting from perception of process and transformation. In the life of the stroke there was more than shape—motion and change were there as well. The growth of the line—its emergence from nothing, its speed, rhythm, length and directional changes—presented another key to the understanding of the world . . . .

"When a figure is an irregular three-dimensional form—like the body of a human being—we are not confused or led astray by the shifting contour that never remains the same for a moment. We are made to see these endlessly changing aspects as persistent forms. In our heads, we build images of the moon, of animals, of trees, choosing from our remembered perceptions the contours which are significant to us. Perception of the boundary line enables man to populate his inner world with the forms and patterns which correspond to the outer world's objects. He begins to understand relations with greater clarity, developing his capacity to control his environment."

—Gyorgy Kepes, *The New Landscape in Art and Science* (Chicago: Paul Theobald, 1956)

A reproduction of the Trajan inscription. From Edward M. Catich, *The Origin of the Serif* (Davenport, Iowa: Catfish Press, 1968)

The uppercase alphabet we use today came from the Romans, who adapted it from the Greeks, who adapted it from the Phoenicians, who adapted it from even earlier precedents about 1000 B.C. to facilitate their commercial activities. The classic Roman version of the alphabet is visible today in the inscriptions on Trajan's Column in Rome, for one example, where it still serves as a standard of typographic excellence.

The specific character of the Roman letters arose from two circumstances: first, the use of a flat lettering brush, which produced variations in the thickness of the parts of the letter; and second, the inscription of these forms on stone, which required a finishing cut across the ends of the vertical strokes with a positive overrun and a rounding-off of the resulting brittle corners. These characteristic variations in thickness, in the oblique "stress" they produce, and in the form of the finishing "serifs" are thus a consequence of both the tools and the surfaces on which they were used. (Other influences on letter forms are seen in the cuneiform marks of the Summerian wedge-shaped stylus in clay, in the variations of thickness in the strokes of the Middle Age reed pen on parchment; and in the infinite flexibility of the sensitive Chinese and Japanese brush on silk and paper.)

The introduction of hand-cut movable type, the subsequent machine production of metal type, and the contemporary use of photographic means to reproduce type have gradually transcended most of these material limitations. Today a seemingly infinite number of idiosyncratic stylistic variations in typefaces are available to us.

With all this technological innovation and stylistic mannerism, however, the primary requirement is still readability. In achieving this we are inevitably constrained to the use of those conventional letter faces which show the clearest differentation between each letter form.

It is possible to classify typefaces under four general headings. This system is based primarily on the formal characteristics of variations in thickness, orientation of stress, and serif type. Such a classification of typefaces enables us to associate styles dating from different historical periods and provides an exercise in the discernment of form qualities (which incidently demonstrates how categorizing and naming can facilitate perception). The four groups are as follows:

1. **Roman.** These are the classical typefaces, incorporating strokes of varying thickness and stress, and some variation in serifs. This group may be subdivided into three historical divisions, demonstrating the exploitation of gradual improvements in printing inks and papers:
Old Style, with moderate variation in weight, oblique stress, and strongly bracketed serifs;
Transitional, with greater variation in weight, nearly vertical stress, and moderately bracketed serifs;
Modern (dating from the late 1700s), showing great variation in weight, vertical stress, and "hairline" serifs.

2. **Egyptian,** or "square serif," is characterized by strokes of nearly equal weight, and heavy, sometimes square or "slab" serifs. Legend has it that these bold typefaces originated to meet the needs of long-distance visual communication in the course of Napoleon's campaigns in the Egyptian desert.

3. **Gothic** faces are also called "sans serif" and in general show an apparent uniform weight, and, most characteristically, no serifs. The name was originally one of opprobrium, for these faces were at one time thought to be crude and grotesque.

4. **Miscellaneous** incorporates all typefaces that do not clearly belong to any of the above categories, and includes the several script typefaces, the "Text" or "Black Letter" faces, and the thousands of "ornamentals."

Books and articles on type and typography are available in great number. A useful selection might include the following: James Craig, *Designing With Type* (New York: Watson-Guptill, 1971); Edmund C. Arnold, *Ink on Paper 2* (New York: Harper and Row, 1972); Rob Roy Kelly, *American Wood Type: 1828-1900* (New York: Van Nostrand Reinhold, 1969); Gerard O. Walter, "Typesetting," *Scientific American,* May 1969; and Ben Rosen, *Type and Typography* (New York: Van Nostrand Reinhold, 1976).

ABCDEFGHIJKLMNOPQRSTUVWXYZ
abcdefghijklmnopqrstuvwxyz   1234567890

Roman   *Old Style*   (Garamond)

ABCDEFGHIJKLMNOPQRSTUVWXYZ
abcdefghijklmnopqrstuvwxyz   1234567890

Roman   *Transitional*   (Caledonia)

ABCDEFGHIJKLMNOPQRSTUVWXYZ
abcdefghijklmnopqrstuvwxyz   1234567890

Roman   *Modern*   (Torino)

ABCDEFGHIJKLMNOPQRSTUVWXYZ
abcdefghijklmnopqrstuvwxyz   1234567890

Egyptian   (Rockwell)

ABCDEFGHIJKLMNOPQRSTUVWXYZ
abcdefghijklmnopqrstuvwxyz   1234567890

Gothic   (Helvetica)

ABCDEFGHIJKLMNOPQRSTUV
WXYZ abcdefghijklmnopqrstuvwxyz   1234567890

Miscellaneous   (Bank Script)

ABCDEFGHIJKLMNOPQRSTUVWXYZ
abcdefghijklmnopqrstuvwxyz   1234567890

Miscellaneous   (Engravers Old English)

ABCDEFGHIJKLMNOPQRSTUVWXYZ
abcdefghijklmnopqrstuvwxyz   1234567890

Miscellaneous   (Hobo)

Materials

You will be assigned two adjacent letters or numerals from the specimens herewith, or from equivalent examples as found in newspaper headlines, magazine displays, or typefaces from art supply stores. In any case the specimens should be about two inches high and selected on the basis of the complexity of the form of the negative space between the two characters. Use a Xerox copy of the original.

1 20″ x 30″ white illustration board

T-square, triangles, scale rule, pencils, etc.

Procedure

You could, of course, use mechanical or optical means to produce this enlargement. But you would then deprive yourself of the opportunity to develop your skill in estimating distances, sizes, and proportions, thus sidestepping a point of the problem.

Grid off the space between the given pair of letters into a system of squares. Using a larger system of squares, transfer the complete, closed bounding contours of this "negative" space, undistorted in form or proportions, but maximally enlarged in size and with 1″ minimum margins, to the board, in either horizontal or vertical format. This contour is then to be lightly drawn freehand in medium-soft pencil in a line of uniform thickness. An algorithm for doing this is now presented in conjunction with the adjacent figure.

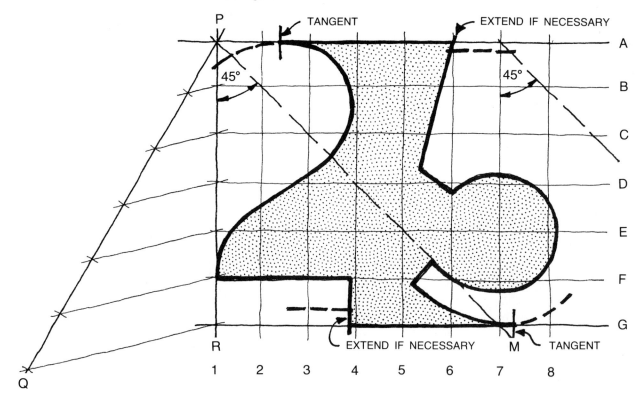

1. Square up your letters or numerals on the drawing board, using the vertical and horizontal elements of your characters, and tape them down.

2. Draw horizontal line PA tangent to the topmost point, and horizontal line RG tangent to the bottommost point of the negative form. (Note that all characters are not necessarily the same height!) *Identify these points of tangency definitely and precisely with a short vertical stroke.* Use a sharp, hard pencil for this, and work very accurately.

3. Now run a check on your understanding of the exact outline of the form to be dealt with. Place a piece of tracing paper over your specimen and, freehand, draw a single, continuous line around what you think is the boundary of the figure. Note again that this is only the space *immediately between* the two characters. Note also that in some cases it may be necessary to extend some straight-line elements of your characters to do this, as shown in the example. When you have done this, check with your instructor.

4. Return to your original specimen and correct your lines on it, if necessary. Next, compare the maximum overall length and height of your *figure.* If necessary, *reorient your specimen on the drawing board so that the minimum dimension is the vertical one,* and redraw lines PA and RG. Then draw vertical line PR tangent to the extreme leftmost point of your (reoriented) figure.

5. Draw line PQ at about 30° to PR and mark off six *equal* segments along it, from point P to point Q.

6. Connect Q with R, and draw lines parallel to QR through the intermediate points (this divides PR into six equal parts).

7. Where these lines intersect PR draw horizontal lines B, C, D, E, and F.

8. Draw line PM at 45° to PR, and where PM intersects these horizontal lines draw vertical lines, 2, 3, 4, 5, 6, and 7. (If necessary repeat this 45° procedure to provide lines 8, 9, etc.) You now have a square grid on the space between your characters.

9. Your problem now is to arrange for the maximal enlargement of your outline figure on the white illustration board, without changing its proportions, and with no margin less than 1″. To do this, use a hard pencil to lay off 1″ margins along the long sides of the horizontal board, and divide the remaining 18″ vertical distance between the margins into six units of 3″ each. Then use these divisions as a basis for a grid of 3″ *squares* on the board. Identify the horizontal lines as A, B, C, D, E, F, and G; and, approximately centering the figure on the board, number the vertical lines 1, 2, 3, 4, 5, 6, 7, etc., to correspond with the equivalent vertical grid lines on your specimen.

10. On the larger grid, plot points that correspond to intersections of the contour with the smaller grid, and "fair in" the enlarged contour on the board, working lightly in pencil, *freehand.*

11. Where the contour is of complex form or changes shape rapidly, introduce subdivisions of ½, ¼, etc., to provide more transfer points on both grids.

You will find that it will help you in checking the fairness of your lines if you place your eye in the plane of the board and sight along the line in question from several different directions. Note that in the case of a "reverse" curve (a curve which changes from convex to concave), there is a point of inflection or even a length of straight line where this occurs, and that both curves will be tangent to each other, or the line, at this point (see the contour near 3D in the example).

There is a matter of some concern at the point where a curve becomes tangent to a straight line, as in the case of a reverse curve, or near 2A, 1F, and 7G in the example. In mathematical terms, at such a point of tangency the finite radius of curvature of the curved line suddenly increases to infinity. In visual terms this abrupt change appears as a "hard" spot, or a discontinuity in the character of the curve. Technically, in the case of railway and highway design, a "transition spiral" is used to ease this abruptness. In our case a recommended procedure is to think of the curve approaching the straight line as the path of a descending airplane approaching a landing strip, on which it will only lightly touch down for a single instant before continuing onwards on a symmetrically reversed upward trajectory. Thus it is suggested that you sketch in your curve symmetrically *past* the point of tangency, taking care to make the curve smooth and continuous. When this is done, you can erase that part of the curve and straight line beyond the point of tangency.

If you are working carefully you will probably notice that those parts of your given forms which seemed to be "straight" at first glance, on closer inspection turn out to be very subtle flat curves; and also that those larger sweeping curves are by no means symmetrical. In discriminating and reproducing these nuances you will heighten your sensitivity.

As mentioned, your final drawing is to be one single, continuous line. This line is to be drawn completely freehand (including all "straight" parts) and is to be done lightly with a medium-soft pencil with uniform width and weight. When you are finished, erase all the construction lines, leaving only the continuous, closed contour line itself.

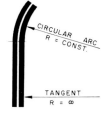

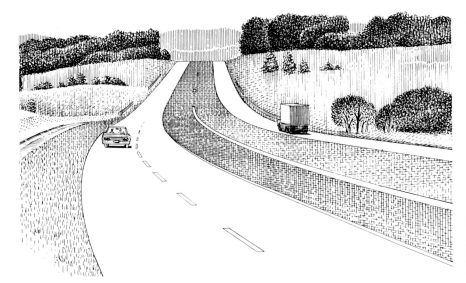

Highway curves with and without spiral transition. From Christopher Tunnard and Boris Pushkarev, *Man-Made America: Chaos or Control* (New Haven: Yale University Press, 1963)

Discussion

The flowing, linear consistency of the lines we are working with here also characterizes those used to delineate the form of objects designed to move with low resistance through water and air, as in the case of ship hulls and aeroframes. Designers involved in this work become very adept in judging the smooth "fairness" of such a "set of lines," and in detecting "knuckles" or abrupt discontinuities in the regular change of shape along the length of a line, and between families of lines.

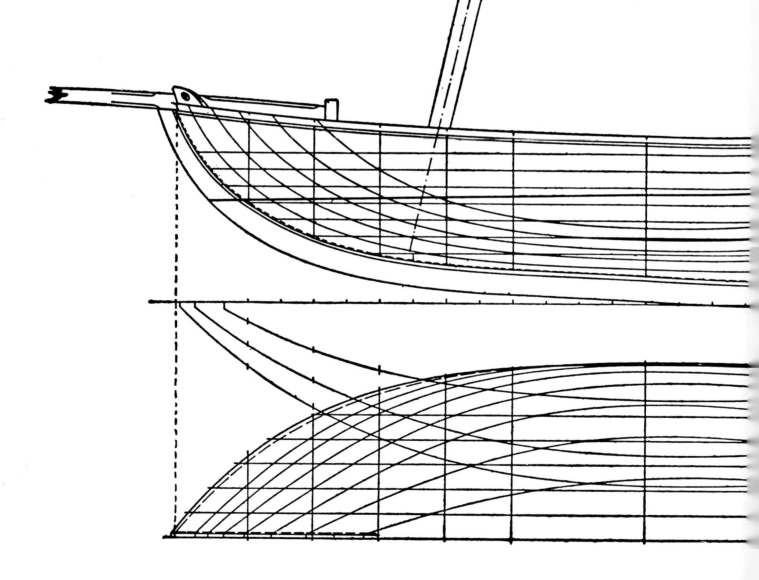

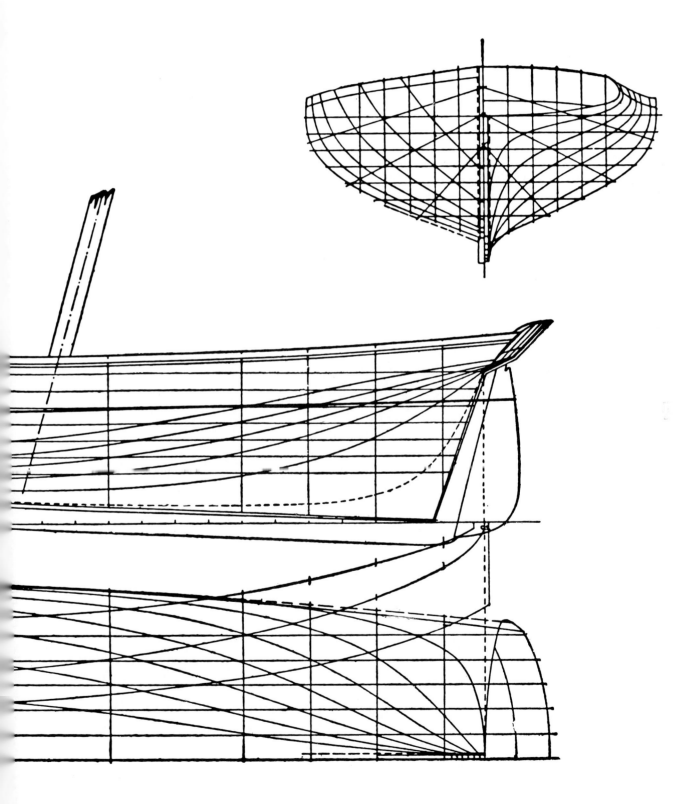

Lines of a schooner yacht, the *Dream,* built at New York in 1833 by Isaac Webb. Reproduced from Howard I. Chapelle's *Yacht Designing and Planning* (New York: W.W. Norton, 1971)

138

Other sets of curved lines with similar characteristics are seen in natural forms and in representations of natural forces: in contour maps of land forms or weather map isobars of barometric pressure; in wood grain patterns and in patterns of trabeculae in sections of bones; in fingerprints and photo-elastic stress patterns; in surface waves from objects moving in a fluid interface; in streamlines about fluid flow obstructions; in lines of force in electric and magnetic fields; and, in general, in any property of a continuous field which varies in direction and/or strength in space.

The expressive eloquence of curvilinear form speaks to us on many scales and in many guises: with the soaring arch of the rainbow and the sweeping sag of the suspension bridge; the sinuous curve of the swan's neck and the stiff flex of the swept wing; the nervous calligraphy of the silhouetted oak and the taut trajectories of the highway interchange; the enigmatic curl of a lip and the soft swell of a teapot. In viewing these forms—and all curved lines—we make a neuromuscular identification with their changes in spatial direction, and from this we perceive various other characteristics, such as certainty, hesitation, agitation, calmness, strength, or weakness. Thus the eternal fascination of handwriting, with its graphic indications of personality, character, and condition of body, mind, and spirit.

For further examples, see Gyorgy Kepes, *The New Landscape in Art and Science* (Chicago: Paul Theobald, 1956); Theodor Schwenk, *Sensitive Chaos* (New York: Schocken Books, 1976); Peter S. Stevens, *Patterns in Nature* (Boston: Little, Brown, 1974); and Peter Pearce, *Structure in Nature Is a Strategy for Design* (Cambridge: MIT Press, 1978). See also Saul Steinberg's linear visualizations of speech and other sounds in *The Labyrinth* (New York: Harper and Bros., 1960).

Bottom left: Yentna glacier, Alaska. Photo by Austin Post, U.S. Geographical Survey

Top: iron filings in the field of a bar magnet

Center: surface waves, generated by a ship. Photo courtesy of Port of Seattle *Reporter,* January 1975

Bottom: topographical contours. From Thomas E. French, *A Manual of Engineering Drawing* (New York: McGraw-Hill, 1941)

Bottom right: sickle grass (*parapholis incúrva*). From A. S. Hitchcock, *Manual of the Grasses of the United States* (Washington, D.C.: U.S. Government Printing Office, 1950)

140

In this problem we used two identical but different-sized coordinate systems as a means of enlarging a form without distorting its shape or proportions. If, however, we transfer the points from the original coordinate system to a *transformed* set of coordinates, we may investigate the metrical relationships between similar forms. See, for example, D'Arcy Wentworth Thompson's classic work on the morphology of organic forms, *On Growth and Form,* in which he plots the profile contours of a human skull on Cartesian coordinates, and shows the equivalent grid of the plots of corresponding points on the skulls of a chimpanzee, a baboon, and a dog. Albrecht Durer (1471-1528) also used transformed coordinates to study variations in facial proportions.

D'Arcy Wentworth Thompson, *On Growth and Form* (Cambridge: Cambridge University Press, 1952); and Albrecht Durer, *Four Books on Human Proportions,* facsimile edition (London: G. M. Wagner, 1970)

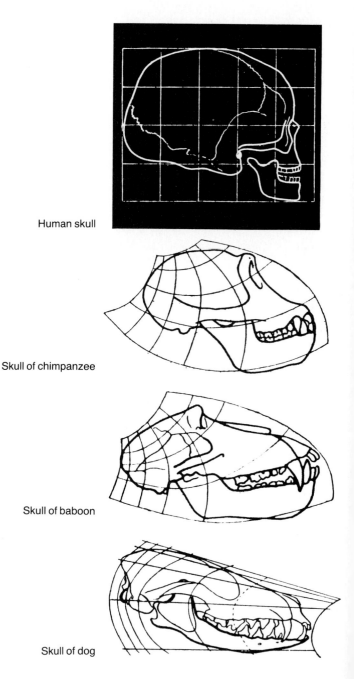

Human skull

Skull of chimpanzee

Skull of baboon

Skull of dog

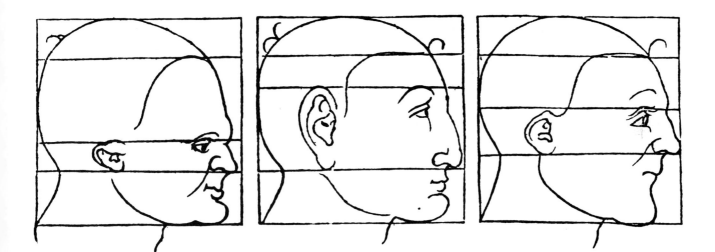

142

The deliberate or unconscious distortion of proportions in designs or free-hand sketches, wherein the size of one or more areas of a composition is increased or decreased relative to the rest, is a major means of expressive communication and the evocation of emotion. Changes from the normal, familiar, or expected serve to focus our attention, point out new relationships, and inadvertently reveal our preoccupations and concerns. Witness the power of the "caricature" (from the Italian, with the sense of overloading, or exaggerating), and of fun-house mirrors. Closely related, in the case of the environment, are the less obvious expressive consequences of the number of basic pattern areas and the range of both pattern-area and texture-element sizes in a given scene. This elusive matter of size relationships is the basis of the subtle subject of "scale," which we will investigate in Problem 17.

For examples of American standards, see Niels Diffrient et al., *Humanscale* (Cambridge, Mass.: MIT Press, 1974); Wesley E. Woodson and Donald W. Conover, *Human Engineering Guide* (Berkeley: University of California Press, 1966); *Architectural Graphic Standards* (New York: Wiley); and *Time Saver Standards* (New York: McGraw-Hill).

Another case of "environmental proportioning" exists in the functional sizing of spaces, furniture, fittings, and equipment relative to the people using them and the activities in which they are involved. Variations in the sizes and capabilities of various age groups of each sex, and conventionalized standards for spatial planning and equipment layout, are discussed in several national publications.

Drawing by Leonardo da Vinci (adapted by Minale Tattersfield)

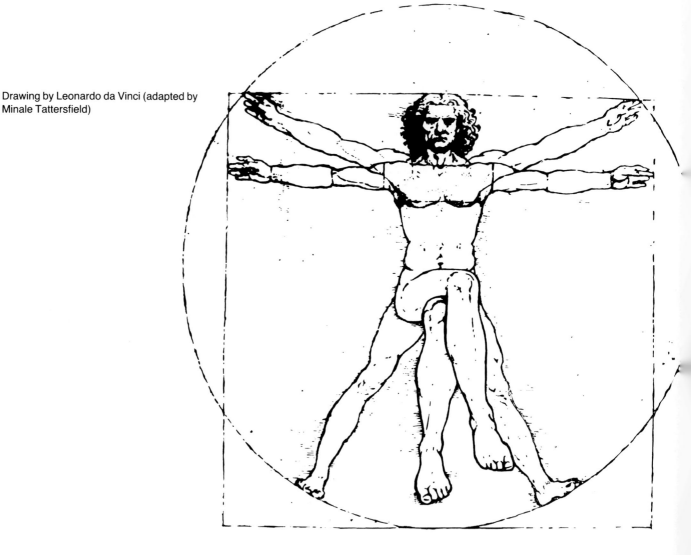

Another area in which we are concerned with proportion is in the sizing of a physical structure and its members. Here the problem is to maintain the stresses in the system below a specified level, and to achieve an efficient use of materials and labor. One must consider the proportional distribution of material in both the individual structural element itself and in the relation of each such element to the larger structural system. For similar systems these proportions will vary with the absolute size of the system. Thompson's *On Growth and Form* provides a fascinating discussion of this matter.

The classic account of a perfect proportioning of the materials of construction in a structural system is given in Oliver Wendell Holmes' poem "The Deacon's Masterpiece, or, The Wonderful One-Hoss Shay." Holmes (1809-94) was an American man of letters, and a professor of anatomy.

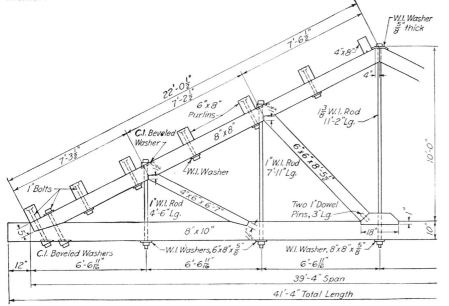

Timber truss, from Thomas E. French, *A Manual of Engineering Drawing* (New York: McGraw-Hill, 1941)

We have hardly exhausted the subject of proportion, for in addition to these several morphological, expressive, operational, and structural aspects on the physical level, there is the functional homeostatic tendency of all living systems to maintain an appropriate equilibrium in their metabolic processes. Beyond this, on the metaphorical level there exist a number of time-honored transcendental considerations of proportion in the realm of metaphysics. Here all the foregoing issues of proportion become emblematic of philosophical truths, principles of order, and rules of conduct. Thus we complete the spiraling circle: physical manifestations are perceived as symbols, and these symbols are used as guiding principles for the subsequent intervention in the environment; and once again we recognize the role of the visual environment as a channel of communication.

For an elaboration of these matters see Gyorgy Kepes, *The New Landscape in Art and Science* (Chicago: Paul Theobald, 1956), and the volume in his "Vision and Value" series entitled *Module, Proportion, Symmetry, Rhythm* (New York: Braziller, 1966).

I *love* you!

I *love* you?

I love *you!*

I love you?

I love you!

I love *you?*

I love *you!*

I love *you?*

Form and Content

It is a common experience in everyday life that much of our routine verbal communication is far from literally explicit. Much or even most information is communicated by the manner in which something is said, rather than by the nominal content of the message itself. Thus, "It's not what you say, but how you say it." For example, consider the different meanings or implications arising from some of the various possible phrasings, intonations, and stresses in the sentence "I love you."

The meaning of these vocal "gestures" (or paralanguage) is often supplemented and modified by facial expression and by physical gestures and body posture. Thus it is possible to say one thing verbally, and yet convey something else by nonverbal means. And of course the social and physical context in which anything is said establishes the entire basis of the meaning. (Can you think of some examples?)

The same phenomena also exist in terms of written communication, or "visible language." The "I love you" examples given here, for instance, use two different typefaces (roman, *italic*) and nonalphabetic signs (?,!) to visually express quite different meanings with the same three words. Newspapers use typeface, size, weight, and position conventions in a similar way to qualify the meanings of the messages on the printed page. There are, of course, many other graphic signs in general use, and, as you recall from Phase B of Problem 4, we find even more fundamental expressive potentials in the relationships of the visual attributes of the graphic forms themselves.

This general phenomenon of nonverbal communication is discussed as "metacommunication" by Ruesch and Kees (1961), and that of vocal gestures as "superfix" by Hall (1959), and is evidence of the interdependence of form, content, and context in communication. Ekman and Freisen (1969) identify five nonverbal means of interpersonal communication, as follows:

1. **Illustrators,** which are actions that assist, explain, or amplify meanings;

2. **Emblems,** which are gestures with standardized meanings which can stand in for speech;

3. **Affect displays,** or the facial patterns that express inner feelings;

4. **Regulators,** or the procedures used to manage conversations; and

5. **Adaptors,** which are customary gestures indicating an emotional state.

See: Paul Ekman and W. V. Friesen, "The Repertoire of Nonverbal Behavior: Categories, Usage, and Coding," *Semiotia* 1 (1969), pp. 49-98; D. S. Thomson, *Language* (New York: Time-Life Books, 1975); J. Ruesch and W. Kees, *Non-Verbal Communication* (Berkeley: University of California Press, 1961); E. H. Hall, *The Silent Language* (Garden City, N.Y.: Doubleday, 1959); E. H. Hall, *Beyond Culture* (Garden City, N.Y.: Doubleday, 1976); J. Liggett, *The Human Face* (New York: Stein and Day, 1974); J. P. Spiegel and P. Machotka, *Messages of the Body* (New York: The Free Press, 1974); Desmond Morris, *Manwatching* (New York: Abrams, 1977).

By means of this problem we propose to further illuminate the subject of visual expression and to involve you in the critical issue of "visual integrity"–or the matter of the "wholeness" or "honesty" of the relationship of form and function. As in the case of the organic forms of nature, when we perceive an isomorphic unity of form and content in works of human origin, our responses at the highest level may approach feelings of awe and ecstasy. For a visual designer, ability in the visual communication of character and meaning is the most essential qualification. The present problem now provides you with an opportunity to acquire an awareness of this issue and develop this ability.

You will be assigned a word such as one from the accompanying list. Your first task is to devise a nonverbal, abstract, nonrepresentational visual expression of one of the meanings of this word. Your next task is to convey the same meaning of the word, this time using only typographic forms, as lettered in an easily readable form and format, which in and of themselves graphically convey the idea or concept. In other words you are to evolve two *visual analogues* for an idea or concept embodied in the word, both of which are self-descriptive. In the first case your visual analogue should "be" this meaning and in the second case your visual analogue should both "say" it and "be" it.

Here is Herb Lubalin's famous example.

M⊗THER
CHILD

"Today . . . we are embedded in a 'second nature' in a man shaped environment which could not grow naturally because it was intercepted and twisted by one-sided economic considerations. The appearance of things in our man made world no longer reveals their nature: images take forms, forms cheat functions, functions are robbed of their natural sources—the human needs. Urban landscapes, buildings with counterfeit insides and fake outsides, offices and factories, objects for use, the packaging of goods, posters, the advertising in our newspapers, our clothes, our gestures, our physiognomy are without visual integrity. The world which modern man has constructed is without sincerity, without scale, without cleanliness, twisted in space, without light and cowardly in colour. It combines a mechanically precise pattern of the details within a formless whole. It is oppressive in its fake monumentality, it is degrading in its petty fawning manner of decorative face lifting. Men living in this false environment and injured emotionally and intellectually by the terrific odds of a chaotic society, cannot avoid injury to their sensibilities, the foundation of their creative faculty."

—Gyorgy Kepes, "The Creative Discipline of Our Visual Environment," *College Art Journal*, vol. 7, no. 1 (Autumn, 1947)

expand	music	attach	couple	quote	apart
orgasm	large	position	pause	words	humility
spray	good	full	new	biography	etymology
enclose	bad	old	closed	trouble	inflation
rupture	unexpected	wall	quote	mail	recession
plunge	face	delight	bigot	puzzle	United Nations
heavy	change	homelike	wall	top	divorce
light	increase	rotten	birth	split	marriage
male	swell	poor	death	sequel	pride
pitfall	limited	pesky	somber	faith	glass
hidden	echo	complacent	hold	submerge	influence
box	typewriter	stop	delight	graph	right
autopsy	mongrel	go	wood	confused	wrong
peace	prison	wait	rain	balance	supercilious
broken	accident	weight	pour	eclipse	transgression
clear	mistake	shelter	rich	tongue	flux
boring	improve	amateur	cheap	detour	ordeal
repetition	minority	professional	dead	ditto	obdurate
clean	empty	good	alive	defect	obtrude
dirty	subtle	bright	love	together	recalcitrant
large	wood	dull	hate	December	contrite
small	bounce	budget	hover	fugue	real
mirror	rhythmic	restrained	cost	discord	false
reflect	weekend	broken	dry	weakness	typography
change	spring	mysterious	wet	strength	shelf
downtown	motley	unclear	free	rising	contour
uptown	clash	pending	female	falling	approximate
sleep	swing	ambiguous	harmony	dominance	pending
wake	bending	seated	heavy	submission	encapsulate
close	folded	occasionally	light	wave	precis
open	take turns	suspect	city lights	sink	market

"Words are signs of natural facts. The use of natural history is to give us aid in supernatural history; the use of the outer creation, to give us language for the beings and changes of the inward creation. Every word which is used to express a moral or intellectual fact, if traced to its root, is found to be borrowed from some material appearance. *Right* means *straight*; *wrong* means *twisted*; *spirit* primarily means *wind*; *transgression*, the crossing of a *line*; *supercilious*, the *raising of an eyebrow*. We say the *heart* to express emotion, the *head* to denote thought; and *thought* and *emotion* are words borrowed from sensible things, and now appropriated to spirtual nature. Most of the process by which this transformation is made is hidden from us in the remote time when language was framed; but the same tendency may be daily observed in children. Children and savages use only nouns or names of things, which they convert into verbs, and apply to analogous acts.

"But this origin of all words that convey a spiritual import—so conspicuous a fact in the history of language—is our least debt to nature. It is not words only that are emblematic; it is things which are emblematic. Every natural fact is a symbol of some spiritual fact. Every appearance in nature corresponds to some state of mind, and that state of the mind can only be described by presenting the natural appearance as its picture. An enraged man is a lion, a cunning man is a fox, a firm man is a rock, a learned man is a torch. A lamb is innocence; a snake is subtle spite; flowers express to us the delicate affections. Light and darkness are our familiar expression for knowledge and ignorance; and heat for love. Visible distance behind and before us, is respectively our image of memory and hope.

"Who looks upon a river in a meditative hour and is not reminded of the flux of all things? Throw a stone into the stream and the circles that propagate themselves are the beautiful type of all influence. . . .

"It is easily seen that there is nothing lucky or capricious in these analogies, but that they are constant, and pervade nature. These are not the dreams of a few poets, here and there, but man is an analogist, and studies relations in all objects. He is placed in the centre of beings, and a ray of relation passes from every other being to him. And neither can man be understood without these objects, not these objects without man. All the facts in natural history taken by themselves, have no value, but are barren, like a single sex. But marry it to human history, and it is full of life. . . .

"Because of this radical correspondence between visible things and human thoughts, savages, who have only what is necessary, converse in figures. As we go back in history, language becomes more picturesque until its infancy, when it is all poetry; or all spiritual facts are represented by natural symbols. The same symbols are found to make the original elements of all languages. It has moreover been observed, that the idioms of all languages approach each other in passages of the greatest eloquence and power. And as this is the first language, so is it the last. This immediate dependence of language upon nature, this conversion of an outward phenomenon into a type of somewhat in human life never loses its power to affect us. It is this which gives that piquancy to the conversation of a strong-natured farmer of backwoodsman, which all men relish."

—Ralph Waldo Emerson, *Nature* (1836)

Ralph Waldo Emerson (1803-82), essayist and poet, was the first philosopher of the American spirit. *Nature* (1836), his first published work, presented the essence of his transcendentalism, which, viewing the external world of physical phenomena as a series of symbols of the inner life, emphasized individual independence and self-reliance, and celebrated the fact that man is a part of nature.

"In times of self-confidence, man was able to domesticate the world and gradually bring it into his human scale. Forests and mountains were once fearsome places; inhabited by wild beasts and demons, they were given a wide berth by the prudent. Later they became part of the familiar, friendly world, peaceful refuges in times of stress. Challenged, the world of nature gave up some secrets of its form and structure and lost its alien and terrifying aspects, if not all its dangers. Man explored his environment with his senses and learned about its form and textures; work and reflection revealed in nature, innate order and susceptibility to human organizing, bringing him a feeling of confidence and power. Sense experiences brought intimacy with nature, awareness of its patterns and the ability to enjoy the natural world. Out of the sensible richness of his environment, man built himself an image, a picture of nature as the great mother—the universal source of life and strength—and of the natural world as a garden—a refuge from stress and the living source of a full human life. He sensed form-patterns in nature, the sun, the moon, a face, an ear of wheat, the shadow of a tree, and used them to break down his isolation within himself. Stored in memory, recreated in imagination, they built a feeling of being connected with the physical environment and with other human beings.

"The sun that warms us, the flowers that please our senses of sight and smell, become clearly apprehended only when we attach significance to them. When we have made *symbols* of them, so that they can evoke emotional response as well as stimulate us by their palpable reality, we can use them to understand both our surroundings and the world at large, individually in our personal images, socially in images we share with men of our time and condition . . . .

"When unprecedented aspects of nature confront us, our world-model inherited from the past becomes strained; the new territory does not belong to it. Disoriented, we become confused and shocked. We may even create monsters, using old, outworn images and symbols in an inverted, negative way. Manipulating them, amplifying them, we invent new Minotaurs and new mazes, until we find new meanings and symbols growing from the new world. We are denied the pleasures of experiencing the sensed form-patterns of this new world until we have traced the paths by which this poetry of form can become meaningful.

"That is our situation today. *The strength of oak, the ferocity of the tiger, the swiftness of the eagle* are expressions which are out of place in the new world of form revealed to us by modern science. They belong to the old world of sense-experiences; they are in scale with it, interrelate some parts of it. Rapid expansion of knowledge and technical development have swept us into a world beyond our grasp; and the face of nature is alien once again. Like the forest and mountains of medieval times, our new environment harbors strange menacing beasts: invisible viruses, atoms, mesons, protons, cosmic rays, supersonic waves. We have been cast out of the smaller, friendlier world in which we moved with the confidence born of knowledge. We try to cope with the exploded scale of things without the standards which would enable us to evaluate them.

"To convert this new environment into human landscape, we need more than a rational grasp of nature. We need to map the world's new configurations with our senses, dispose our own activities and movements in conformity with its rhythms and discover in it potentialities for a richer, more orderly and secure human life. The sensed, the emotional, are of vital importance in transforming its chaos into order. The new world has its own dimensions of light, color, space, forms, textures, rhythms of sound and movement—a wealth of qualities and sensations to be apprehended and experienced. If we relate experience, image to image, we can bring our environment into focus and become aware of the new order on the sensed and emotional levels rather than on the rational level alone. Reoriented, we shall then be in a position to cope with the new world of forms . . . .

"Where our age falls short is in the harmonizing of our outer and our inner wealth. We lack the depth of feeling and the range of sensibility needed to retain the riches that science and technique have brought within our grasp. The images and symbols which can truly domesticate the newly revealed aspects of nature will be developed only if we use all our faculties to the full—assimilate with the scientist's brain, the poet's heart, the painter's eyes. It is an integrated vision that we need; but our awareness and understanding of the world and its realities are divided into the rational—the knowledge frozen in words and quantities—and the emotional—the knowledge vested in sensory images and feelings. Artists and poets on the one hand, scientists and engineers on the other, appear to live in two different worlds. Their common language, their common symbols, do not exist.

"To develop a vision which brings the inner and outer worlds together, we need common roots once more. We are like Antaeus of old, whose strength, ebbing whenever he lost contact with the Earth, his mother, became renewed each time he touched the ground. Spun out of our heads, science and art remain anemic and without root, and need strengthening contact with nature once again. The natural world remains the common basis for all of us, even though it is changed beyond recognition from the world of nature known to our fathers. It still starts for us where we come in contact with it—through our senses. Science has opened up resources for new sights and sounds, new tastes and senses. If we are to understand the new landscape, we need to touch it with our senses and build the images that will make it ours. For this we must remake our vision."

—Gyorgy Kepes, *The New Landscape in Art and Science* (Chicago: Paul Theobald, 1956)

Gyorgy Kepes (1906-) is a painter, designer, writer, and educator. Born in Hungary, he collaborated with Laszlo Moholy-Nagy on film, stage, and exhibition design in Berlin and London. Professor of visual design at MIT, he eloquently stated the case for the symbiosis of art and science, and founded and directed the MIT Center for Advanced Visual Studies. His lyrical work as a painter and designer is internationally acclaimed, and many examples are in permanent museum collections.

Photograph by Béla Kalman, EFIAP

Materials

2 15″ x 20″ boards (white or colored, with or without texture) in horizontal format

Paint set, as specified in Introduction C: Program and Procedure

Brushes, drafting paper, colored construction paper, scissors

Procedure

Consult several unabridged or large dictionaries and copy out into your notebook the full exposition of your assigned word, including its etymology or derivation, and illustrating the changes in form and subtle shifts in meaning or association over time. Be sure to include all the *senses* of the word, noting that the order in which they appear usually reflects the range from most to least common use. A full understanding of all these meanings of the word is, of course, indispensable for a successful use of the word in this problem. You are free to use any one of the common senses of the word, and thus may be better able to come up with an apt solution if you are aware of all the possibilities.

By having a clear, complete copy of this key information available in your "job file" notebook (instead of some random fragments scribbled on a scrap of paper) all essential information will be readily available to you throughout the cycles of the design process.

Phase A

This will require the development of a *non*verbal abstract expression of one of the senses or meanings of your assigned word. Your task will be to use one or more *nonrepresentional* forms, perhaps cut out of colored construction paper and rubber-cemented on a 15″ x 20″ board in horizontal format, to convey that sense or meaning. Here you must investigate all the expressive potentials of size, position, shape, number, color, texture, direction, and surface quality in the context of the 15″ x 20″ field. Refer to your studies of this in Problem 4, and work methodically to prepare and compare alternatives of variations in each of the above attributes. Put these comparisons up on the wall, where your colleagues can view them and tell you what *they* think the designs "say." After your ideas have evolved through this iterative process, select one design for presentation.

"The impact of the forces transmitted by a visual pattern is an intrinsic part of the percept, just as shape or color. In fact, expression can be described as the primary content of vision. We have been trained to think of perception as the recording of shapes, distances, hues, motions. The awareness of these measurable characteristics is really a fairly late accomplishment of the human mind. Even in the Western man of the twentieth century it presupposes special conditions. It is the attitude of the scientist and the engineer or of the salesman who estimates the size of a customer's waist, the shade of a lipstick, the weight of a suitcase. But if I sit in front of a fireplace and watch the flames, I do not normally register certain shades of red, various degrees of brightness, geometrically defined shapes moving at such and such a speed. I see the graceful play of aggressive tongues, flexible striving, lively color. The face of a person is more readily perceived and remembered as being alert, tense, concentrated rather than as being triangularly shaped, having slanted eyebrows, straight lips, and so on. This priority of expression, although somewhat modified in adults by a scientifically oriented education, is striking in children and primitives, as has been shown by Werner and Kohler. The profile of a mountain is soft or threateningly harsh; a blanket thrown over a chair is twisted, sad, tired.

"The priority of physiognomic properties should not come as a surprise. Our senses are not self-contained recording devices operating for their own sake. They have been developed by the organism as an aid in properly reacting to the environment. The organism is primarily interested in the forces that are active around it—their place, strength, direction. Hostility and friendliness are attributes of forces. And the perceived impact of forces makes for what we call expression . . . .

"Evidently, then, expression is not limited to living organisms that we assume to possess consciousness. A steep rock, a willow tree, the colors of a sunset, the cracks in a wall, a tumbling leaf, a flowing fountain, and in fact a mere line or color or the dance of an abstract shape on the movie screen have as much expression as the human body, and serve the artist equally well. In some ways they serve him even better, for the human body is a particularly complex pattern, not easily reduced to the simplicity of shape and motion that transmits compelling expression. Also it is overloaded with nonvisual associations. The human figure is not the easiest, but the most difficult, vehicle of artistic expression.

"The fact that nonhuman objects have genuine physiognomic properties has been concealed by the popular assumption that they are merely dressed up with human expression by an illusory 'pathetic fallacy,' by empathy, anthropomorphism, primitive animism. But if expression is an inherent characteristic of perceptual patterns, its manifestations in the human figure are but a special case of a more general phenomenon. The comparison of an object's expression with a human state of mind is a secondary process. A weeping willow does not look sad because it looks like a sad person. It is more adequate to say that since the shape, direction, and flexibility of willow branches convey the expression of passive hanging, a comparison with the structurally similar state of mind and body that we call sadness imposes itself secondarily. The columns of a temple do not strive upward and carry the weight of the roof so dramatically because we put ourselves in their place, but because their location, proportion, and shape are carefully chosen in such a way that their image contains the desired expression. Only because and when this is so, are we enabled to 'sympathize' with the columns, if we so desire. An inappropriately designed temple resists all empathy.

"To define visual expression as a reflection of human feelings would seem to be misleading on two counts: first, because it makes us ignore the fact that expression has its origin in the perceived pattern and in the reaction of the brain field of vision to this pattern; second, because such a description unduly limits the range of what is being expressed. We found as the basis of expression a configuration of forces. Such a configuration interests us because it is significant not only for the object in whose image it appears, but for the physical and mental world in general. Motifs like rising and falling, dominance and submission, weakness and strength, harmony and discord, struggle and conformance, underlie all existence. We find them within our own mind and in our relations to other people, in the human community and in the events of nature. Perception of expression fulfills its spiritual mission only if we experience it in more than the resonance of our own feelings. It permits us to realize that the forces stirring in ourselves are only individual examples of the same forces acting throughout the universe. We are thus enabled to sense our place in the whole and the inner unity of that whole."

—Rudolf Arnheim, *Art and Visual Perception* (Berkeley: University of California Press, 1954)

Phase B

Display type is usually 14 points or larger in size. Examples may be found in such references as: W. T. Berry, A. F. Johnson, and W. P. Jasper, *The Encyclopaedia of Type Faces* (London: Blandford Press, 1958); J. I. Biegeleisen, *Art Director's Work Book of Type Faces* (New York: Arco, 1963); Aaron Burns, *Typography* (New York: Reinhold, 1961); J. Craig, *Designing With Type* (New York: Watson-Guptill, 1971); Theo Crosby, Alan Fletcher, and Colin Forbes, *A Sign Systems Manual* (New York: Praeger, 1970); Rob Roy Kelly, *American Wood Type, 1828-1900* (New York: Van Nostrand, 1968); John Lewis, *Printed Ephemera* (Ipswich: W. S. Cowell, 1962); John Lewis, *Typography: Basic Principles* (New York: Reinhold, 1964); E. Rondthaler, *Alphabet Thesaurus* (New York: Reinhold, 1960); Ben Rosen, *Type and Typography* (New York: Reinhold, 1963).

On the design of typefaces, see Herbert Bayer, *Herbert Bayer: Painter, Designer, Architect* (New York: Reinhold, 1967); and Herbert Spencer, *The Visible Word* (New York: Hastings House, 1969).

Next, refer to several collections of "display" typefaces. You may be somewhat daunted to discover the enormous variety of typefaces that are available, and will probably surmise that the situation here is similar to that in industries where manneristic novelty is the means of promoting an artificial obsolescence. But you will probably also discover that these stylistic differences are the associative means by which a given typeface is able to evoke a period, an era, a personage, or a situation. Obviously you should capitalize on these culturally determined connotations, if possible.

You are in general restricted to the use of existing typefaces and/or typographical elements, and should not invent or design a new one (which is a special design problem in itself). You will soon become aware that each typeface (like a person's face) possesses a unique physiognomy, suggestive of character or mood. For example, consider the adjacent examples: which typeface do you think is most appropriate for each word? Or, to put the matter the other way, what are the different connotations of each word for each of the three typefaces?

SENATE   SENATE   SENATE

GARDEN   GARDEN   GARDEN

QUARRY   QUARRY   QUARRY

Remember: you are restricted to the use of *only* typographic forms in this phase. At this point you are probably brimming over with ideas, and you should now manifest them in the form of small freehand "thumbnail sketches" (but in the required horizontal format and same proportions as the 15″ x 20″ board), using soft or colored pencils or felt-tip pens. From the dozens of these sketches you should then select the most promising ideas, and, taking each of them in turn, enlarge the individual letters to full size on *separate* pieces of white tracing paper. These then can be easily moved about over a second piece of 15″ x 20″ paper or board to study the possibilities resulting from variations in position and direction. They may also be interchanged with additional letters of different sizes, shapes, colors, and textures for a full investigation of alternatives. It is a good idea to work on two such studies simultaneously, side by side; in this manner you can very quickly simulate and compare *hundreds* of possibilities. When you discover a promising layout, trace it on a superimposed piece of tracing paper, render it, and put it up on the wall. *Throughout your work on this problem be sure to apply your discoveries of expressive potentials from Phase 1, and from Problem 4.*

These simulations or dress rehearsals should be continually displayed for discussion and comparative evaluation by you and your colleagues. Remember that success in design depends on your willingness to *actually manifest* (not just think about) these simulations—to physically produce them in multiple and systematic variations and to display them side by side. There is *no* substitute for this work, and *everything* hinges on doing it well and prolifically.

In testing these designs, try thinking of them as 15″ x 20″ billboards located alongside a highway, and ask yourself if the message could be grasped by someone passing at a speed of fifty-five miles an hour; in other words, with a glance. For another test, consider whether a person who does not read English could get the sense of your meaning from just seeing your design. Are there any alternative meanings? Is your design ambiguous, because of several possible interpretations?

Be sure to watch out for the "death-grip" syndrome; it is often fatal to beginning designers. This occurs when a student starts to panic over an apparent lack of ideas and persists in elaborating the first even halfway possible solution in trivial detail, to the neglect of further explorations. The remedy for this affliction is first to put in a period of solid work on the problem, and then, if stagnation sets in, to drop it for at least several hours and immerse yourself in some other activity. When you return to the problem at a later time you will most probably find yourself unblocked and full of new ideas. By managing your time so as to take advantage of this tendency of the subconscious mind to develop further perspectives and additional associations on a problem while you are consciously engaged in something else, you can avoid limiting yourself to low levels of achievement.

"One of my first typographic design commissions was for the renowned European architect, Eric Mendelsohn. When I presented my laborious layouts to him he glanced at them, shook his head and roared, 'You suffer from the same fault as the rest of your countrymen. You do not sketch enough!' He took a roll of cheap yellow tracing paper, quickly drew some lines with a soft pencil at very small scale, ripped off the sheet and handed it to me. 'There is your design! Better, isn't it?' I had to admit that it was, despite the days I had spent on my meticulous rendering. And I never forgot the lesson: to realize the power of a quick small sketch in forming a broad concept."

—Adrian Wilson, *The Design of Books* (New York: Reinhold, 1967)

Discussion

The twenty-six letters of our alphabet are phonograms, or graphic signs denoting the sounds of our spoken language. What about other kinds of written, or "visible," language? In the case of the Chinese language, the written characters are derived in many cases from pictographs or ideographs, as schematic representations of objects or ideas. Over the centuries, the inevitable practical simplifications have obscured some of the original graphic literalness, but the etymology of these characters is very rich in expressive concepts.

Can you think of some contemporary systems of pictographs or ideographs? Besides such examples as the international traffic-sign code there are of course those of the several branches of science and engineering, in which the entities, issues, and concepts of these specialized fields are made visible for communication and manipulation. In fact, it may be said that from the days when human beings first used knotted strings and notched sticks as aids to memory and for record-keeping purposes, the invention of such systems of notation has always been a key factor in our survival and development as a social species.

Having developed and presented a "visual analogue" of the idea or meaning embodied in a given word, in which the graphic presentation of this word both "says" it and "is" it, you are now challenged, as an application of your new skills and insights, to undertake the design of a poster announcing a lecture, exhibit, concert, or performance of some person well known in his or her field. Your subject could be a scientist, artist, writer, politician, historian, athlete, musician, or whatever; and your challenge is to develop a vivid visual expression of the essence of this person, his or her subject, field, or achievement, and to graphically communicate this essence as a visual synecdoche, on a nonverbal level. Here also you should strive for a succinct and strong presentation, capable of being comprehended at a glance.

PICTOGRAPHS

人 **person**
standing with legs apart

女 **woman**
seated figure

山 **mountain**
three peaks

日 **sun**
circle and dot

月 **moon**
crescent

田 **field**
divided plain

車 **vehicle**
wheels, axle, and body

目 **eye**
eyelids and pupil

囚 **prisoner, convict**
person in enclosure

木 **tree, wood**
trunk and branches

川 **river**
flowing stream

IDEOGRAPHS

上 **up, above, superior**
something over

下 **down, below, inferior**
something under

安 **peaceful, tranquil**
woman under roof

見 **to see, look, or show**
eye on legs

明 **bright, clear**
sun and moon

姦 **adultery, or boisterousness**
three women

峠 **mountain pass, or climax**
mountain, up, down

林 **grove**
two trees

森 **forest**
three trees

从 **to follow, or obey**
two persons in line

旦 **dawn**
sun above horizon

Here are some examples. For more, see Chiang Yee, *Chinese Calligraphy* (Cambridge, Mass.: Harvard University Press, 1934); G. D. Wilder and J. H. Ingram, *Analysis of Chinese Characters* (New York: Dover, 1974); Oreste and Enko Vaccari, *Pictorial Chinese-Japanese Characters* (Rutland, Vt.: Charles E. Tuttle, 1954). See also William S-Y Wang, "The Chinese Language," *Scientific American,* February 1973.

For some comments on Egyptian hieroglyphics see R. L. Gregory, *The Intelligent Eye* (New York: McGraw-Hill, 1970); and for a review of contemporary signs and symbols refer to Henry Dreyfus, *Symbol Sourcebook* (New York: McGraw-Hill, 1972).

Toyo Sesshu (1420-1506), *Monkeys and Birds in Trees*, six-fold screen, ink on paper, 160.6 cm × 366 cm. Courtesy of the Museum of Fine Arts, Boston

Visual Organization

With this problem we reach the midpoint of our program, and now summarize our work to date as a preliminary to its consolidation in the present exercise.

The preceding problems have introduced the concept of the basic pattern area (BPA) as the elementary sensory unit of the optically differentiated visual field, and much of our work has been concerned with various aspects of the number, position, size, direction, shape, color, texture, and surface-quality attributes of these basic pattern areas as they appear in the visual field. We have also considered the process of perception, which is the interpretative activity of the viewer in ascribing meaning to these optical differences in the visual field, in the context of his or her prior experiences and present circumstances, expectations, and interest. We have noted that the process of perception involves the tentative association of some of these basic pattern areas into a "figure," in a reciprocal and reversible relationship with the rest of them, which remain as a "ground." But what determines which basic pattern areas will be taken together, and seen as the constituents of this figure? In this problem we will investigate the principles that underlie this visual organization of the basic pattern areas.

Here we have two world-famous paintings: one from the fifteenth century gently portraying a humorous subject, and one from the twentieth century making a biting indictment of inhumanity; but both illustrating the application of the laws of visual organization.

Pablo Picasso (1881-1973), *Guernica* (1937, May–early June), oil on canvas, 11'5½'' 25' 5¾''. On extended loan to the Museum of Modern Art, New York, from the artist's estate

158

The Gestalt school of psychology originated in Germany in the early part of the twentieth century, and has been most influential in connection with these principles of organization as related to the perception of wholes. For further examples and discussions see, Gyorgy Kepes, *The Language of Vision* (Chicago: Paul Theobald, 1948); Rudolf Arnheim, *Art and Visual Perception* (Berkeley: University of California Press, 1974); R. L. Gregory, *The Intelligent Eye* (New York: McGraw Hill, 1970); and Gaetano Kanizas, "Subjective Contours," *Scientific American*, April 1976.

The conditions that facilitate the organization of a heterogeneous visual field have been identified as "proximity," "similarity," "continuance," and "closure" by the Gestalt psychologists, and formulated as "laws." (Refer again to the comments of Von Foerster in Problem 5 on this matter of natural laws.)

Proximity. The Law of Proximity states that the relative closeness of some units to each other as compared to others at a greater distance will cause the closer elements to be seen together as a new entity. The greater the relative physical proximity, the stronger the tendency for a visual association. This is the simplest condition for relating discrete elements into larger wholes.

Similarity. The Law of Similarity concerns the tendency of commonalities in the attributes of a number of separate elements to relate them as a group. Similarities of form, size, direction, color, or texture will serve to associate a variety of discrete units into a new and larger whole. Note that this organizing tendency may be in competition with the Law of Proximity and, if so, will produce a perceptual "tension" in the visual field.

Continuance. The Law of Continuance refers to the relating tendency of similarities in the *changes* in the attributes of a series of adjacent basic pattern areas. These similarities may be a progression of graded changes in size, shape, direction, hue, value, chroma, or texture. Continuance also applies to consistencies in the direction and linear character (straight, curved, jagged, wavy) of the "in-lines" (lines within) or outlines (bounding contours) of the adjacent basic pattern areas.

Closure. The Law of Closure deals with our perceptual tendency to group certain visual elements and, by "filling in" the gaps between them, to establish one simple larger form. This completion of latent connections to produce new virtual forms takes place in two, three, or four dimensions.

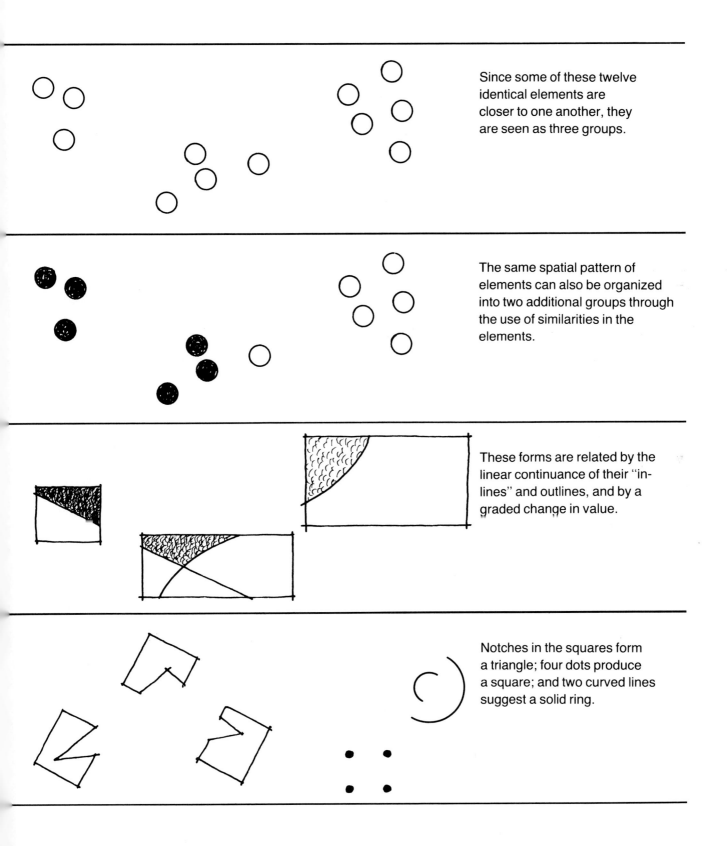

Since some of these twelve identical elements are closer to one another, they are seen as three groups.

The same spatial pattern of elements can also be organized into two additional groups through the use of similarities in the elements.

These forms are related by the linear continuance of their "inlines" and outlines, and by a graded change in value.

Notches in the squares form a triangle; four dots produce a square; and two curved lines suggest a solid ring.

At this point it will be useful to refer to the results of your algorithm from Problem 5. In the aleatory patterning of the triangular basic pattern areas, you may be aware of a number of larger forms, whose existence can now be explained in terms of the above four laws. Also, please reflect on your studies in camouflage and display in Problem 1.

You will be challenged now to consciously apply these laws in the design of two adjacent facing pages, or a "double-page spread," as for a book or magazine. Here you will have an opportunity to organize a number of graphic elements in an expressive and coherent visual design. In the process you will become familiar with some typographic concepts and new simulation techniques.

Materials

1 15″ x 20″ white illustration board in horizontal format ("trim size"). Indicate gutter by means of a single vertical line down the center.

3 black-and-white photographs with area ratios of 1:4:8. These may be clipped from magazines, with size and subject matter decided by you. Tolerance of variations in relative size is limited to about ±3 percent.

Simulated body text: 15 column-inches (total vertical length), on 18 pica measure (line width)

1 display heading related or not to photo content

3 short simulated captions (one for each photo)

Your name (as "author")

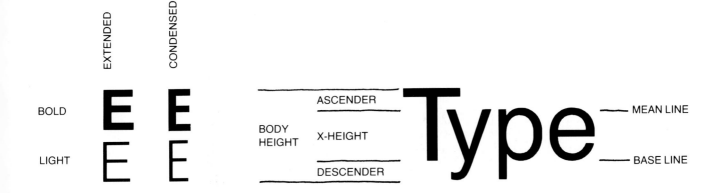

Art. Illustrations and artist-prepared materials used in a layout.

Ascender. That part of the lowercase letters b,d,f,h,k,l, and t which extends above the mean line. (See Descender.)

Base Line. The imaginary horizontal line on which all letters stand. (See Mean Line.)

Bleed. Said of type or art when it extends beyond the trim line.

Body Size. The vertical dimension of the typeface, measured in points, usually including x-height, ascenders, and descenders.

Body Type. The main typeface used in a text, usually less than 14 points in size.

Bold Face. A thicker version of a typeface. (See Light Face.)

Caps. The "uppercase," or capital letters. (See L.C.)

Characters. The individual letters.

Comprehensive. A complete simulation of a layout of body type, display headings, and art.

Condensed. A narrow version of a given typeface. (See Extended.)

Copy. Any matter to be set in type.

Descender. That part of the lowercase letters g,j,p,q, and y which extends below the baseline. (See Ascender.)

Display Type. Typeface usually 14 points or larger, commonly employed for headings, titles, etc.

Extended. A wider version of a given typeface. (See Condensed.)

Face. The style or design of a given alphabet.

Flush. Body type set without indentations.

Gutter. The center of an open book or magazine where the two facing pages adjoin at the binding.

Heading. Bold face or display type, as used for titles, etc.

Italic. The version of a typeface in which the characters slant to the right. Sometimes called cursive, or oblique. (See Roman.)

Justified. A line of type word-spaced to a given measure.

L.C. The "lowercase" or small letters. (See Caps.)

Leading (pronounced "ledding"). Line spacing, or vertical spacing between lines of type. In general, to insure good readability, for a given x-height the leading should increase as the measure increases.

Letterspacing. Adjustment of horizontal distances between individual letters so as to achieve a uniform appearance within a word.

Light Face. A thinner version of a typeface. (See Bold Face.)

Line Spacing. (See Leading.)

Mean Line. The imaginary horizontal line along the top of the lowercase letters without ascenders. (See Base Line.)

Measure. The length of a line of type, usually expressed in picas.

Pica. A unit of typographic measurement equivalent to 1/6 of an inch.

Point. A unit of typographic measurement equivalent to 1/72 of an inch.

Roman. The version of a typeface in which the characters are vertical. (See Italic.) Also, a category of typefaces.

Serif. Finishing strokes crossing or projecting from the ends of the main elements of a letter.

Solid. Said of lines of type set with no leading.

Text Type. (See Body Type.)

Trim Line. The line along which pages will be cut to their final dimension.

Wordspacing. Adjustment of horizontal distance between words so as to justify a line of type.

X-Height. The vertical distance between the base line and the mean line; or the height of lowercase letters not including ascenders and descenders.

Successful simulation
of text type depends
on a close matching
of the x-height of the
given typeface, and
on a good approximation
of the "weight," or
tone, of the block of
text as a whole. Here
are three alternatives,
all of the same x-height
but differing in weight:
all shown flush left
and ragged right to
match the original.

Procedure

Prepare at least three sets of photos (with each set differing in size from the next, but all conforming to the required area ratios) so that you will be able to find the proportions that permit the best interaction of white space in your layout. Photos may bleed at any edge.

Prepare several sets of the required amount of simulated text (on white tracing paper) using one of the methods shown in the adjacent figure. Note that successful text simulation depends on a close matching of the x-height of the typeface. The 15″ of text may be justified, flush left or right, or indented, as you prefer (you should simulate and test all possibilities). It may also be broken up into two, three, or four equal-length blocks of 7½″, 5″, or 3¾″, respectively. Text must have a ½″ minimum margin at any edge, including the gutter. Adjacent blocks of text may be spaced 2 picas apart except across the gutter. Prepare several sets of display headings on white tracing paper, experimenting with different typefaces, sizes, and weights, and applying what you learned in the preceding problem. Prepare several sets of one-line photo captions, in body-type size; and your name, in a variety of sizes. You now should have several sets of:

three photos,

two (or more) blocks of body type,

one line of display type,

three photo captions,

your name.

You are now challenged to develop an arrangement of one set of all these elements (and the negative spaces!) on *both pages together as one whole,* in which all elements, positive and negative, are sized and positioned in functional relationships, a unity of opposites, and in an overall expressive configuration.

Note that if there were no editorial content, and no conceptual connection of the various elements, then a more-or-less evenly spaced, random arrangement of generally equal-size elements on the double-page spread would clearly communicate this high-entropy situation. In your case, however, there are very definite functional relationships between all these elements, and (as indicated by the given size-ratios of the photographs) a very specific hierarchy of relative importance.

Thus: each caption relates to one photo, and this relationship can be indicated by the *proximity* of that caption to that photo; all blocks of body-type are part of the same text, and this relationship can be communicated by their *proximity* to one another, and by their *similarity* in size and/or shape and/or position and/or direction; the several photos illustrate the copy, and this connection can be shown by their *proximity* to this copy, by a *continuance* of the "in-lines" and the outlines of the photographs from one to another and to those of the copy elements, and by a *closure* of all these elements; and finally, the display type and your name relate to all the elements, as indicated by *proximity, similarity, continuance,* and *closure.*

Beyond this visually literate structuring of the functional relationships, there are the superordinate matters of the nonverbal identification of the main subject (as indicated by the relative sizes of the elements of a set); and the visual expression of an appropriate mood or character (strong, active, gentle, calm, solemn, dignified, animated, gay, serious, heavy, light, frivolous, etc.) which you will achieve by applying what you learned in the previous problems.

Having prepared simulations of all the required elements on separate pieces of white tracing paper, you will find your design work will be greatly facilitated if you study your layouts by shifting these elements around directly on the 15″ x 20″ illustration board (be sure to show the gutter as a definite solid line drawn on the board). By this means you will be able to quickly simulate a large number of layouts. And remember: you are to work with the double-page spread as a whole, not with each page separately.

When you discover what seems to be a workable layout, place a new sheet of tracing paper over the arrangement and prepare a complete simulation on this one piece of tracing paper. This "comprehensive" *must* be a complete simulation, not an outline drawing; it should represent all text, display headings, captions, and photos (including their black, white, and gray tones). At first glance it should be indistinguishable from your final production.

You should prepare at least six such comprehensives, each manifesting a basically different design idea and not just a minor variation of the same idea. When you have done this, you will be able to select one for further refinement. Your final presentation should incorporate the three photos, rubber-cemented to the board, and all other material drawn freehand directly on the board, using pen or pencil as you prefer. Do not use transfer or rub-on type for this problem; these prefabricated aids are fine for other times and purposes, but give you no opportunity to develop your own skills. Submit the appropriate comprehensive, along with your final presentation, *just as it was before you started on your final presentation,* so that we may admire your growing skill in simulation.

And here are some words to remind you of the possibilities:

relate	subtract
add	interchange
omit	lower
exaggerate	higher
understate	wider
invert	longer
reverse	shorter
transpose	narrower
substitute	select
cycle	enlarge
repeat	reduce
divide	increase
rhythm	exchange
vary	relocate
rotate	combine
incline	associate
juxtapose	merge
contrast	compare
break up	separate
transform	oppose
translate	upend
condense	horizontal
expand	vertical
free	curve

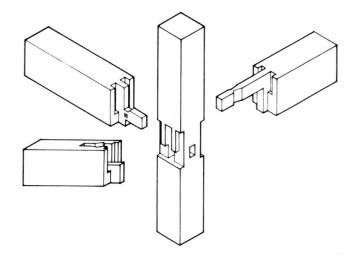

Sampo-zashi post-and-beam connection. From Kiyosi Seike, *The Art of Japanese Joinery* (New York: Weatherhill/Tankosha, 1977)

Discussion

The word *harmony* may be defined as "a state of order, agreement, or aesthetically pleasing relationships among the elements of a whole." It derives from the Greek words *harmos,* meaning "a joint, or a joining," and *harmozein,* "to join, to fit together." In this problem we have been involved with the visual joining or fitting together of the basic pattern areas as the elements of the visual field. Just as a random grouping of the elements of a physical structure such as beams, columns, girders, and slabs will not produce a serviceable bridge or building, neither will an unorganized collection of perceptual elements result in a purposeful or coherent visual statement. Only when the elements, physical or perceptual, are properly joined and related to each other does the structure become serviceable. To test your understanding of the laws of visual organization place a sheet of tracing paper over the reproductions of the Sesshu and Picasso paintings presented earlier, and using a different colored pen or pencil for each of the four laws, diagram how they operate, in each case.

A random or accidental patterning of visual elements can only give evidence of the process that produces it. As visual designers interested in conveying ideas or information, expressing feelings or moods, and communicating intentions and attitudes, we need to be aware of the principles of perceptual organization, and skilled in the art of applying them. In this problem you tried out these skills in terms of the elements on a double-page spread. You could now continue this study of organization in a sequence of such spreads, in which visual relationships flow and develop as one turns the pages in a magazine, book, or brochure—or as one watches a film in which the visual elements both within and between the shots are rhythmically articulated and developed over time.

A conjunction of wood and masonry in a building designed by Greene and Greene, architects (Thorsen residence, Berkeley, California: c. 1910). The transitions and connections are eloquently expressed by the similar shape and direction of the concrete cap and wooden sill, and the similar forms and opposite directions of the bricks and shingles.

Compare the films *Go Slow on the Brighton Line* and *Pacific 231*, both concerned with a trip by railway. The first film is composed of essentially one continuous shot, with continuity resulting from a use of the same camera position and direction over an uninterrupted period of time. The second film, however, is composed of a myriad of shots taken from a variety of positions, in different directions, and at different times. Here continuity is a consequence of the editing or connections of the many separate pieces of film in terms of the similarities, oppositions, progressions, or rhythms of such shot-attributes as direction, movement, speed, size, length, distance, position, number, content, light value, and so on.

Joris Ivens' famous film-poem *Rain*, on a passing shower in Amsterdam, offers another good example for an analysis of visual connections. See also the designer's comments on this film in Joris Ivens, *The Camera and I* (New York: International Press, 1969).

166

Descriptions and analyses of environmental sequences will be found in Donald Appleyard et al., *The View from the Road* (Cambridge, Mass.: MIT Press, 1964); and in several articles by Philip Thiel: "To the Kamakura Station," *Landscape*, Fall 1961; "An Experiment in Space Notation," *Architectural Review*, May 1962; "An Old Garden, a New Tool, and Our Future Cities," *Landscape Architecture*, July 1962; and "Processional Architecture," *AIA Journal*, February 1964.

For a challenge in making visual connections in three dimensions, collect a number of naturally faceted stones of varied sizes, and arrange three or four of them on a level surface, so that they relate visually when seen from any direction. Or, build a 12″ or 18″ open-frame cube of wire or light wood, and "invisibly" support within it three or four small objects of varied natures. Here again the problem is to create effective visual relationships between the elements when viewed from all sides. Finally, consider the prospect of moving through such a three-dimensional form relationship: adding the dimension of time, and thus arriving at the challenge of exhibition design, architecture, or urban design.

Drawings by Victor Steinbrueck

"A marvelous and wonderful thing has occurred in downtown Seattle with the placing of the Isamu Noguchi stone sculpture (Landscape of Time) in the brick terrace of the General Services Administration Building on 2nd Avenue between Marion and Madison Streets. Noguchi has transformed an already pleasant space, designed by architect Fred Bassetti, into a very special aesthetic experience.

"Creating from and beyond the great Japanese traditional art of selecting, grouping, and composing stones, Noguchi has sensitively incised the five granite stones, modulating their interrelations by introducing a man-made aspect to their timeless natural quality. The stones are always composed and in balance to each other from every viewpoint while their unassuming uniqueness and harmony with their surroundings evokes a great sense of repose in spite of the nearby street traffic. Their quality is both gentle and overwhelming. They have much to offer for those who can accept. Downtown has become a better place."

—Victor Steinbrueck, in *The Arts: Newsletter of the Seattle and King County Arts Commissions*, October 1975

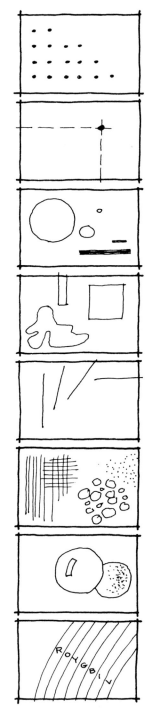

Color Attributes

With this exercise we move to a consideration of another aspect of the basic pattern area: that of color. You will be introduced to a systematization of three attributes of the appearance of color in the surface mode, and have an opportunity to discriminate them firsthand.

To begin let us imagine that we have gathered together a large number of differently colored objects: stones, bricks, boards, flowers, leaves, paper, carpet, clothing, ceramics, metals, and so on. What we want to do now is to find a way by which we can describe the many differences in the colors we see before us.

"If we are asked the color of an object such as a sweater, our first reaction may be to say, for example, that it is red. By this means, we identify the *hue* of the object, that is, whether it is red or yellow or purple.

"However, we are all conscious, at least in a vague way, that this description is inadequate. In an effort to be more specific, we may say that the sweater is light red or dark red. When we do this, we are describing the *brightness* of the color. If we stop to think about it, we realize that this characteristic of a color is independent of hue, that is, we can have two colors which are of the same hue but of different brightness.

"We might also say of the sweater that it is a dull red or a bright, vivid, or brilliant red. Here we are attempting to describe still another characteristic of a color, that is, its *saturation*. The saturation of a given color may be regarded as a measure of the extent to which it departs from a neutral gray of the same brightness.

"Thus any color perception has three characteristics, any one of which can be varied independently of the other two. In psychological usage, the correct term is *attributes*, because we are really describing sensations, not the object or the physical stimuli reaching the eye.

"While we experience little difficulty in detecting hue differences, we frequently become confused in judging brightness and saturation differences—we cannot decide whether two colors differ only in brightness or whether their saturation is also different. . . . The confusion between saturation and brightness is typified by the frequency in which the word 'bright' is used in everyday speech to describe a highly saturated color.

"Frequently we attempt to describe a color more or less completely by a single term, sometimes the name of some object which is more or less familiar to everyone. For example, pink, cherry, cerise, dusty pink, rose, scarlet, vermilion, crimson and rust are all used to describe various reds. The difficulty is that each term means one thing to one person, another to another person. We would all agree that pink describes a red which is high in brightness, fairly low in saturation, and slightly bluish in hue. Even within these limitations, however, there are many possibilites; we would certainly not think of buying yarn to complete a half-finished sweater, specifying only that it was to be pink. Instead, we would match the two yarns directly, and with some experience in the ways of color, we would also make sure that the two samples matched both in daylight and in artificial light.

Depending on the attitude of the observer, color can be perceived in five different "modes." As codified by the Committee on Colorimetry of the Optical Society of America in *The Science of Color* (New York: Thomas Y. Crowell, 1953), they are:

the **illuminant** mode, in which color is perceived as belonging to a source of light,

the **illumination** mode, in which the presence of illuminated objects reflecting light and casting shadows provides a basis for the perception of color,

the **surface** mode, in which color is perceived as belonging to a surface, based on the presence of a physical surface from which light is reflected,

the **volume** mode, involving the passage of light through a more-or-less uniform and transparent substance such as smoke or haze, and

the **film or aperture** mode, in which a color is seen through an aperture, as in a mask, isolated from and unrelated to other colors. This mode provides an experience closest to pure color sensation.

Because of this confusion, in our work with color as perceived in the surface mode, we will use the term "lightness" or *value* to refer to this attribute. Technically, brightness refers to the perception of luminance, which is the effective intensity of the light reaching the eye; while lightness refers to the perception of reflectance, which is the fractional part of the light reflected from a surface under given conditions. Reflectance is a characteristic of the surface for a given light, and luminance is a characteristic of the light itself.

"The need for an accurate language of color becomes acute when, as often happens, circumstances do not permit direct comparisons. Actually, we do not have a universal language, but we do have systems of color specification and notation which answer most of our needs. The importance of such systems to manufacturers of dyes, pigments, paints, inks, papers, etc., and to many workers in science and industry can hardly be overestimated.

"In the United States, the best-known and most widely used system of color notation is that developed by Albert H. Munsell. Essentially, this system is an orderly arrangement into a three-dimensional solid of all the colors which can be represented by actual surface samples prepared from stable pigments. . . .

"The various hues are spaced horizontally around a circle in such a manner that they appear approximately equidistant to a normal observer, provided he examines them under illumination of the correct quality. The circle . . . is divided into ten Major Hues, consisting of five Principal Hues (Red, Yellow, Green, Blue, and Purple) and five Intermediate Hues (Yellow-Red, Green-Yellow, Blue-Green, Purple-Blue, and Red-Purple). Each of these ten Major Hues is number 5 of a hue series of 10 numbers. Thus the complete hue circle consists of 100 hues, 40 of which are represented by actual samples in the *Munsell Book of Color*. This book is supplied as a Matte Finish Collection and a Glossy Finish Collection; a number of abridged collections designed for special purposes are also available.

"Extending vertically through the center of the hue circle is the scale of reflectances, known as *values* in the Munsell System. Number 10, at the top of the value scale, is a theoretically perfect white (100 percent reflectance); number 0, at the bottom, is a theoretically perfect black (0 percent reflectance). In between, there are value steps represented by actual samples.

". . .the value scale deserves more than passing notice. Superficial reasoning would indicate that the midpoint of the scale should have a reflectance of 50 percent, that is, it should reflect 50 percent of the light falling on it. However, the eye tends to see as equal tone steps not equal differences in reflectance (e.g., 10, 20, 30, and 40 percent, where there is a constant difference of 10 percent), but rather equal ratios of reflectance (e.g., 10, 20, 40, and 80 percent, where the ratio of each reflectance to the preceding one is 2). As a result, the gray which impresses the eye as falling midway between white and black actually has a reflectance of about 18 percent. . . .

"Radiating out from the scale of values, which is the central core of the color solid, are the steps of saturation, known as *chroma* in the Munsell System. Here again the steps appear approximately equidistant to a normal observer. The numbers extend from 0, which is the neutral gray, to numbers as high as 16, depending on the degree of saturation attainable with a given hue at a given value level. Because of variations in attainable saturation with hue and value, the color solid is not symmetrical. For glossy samples, the highest chroma of 5 Red is 14, whereas the highest chroma of 5 Blue-Green, opposite Red, is only 8. Yellow reaches its maximum chroma at a high value; Purple-Blue, opposite Yellow, reaches its maximum chroma at a low value. The Munsell System has the advantage over some other systems that if a new pigment is produced which permits samples of higher saturation to be prepared, there is no difficulty in adding the new samples to the appropriate hue chart."

Excerpted from *Color As Seen and Photographed*, Kodak Data Book E-74H, second ed. (Rochester, N.Y.: Eastman Kodak Company, 1972)

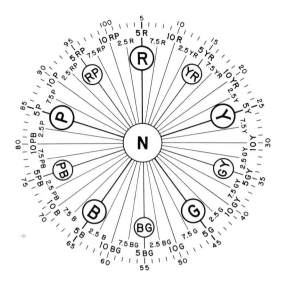

FIGURE 1 The Munsell hue circle

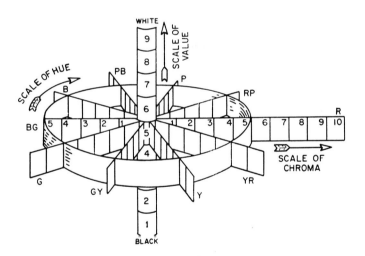

FIGURE 2 Munsell hue, value, and chroma scales in color space

Munsell Color (Macbeth Division of Kollmorgan Corporation, 2441 N. Calvert St., Baltimore, Md., 21218) describes the system as follows:

"The system of color notation, developed by A. H. Munsell, identifies color in terms of three attributes: hue, value and chroma. This method of color notation arranges the three attributes of color into orderly scales of equal visual steps; the scales are used as dimensions or parameters for the accurate specification and description of color under standard conditions of illuminating and viewing.

"The hue (H) notation of a color indicates its relation to a visually equally-spaced scale of 100 hues. There are 10 major hues (5 principal and 5 intermediate) positioned ten hue steps apart within this scale. The hue notation in general use is based on the ten major hue names: Red, Yellow-Red, Yellow, Green-Yellow, Green, Blue-Green, Blue, Purple-Blue, Purple and Red-Purple.

"Any one of several symbols may be used for the notation of hue, as shown in Figure 1. Hue initials for the ten major hue families, shown in the inner circle, may be used alone for rough identification of hue. Numerals from 1 to 100, as shown in the outer circle, may be used alone for statistical records, cataloging and computer programming. The combination of

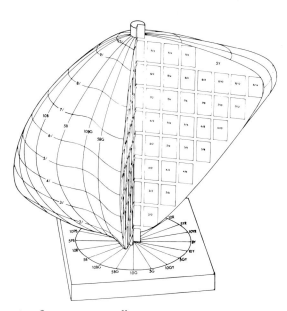

FIGURE 3 Munsell color solid with one quarter removed

numerals with the hue initials is considered the most descriptive form of the hue notation. This combination is shown between the inner and outer circles in Figure 1, and this is the form used on the 40 constant hue charts displayed in the *Munsell Book of Color*.

"The value (V) notation indicates the degree of lightness or darkness of a color in relation to a neutral gray scale, which extends from absolute black to absolute white. The value symbol 0/ is used for absolute black; the symbol 10/ is used for absolute white. The symbol 5/ is used for the middle gray and for all chromatic colors that appear half-way in value between absolute black and absolute white. Figs. 2 and 3.

"The chroma (C) notation indicates the degree of departure of a given hue from a neutral gray of the same value. The scales of chroma extend from /0 for a neutral gray out to /10, /12, /14, or farther, depending upon the strength (saturation) of the sample to be evaluated. A color classified popularly as 'vermilion' might have a chroma as strong as /12 or as vivid as /16, while another color of the same hue and value, classified popularly as 'rose,' might have a chroma as weak (grayed) as /4. Figs. 2 and 3.

"The complete Munsell notation for a chromatic color is written symbolically: H V/C. The complete notation for a sample of 'vermilion' might be 5R 5/14, while the notation for a sample of 'rose' might be 5R 5/4. When a finer division is needed for any of the attributes, decimals are used; for example: 2.8R 4.-5/12.4.

"The notation for a neutral (achromatic) color is written: N V/. The notation for a sample of black, a very dark neutral, might be N 1/; the notation for a sample of white, a very light neutral, might be N 9/, while the notation for a gray, visually half-way between these two, would be N 5/.

"The chroma symbol /0 may be used in the notation for neutral colors but it is customary to omit it. Blacks, grays, and whites of chroma weaker than /0.3 are customarily notated as neutrals; if a more precise notation is required, the form used is: N V/(H,C). In such cases, the symbol for one of the ten major hues is used with the chroma; thus, a light gray of a slightly yellowish appearance might have a notation of N 8/(Y,0.2). It is perfectly correct, of course, to use the regular H V/C form to describe all colors, using N V/O for absolute neutrals.

"The Munsell scales of hue, value and chroma can be visualized in terms of a color solid, or color space. The neutral value scale, graded in equal visual steps, from black at the bottom to white at the top, forms the central vertical axis. The hue scale is positioned in equal visual steps around the neutral axis. Chroma scales radiate in equal visual steps from the neutral axis outward to the periphery of the color space. Figs. 2 and 3. Color space as defined by the Munsell color solid is quite irregular, roughly conforming to the shape dictated by absolute limits of reflecting materials.

"The scales shown in Figures 1, 2 and 3 are intended to illustrate the concept of three dimensional color space; they are not limited to the notations shown. By the use of decimals, each scale may be divided into increments as small as may be required for the most accurate color notation. The chroma scales may be extended to include the chroma notation of all material samples. The value scale is limited by the end points (absolute black and absolute white); these are not achievable in material form. The hue scale forms a closed circle."

Now, let's test your ability in discriminating these concepts of hue, value, and chroma with actual color samples. For this you will need the materials listed below. In case you have some form of color blindness and are not aware of it, be sure to check your work at each stage with two or three of your colleagues.

Materials

Munsell 11-chart student set

Sheet of white paper

Knife

Procedure

Select any one of the eleven Munsell charts and the corresponding envelope of color chips. Empty the envelope carefully onto a clean sheet of white paper and count the chips to see if the number corresponds with that on the envelope. Note that in some cases two color chips may adhere to each other, causing you to think that one is missing. Check them carefully before you file a complaint!

Each chip belongs in one of the x-marked locations on the hue chart. Your problem is to position them on the chart so that each x is covered *and* so that the values and the chromas also are arranged in the proper order. A knife blade is useful in picking up the chips to transfer them to the position on the chart. Slip it under the chip with your finger on top of the chip (this way there is less chance of bending the chip).

When you believe all your color chips are properly positioned, check your work with your instructor, or two or three of your colleagues. When you are sure you have the correct arrangement, either replace all the chips carefully in the proper envelope for subsequent use in the same exercise by another colleague or, since we will be using a set of the assembled charts later in Problem 11, cement the chips in place on the chart using the double-coat rubber-cement technique.

Continue this operation until you have arranged the chips on each of the ten hue charts and on the eleventh hue value/chroma chart.

About 8 to 10 percent of the male population suffer from marked color blindness, and 4 to 5 percent of the total population possess some degree of seriously abnormal color vision. See W.A.H. Rushton, "Visual Pigments and Color Blindness," *Scientific American*, March 1975.

Discussion

It must not be assumed that the use of an alphanumeric system of color notation (such as the Munsell system) is intended as a replacement for the more commonly used names of colors found in the natural language. Any objective system of color specification should be understood as necessary only when we want to analyze color in technical and professional terms (as we do here). The poetic and allusive names of colors are of course most effective in conjuring up subjective associations in the use and appreciation of color. See, for example, the adjacent list; perhaps you will recognize some specially evocative terms in it.

For a little experiment, take any dozen or so of these words and find what you think are examples of them in the Munsell charts. Then compare your identification of each (in alphanumeric terms) with that of several of your colleagues, or with those in A. H. Munsell, *A Color Notation* (Baltimore, Md.: Munsell Color Co., 1967), which is included with each Munsell student set. You will probably discover some interesting individual differences in color images.

Another challenging exercise is to start a collage/mural of color-samples collected from all possible sources in your daily world, and to continue it collectively with your colleagues over a period of time. Swatches of paper, cloth, metal, foil, tree bark, cardboard, paint samples, leather, and so on, all trimmed to about the same size and shape and mounted on the studio wall will provide an enriching enlargement of your color horizons, as well as suggest some of the color nuances that result from the various surface qualities of the samples.

See B. Berlin and P. Kay, *Basic Color Terms: Their Universality and Evolution* (Berkeley: University of California Press, 1969), A. Maertz and M. Rea Paul, *A Dictionary of Color* (New York: McGraw-Hill, 1950), and Kenneth L. Kelly and Deane B. Judd, *Color: Universal Language and Dictionary of Names* (Washington, D.C.: Department of Commerce, 1976).

adobe	chocolate	gamboge	magenta	pistachio	sienna
alabaster	cinnamon	geranium	mahogany	pitch	silver
alfalfa	citron	gilt	maize	platinum	sky blue
alice blue	claret	ginger	mandarin	plum	slate
almond	cocoa	glacier blue	maple	port	smoke
amber	coffee	gold	maroon	powder blue	soot
amethyst	copper	grass green	mauve	primrose yellow	spinach green
apple green	coral	grotto blue	mist	prune	steel gray
apricot	cordovan	gunmetal	moss	puce	straw
aquamarine	cork		mulberry	purple	strawberry
auburn	cornflower	havana brown	mustard	putty	sulphur
azure	cream	hazel			
	crimson	heather	navy	raspberry	tan
beige		heliotrope	nickel	raven black	tangerine
biscuit	daffodil	henna	nile green	red	taupe
bisque	delft blue		nude	robin's egg blue	terra cotta
blond	dove gray	indian red	nut brown	rose	toast
bottle green	drab	indigo		ruby	tobacco brown
bronze	dun	ivory	ochre	russet	tomato red
buff			olivo		turquoise
burgandy	ebony	jade	orange	sable	tuscan red
	ecru		orchid	saffron	
canary	emerald	khaki		sage	ultramarine
cardinal		killarney green	pea green	salmon	umber
carmine	fawn		peach	sapphire	
cerise	fern	lavender	peacock blue	scarlet	vermilion
cerulean	flax	lead	pearl	sea green	violet
charcoal	flemish blue	lemon	pecan	seal brown	viridian
chartreuse	flesh	lilac	peppermint	sepia	
cherry	fuchsia	lime	pewter	shamrock green	walnut
chestnut	fudge		pink	sherry brown	wisteria

B = black
W = white
S_1 = given swatch no. 1
S_1^* = your match of it
S_2 = given swatch no. 2
S_2^* = your match of it

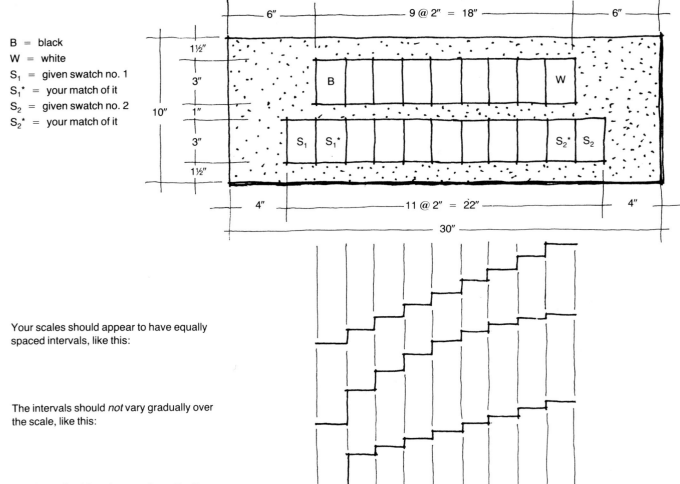

Your scales should appear to have equally spaced intervals, like this:

The intervals should *not* vary gradually over the scale, like this:

And there should *not* be any discontinuities in intervals, like this:

Color Scales

Here you will be challenged to apply your newly heightened sensitivity to color nuances by mixing and matching color pigments to produce a pair of evenly graded color scales. In each case the problem will be to achieve identical apparent intervals from one step to the next over the whole length of the scale. In doing this you will have an opportunity to develop some skill in the practical craft of painting.

Materials

1 10″ x 30″ white illustration board (cut from 20″ x 30″ board)

Paint set (as specified in Introduction C: Program and Procedures)

Drafting gear

2 color swatches, each 2″ x 3″, of approximately complementary hues and equal values

Procedure

Lay out the illustration board as diagrammed, and first paint a "gray scale" in which each element is at the same apparent interval from the next—that is, in which the change from one unit to the next appears to be the same. In painting this gray scale, you should start at the white end and progress by adding a small amount of black to make each successive unit. The consistency of your paint is important. If it is too thin it will not "cover" adequately, and if too thick, it cannot be applied smoothly. A consistency like that of heavy cream is about right. If you spill any paint on your clothes, be sure to wash it out at once because once it dries it cannot be removed.

You will also find that the appearance of some pigments changes a bit in drying. When your work is dry, check it by mounting the panel on a vertical surface and viewing it from some distance. Compare your results with those of your colleagues by overlapping the boards so that the scales are adjacent. You may have to do some repainting, in a "trial and error" (hypothesis, simulation, and evaluation) procedure, to produce a satisfactory scale. Keep in mind that all this work is essentially a training program for your own development, and that such basic skills are only won by significant effort.

For a discussion of the psychology of perception of evenly stepped graduated color scales, see chapter 20 of Josef Albers' *Interaction of Color* (New Haven: Yale University Press, 1971). We are dealing here with the so-called Weber-Fechner law, which states (as an approximate rule) that equal apparent differences arise from physical stimuli which differ, not by equal amounts, but by equal ratios.

Look carefully at your gray scale. Does each element appear to be "flat," or uniform in value from edge to edge? (See Floyd Ratliff, "Contour and Contrast," *Scientific American,* June 1972.)

For the next scale you will use the two different 2" x 3" color swatches. Taking them one at a time, mix paint to match each as closely as possible, and then paint the two spaces indicated on the board. Now mix and paint a chromatic series of colors which progresses with uniform hue, value, and chroma intervals from one to the other.

This exercise will be a bit more difficult, since you now have to deal with hue and chroma as well as value. Visualizing your two given colors as two points in the Munsell color solid, you will realize that there are an infinite number of possible paths between them. If you choose to go through or near the vertical neutral axis, you will then incorporate some achromatic or low chroma elements in your scale. A more difficult alternative is to go around the neutral axis—the "great circle route"—maintaining a higher chroma. If you choose to go through the "poles" (white or black) you will be dealing with only tints and shades of your colors, and this is perhaps too easy.

Be sure to protect your given paint swatches from soiling: keep them covered when you are not using them, and cement them in place only after you have completed all the painting. It is also a good idea to keep your whole board covered with a taped-on sheet of tracing paper except when you are working on it.

Do not use any masking tape in any of this work: develop your brush control instead. And be sure to do all your work under the same conditions of illumination.

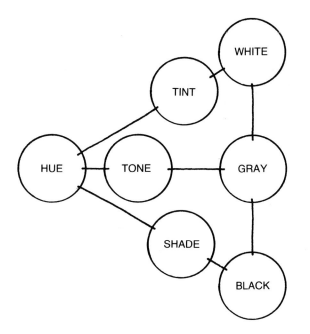

Tints are the result of the subtractive mixing of a hue with white.

Shades are the result of the subtractive mixing of a hue with black.

Tones are the result of a subtractive mixing of a hue with black *and* white (or gray).

"At least one American artist has an entire city as his canvas.

"From the Governor's suite to the Boston Garden, his art work is stared at, rained on, eaten on, and sat on daily. Million-dollar contracts are signed next to it. Carl Yastrzemski blasts doubles off it.

"Robert Rossi is an unusual paint mixer and he does more of it than anyone in Boston. His job is as simple as sky blue and as subtle as hot-dog pink.

"Over the last 17 years he has brewed enough latex and oil in the Newbury Street basement of Johnson's Paint Company to cover downtown with a good coat and still have a few thousand gallons left over for the Tobin Bridge.

"A list of his patrons reads like a Who's Who in Boston and runs the gamut of distinguished institutions from MIT and Bloomingdale's to the Prudential Center and Kentucky Fried Chicken.

"Mr. Rossi mixed the yellow that circles the Bruins' hockey rink, the red on the Lobsters' tennis courts, and the spruce green that covers Fenway Park's left-field wall. His mixtures have been used in the mansions of Grosse Point, Michigan, and on school blackboards in Dallas, Texas.

"Stockbrokers leave him free advice on playing the market when they come in to pick up the paint for their living rooms.

"Like most modern paint establishments, Johnson's employs a computerized 'color robot' for standard hues (like fire-engine red and cloud white). The tough stuff is left for the indefatigable Mr. Rossi, who is said to be the last full-time paint mixer left in Boston.

"He is daily deluged with requests that include matching the inside of a watermelon, the outside of a purple jelly bean, women's shoes, men's ties, and beach sand. One couple recently dropped by with a submarine sandwich and asked him to duplicate its colors right down to the tints of the baloney, mustard, and the bulkie roll.

" 'I can match anything. Just show me a paint chip,' grins Mr. Rossi as a customer impishly tries to stump him with a request for the 'blue in the Shaker's meeting house at Sabbathday Lake, Maine.'

"Surrounded by tiers of drooling paint pots and a spattered floor that would rival Kandinsky's best, he is absorbed by his alchemy. He carefully pours, stirs, and lifts his mixing stick to let the paint dribble back into the gallon bucket.

"Mr. Rossi shuns the refinement of paint brushes. He casually dips his index finger into the bucket and smears the gooey mixture on the end of a white cardboard strip, which he then places under a hair dryer to speed the process. Excess paint is hurriedly wiped on the pants pocket of his army fatigue trousers, already crusted with a glaciered spectrum of previous mixtures.

"He rambles to a nearby window and holds the original and his counterfeit up to the light. His clear brown eyes are the judge. 'A little too gray,' he surmises, returning to his laboratory.

"Mr. Rossi has no Rembrandts or Botticellis in his family tree. In fact, he was studying to become a radio repairman when he answered Johnson's newspaper ad 17 years ago and began his apprenticeship with such master mixers as Lloyd Larsen, Helmut Friend, and John Johnson, the company's founder.

"It took years and years of blending paint to learn that apple leaf is just the right portions of canary yellow, chrome green medium and burnt umber, and that combining radiant red, bermuda blue, and lamp black produces a delectable eggplant purple.

"Oddly enough, says Mr. Rossi, the recipes for such delicious hues are not the most difficult. It is the subtle off-whites and pastels, he explains, that require the delicate touch. And watch out for the golds that change depending on the direction and source of lighting (daylight, incandescent, or fluorescent), he warns.

"Many of history's great artists have been plagued by a view of the world as a giant painting and never seemed able to escape the realm of their paintbrush. Not Mr. Rossi. He leaves his work (and his colors) behind in a pile of speckled paint clothes and retreats to the refuge of his Cape Cod-style home in a Boston suburb. There he gets away from it all— the watermelon reds, the eggplant purples, the hot-dog pinks—and bathes in the chromatic quietude of pale green wallpaper."

—Stewart Dill McBride, "Boston Paint Mixer Leaves His Mark on City," *The Christian Science Monitor,* 10 December 1975

Discussion

When your work is displayed on the wall in association with that of your classmates, and viewed from a distance of about ten to twenty feet, you can get a better idea of your degree of success in matching colors and in painting evenly-graduated color scales. This problem is closely analogous to the exercises performed by musicians and athletes who also must develop an almost instinctive ability to discriminate and generate nuances of response.

Certainly you became aware of the iterative process of hypothesizing, simulating, and evaluating pigment mixtures in the "trial and error" attempt to match and mix specific colors. Perhaps you also discovered how pigments change color in drying?

In this problem we used what is termed "subtractive" color mixing. Subtractive color mixing commonly occurs when several pigments are physically mixed on a surface, or when translucent colored filters are superimposed in front of a light source. If cyan (blue-green), magenta (blue-red), and yellow are used in the proper proportions, they will mix subtractively to produce red, green, and blue secondaries, and in triple combination an achromatic color of lower value. In any subtractive color mixture the chroma of the resulting color is usually lower than that of the original colors.

There is, of course, such a thing as "additive" color mixing. It occurs when viewing a surface simultaneously illuminated by two or more colored lights. If red, green, and blue primaries are used in the proper proportions, they will mix additively to produce cyan, magenta, and yellow secondaries, and in triple combination, an achromatic color sensation of a higher value.

Subtractive color mixing

You can investigate this by using three PAR dichroic spotlights, obtainable from a lighting equipment supply store. Project them two and three at a time on a white surface such as a movie screen, in a dark room, and vary their relative distance from the surface. Be sure to intercept the beams with some opaque object. Can you explain the resulting color shadows?

Additive color mixing also occurs when small areas of two or more colors are closely juxtaposed in separate, finely textured patterns which, when viewed at the proper distance, blend optically to produce a color sensation different from that produced by the original colors viewed separately. This type of additive color mixing was used by such nineteenth century French Neo-Impressionist "Pointillist" painters as Seurat, Signac, Monet, Sisley, and Pissarro, who "mixed" their colors "on the retina of the observer" by applying pigment to their canvasses in small, closely spaced dots or strokes of paint. In so doing, these painters were utilizing the results of a number of scientific investigations in the perception of color, generally summarized in 1828 by the great French chemist M. E. Chevreul as the "laws" of "simultaneous and successive contrast," in which a change in any part of a visual field causes a change in the rest of that field. These painters used this principle in an attempt to achieve higher apparent chromas with their paints, and to produce a shimmering, luminous quality in their impressionistic representations of the momentary effects of light in the illumination of space and form. A contemporary application of additive color mixing also occurs of course in color television, where a minute mosaic of red, green, and blue phosphor dots on the surface of a cathode-ray tube is excited to fluorescence by a variable stream of electrons.

Red, green, and blue Sylvania 150 watt PAR-38 Dichromatic Color Spots are recommended. These lamps use thin dichroic interference coatings on the inside surfaces of the lens to provide 30° beams of pure hue.

See William Innes Homer, *Seurat and the Science of Painting* (Cambridge, Mass.: MIT Press, 1978).

This is, of course, of a piece with the issues discussed in terms of "illusions" in Problem 1. But note that of all the visual attributes, that of color is the most "relative" of all.

Additive color mixing

You can continue your color solfeggio with a painted demonstration of both additive and subtractive color mixing. Use the layouts suggested in the diagram, on a medium-gray board (or studio wall); and, for convenience, Liquitex acrylic Napthol Crimson (red), Ultramarine Blue (blue), and Permanent Green Light (green) for the additive primaries; and Cadmium Yellow Light or Medium (yellow), Acra Violet (magenta), and Phthalocyanine Blue (cyan) for the subtractive. You may have to adjust some of these pigments to the same value by tinting or shading them, and experiment with the proportions to achieve an optimum result.

Another challenge is to investigate the interaction of color with variations in texture and surface finish. For this study lay out nine 16″ x 32″ panels on one sheet of ½″ or ¾″ plywood, and prepare four 8″ x 16″ bands of physical textures on each panel. These textures should be "granular" (see Problem 3) and include one band each of smooth, fine, medium, and coarse textures. This may be achieved by gluing sand, pebbles, and gravel on the panels. Then, using flat matte paint, prime and color one panel in black, one in middle gray, and one in white; three panels in a cool hue (with one high, one middle, and one low value); and the remaining three panels in a warm hue (again with one high, one middle, and one low value). Finally, "glaze" half of each panel in an 8″ x 32″ strip with clear lacquer or varnish so that each four-textured monochromatic or achromatic panel is half matte and half glossy.

If all these panels are studied together, under a variety of lighting conditions (see Problem 3b: Texture Archetypes: Conclusion) you will be able to make some generalizations on the subject.

For "warm" and "cool" hues, see Problem 11.

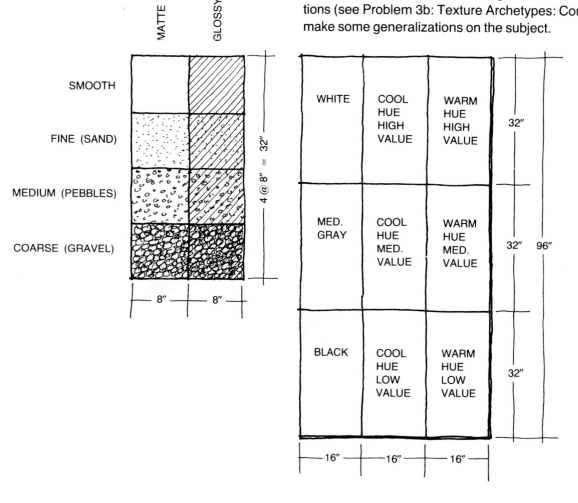

Achromatic colors are those without the attributes of hue and chroma; in other words, the blacks, grays, and whites of the vertical scale at the center of the Munsell color solid.

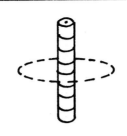

Monochromatic colors are those of the same hue but of differing value and saturation; in other words, colors on any single vertical hue plane of the Munsell color solid.

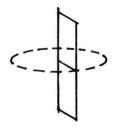

Analogous colors are those whose hues are closely related, such as blue and green, or red and orange; in other words, those colors on adjacent vertical hue planes of the Munsell color solid.

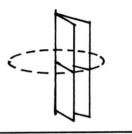

Complementary colors are those on diametrically opposite vertical hue planes of the Munsell color solid. When mixed subtractively, complementary colors will tend to produce an achromatic color of lower value.

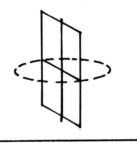

High Key refers to a color composition in which all colors are of a high value: in other words, those at the upper third of the Munsell color solid.

Low Key refers to a color composition in which all colors are of a low value; in other words, those colors at the lower third of the Munsell color solid.

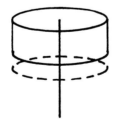

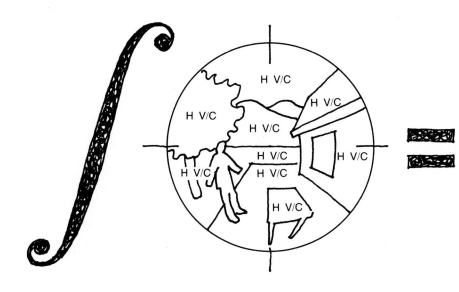

Color Analysis of Scene

In Problem 9 we became familiar with the use of the Munsell system as a means for the standardized description of the color of a given basic pattern area (BPA), in terms of alphanumeric values of "hue," "value," and "chroma." Our question now is, How can we describe the color effect of a *combination* of basic pattern areas, such as those which are associated in a painting, or in an environmental scene? Obviously we could match the color of each basic pattern area with the nearest Munsell color chip, and present the result of this survey in a diagram with each basic pattern area identified by the corresponding Munsell notation. But this stops short of characterizing the color effect of the whole, and as visual designers we are concerned with the overall color impression of both existing and proposed environments.

This problem introduces a procedure for the description of the color attributes of a given *scene.* It is based on the assumption that an existing scene, or a proposed one, is available in a full color, fish-eye representation; however, for the present purposes we will use a rectangular color reproduction from a magazine as a substitute. The subject is not important as long as the picture contains at last ten color BPAs differing in hue, value, and chroma, but if it represents an exterior or interior scene, so much the better.

It should be noted that the relationship between an actual scene in the "real world" and the representation of this scene in a two-dimensional rendering is not a simple one. Although to a large extent the patterns of radiant energy reaching the observer's eyes in each case may evoke similar responses, these patterns result from very different circumstances. For one example: in the real-world scene each environmental surface usually receives a different amount and kind of illumination, whereas in the two-dimensional representation all the surfaces are illuminated only by the ambient viewing light. Other differences are discussed in Ralph Evans, *An Introduction to Color* (New York: Wiley, 1948).

The procedure used here does not presume to suggest that there is a point-by-point identity between the colors of environmental surfaces and the colors of these surfaces as rendered in two dimensons; it is only intended for the introduction of a series of conceptualizations by means of which our perceptions of a given scene (in terms of either the real world or its representation) may be more adequately characterized. For examples of applications of this approach see: Luigi Moretti, "Colore di Venezia," *Spazio,* October 1950; Jean Philippe Lenclos, "Couleurs et Paysages," *L'Architecture d'Aujourd'hui,* November 1972; Gilles de Bure, "The Powerful Hum of Color," *Architecture Plus,* October 1973; Jean Philippe Lenclos, "Living in Color," in Tom Porter and Byron Mikellides, *Color for Architecture* (New York: Van Nostrand Reinhold, 1976); Masao Inui, "Colour in the Interior Environment," *Lighting Research and Technology,* vol. 1, no. 2 (1969).

Materials

1 15″ x 20″ white illustration board

Paint set

Rubber cement; protractor

Color reproduction, as described above: about 6″ x 8″

Munsell color charts

Gray paper, approximately middle value: two sheets, each about 8″ x 10″

Procedure

Trim the reproduction to 6″ x 8″ and cement it in position on the upper left-hand side of the illustration board, as indicated in the figure. Using tracing paper, or a transfer grid, reproduce the outlines of all the color BPAs of your original in an equivalent 6″ x 8″ area on the board. Your first task is then to paint in these areas directly on the board to produce as close a match as possible with the original.

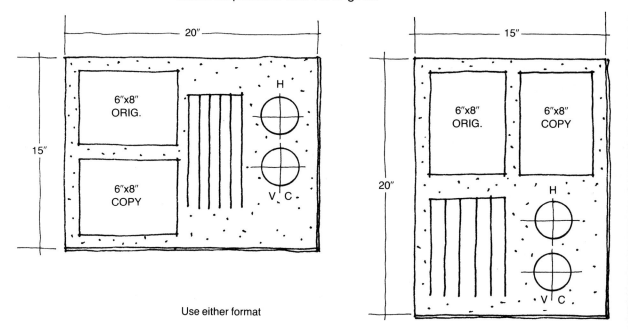

Use either format

It is suggested that you test your color mixes on some scrap pieces of board. A sample of your trial mixture (your hypothesis) can be applied to such a strip (a simulation) and compared in juxtaposition with the area to be matched (an evaluation). Remember that paints change in appearance in drying, and be sure to do all this work under the same lighting conditions.

Your criterion of success for this work is that when the board with your original and your copy are seen from a distance of about ten feet, you should not be able to tell the original and copy apart. At this point you may feel that this is an impossible challenge, but be prepared to be (delightfully) surprised.

Next, superimpose a top-hinged piece of tracing paper over the original color item, and on it outline and number consecutively all the color BPAs larger than 1 percent of the total picture area. (By dividing each side of the 6″ x 8″ reproduction into ten equal parts, and drawing the resulting 10 x 10 grid on the tracing paper, each of the resulting one hundred units represents 1 percent of the total area. Note also that the diagonal of a 6″ x 8″ rectangle is 10″ long.) As a matter of practical convenience, for the purposes of this illustrative exercise, limit the number of BPAs to about twenty, more or less, by aggregating them where possible and by ignoring those smaller than 1 percent of the total picture area. To make this easier, you might imagine the picture as being projected somewhat out of focus, or, alternately, as if you were "blocking out" or approximating its major color areas in making a painting. Please note also that at this point you are dealing with patches of color on a two-dimensional surface—not with walls or rugs or grass or any environmental surfaces.

Then prepare a five-column table, located as shown in the figure, with the columns labeled from left to right as follows:

/ BPA No. / % Area / Hue / Value / Chroma /

Your task now is to estimate the percentage of the total area occupied by each BPA, and to identify its color attributes in terms of the Munsell H-V/C notation. To do the former, use as a guide the 1 percent squares you have ruled. Note that they should all add up to 100 percent.

To identify the color attributes of each BPA, prepare two 8″ x 10″ pieces of middle-value achromatic gray construction paper, each with a single rectangular aperture cut in the center, slightly smaller than the size of a color chip on the Munsell charts. Place one of these aperture sheets over the BPA in question and use the other mask to cover in turn a number of color chips in your Munsell charts. Try to juxtapose the two apertures, so that you can see them together. By this means you can determine the closest match of that BPA with one of the Munsell chips. When you have done this, enter the Munsell notation of this chip in the appropriate position in the table, and repeat the procedure for each of the BPAs.

In some cases you may not be able to find a reasonably close match with one of the Munsell student set color chips. Lacking the use of the more extensive charts of the complete *Munsell Book of Color*, your option is to interpolate between the ten-hue student charts, and the value/chroma chips on them.

If you have simplified your identification of BPAs to limit their number, some of them may not have a "flat" or uniform color area. Here again try to imagine them as being out of focus (try squinting at a typical or representative part in the aperture to simulate this effect) and match this to the nearest Munsell equivalent. This procedure is also recommended in the case of patterned or textured BPAs.

188

For a discussion of descriptive statistics see Geoffrey Broadbent, *Design in Architecture* (New York: Wiley, 1973).

The final step is to summarize the frequency distribution of these color attributes by plotting them on two polar histograms like the ones shown in the accompanying diagrams. The central tendencies revealed by these plots provide an overall characterization of the matched colors in the original reproduction.

In the hue histogram the ten major hues are laid out at 36° intervals in the order shown. The total percentage of any given hue is indicated, as a solid line in a bar graph, on the radius at that hue, with 0 percent at the circumference and 100 percent at the center. The total achromatic area, however, is plotted as a circle of the appropriate radius with 0 percent at the center and 100 percent at the circumference.

In the value/chroma histogram the left side of the circumference represents the value scale extending from 0 at the bottom to 10 at the top, at 18° intervals. The chroma scale extends from 0 at the bottom to 16 at the top, at 22.5° intervals. As in the case of the hue histogram, the total percentage of any given value or chroma is also indicated as a bar on the radius at the appropriate point with 0 percent at the circumference and 100 percent at the center.

Adapted from P. Moon and D. E. Spencer, "Area in Color Harmony," *Journal of the Optical Society of America,* vol. 34, no. 2 (February 1944)

Adapted from Ralph Evans, *An Introduction to Color*

From an inspection of the central tendencies in the hue histogram we can then characterize the type of color combination, and also hypothesize the resulting psychological "temperature feeling." From an inspection of the central tendencies of the value and chroma histograms we can hypothesize the resulting psychological "mood feeling," in accordance with the accompanying diagrams.

Note that it is quite possible that your histograms may show no clear central tendencies. All this means is that the scene you are analyzing has no specific color combination, "temperature feeling," or "mood feeling."

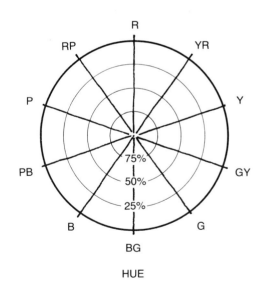

HUE

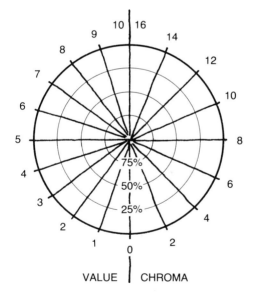

VALUE | CHROMA

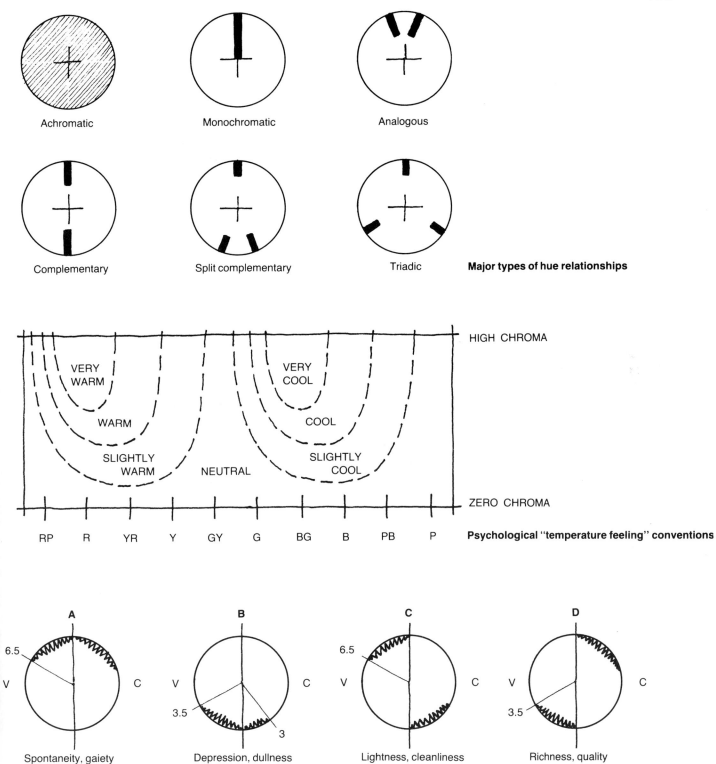

Achromatic

Monochromatic

Analogous

Complementary

Split complementary

Triadic

Major types of hue relationships

HIGH CHROMA

VERY WARM

VERY COOL

WARM

COOL

SLIGHTLY WARM

NEUTRAL

SLIGHTLY COOL

ZERO CHROMA

Psychological "temperature feeling" conventions

RP R YR Y GY G BG B PB P

A

6.5

V C

Spontaneity, gaiety

B

3.5

V C

3

Depression, dullness

C

6.5

V C

Lightness, cleanliness

D

V C

3.5

Richness, quality

Hypothetical psychological "mood feeling"

As will be seen in Problem 13, there are many factors other than color acting to qualify the subjective impression of "temperature feeling" in a given scene.

Johannes Itten, in *The Art of Color* (New York: Reinhold, 1961), demonstrates how the "temperature feeling" of a given color area may change as a result of being placed in a different context, and Ralph Evans (*An Introduction to Color*, pp. 314-15) describes how the subjective impression of a predominant hue in a given scene depends not on a majority of the areas in that scene having that hue, but rather "all colors in the scene are shifted toward this hue from their most probable color in everyday life."

These hue, value, and chroma effects are included under the general heading of "adaptation"; more specifically, "lateral adaptation," or "simultaneous contrast." Discussions of these and the other effects may be found in the following references:
R. Arnheim, *Art and Visual Perception* (Berkeley: University of California Press, 1954); J. Beck, "The Perception of Surface Colors," *Scientific American,* August 1975; R. Evans, *An Introduction to Color* (New York: Wiley, 1948); W. Faulkner, *Architecture and Color* (New York: Wiley-Interscience, 1972); R. M. Hanes, "The Long and Short of Color Distance," *Architectural Record,* April 1960; J. Itten, *The Art of Color* (New York: Reinhold, 1961); E. H. Johns and F. C. Sumner, "Relation of the Brightness Differences of Color to their Apparent Distance," *Journal of Psychology* 26 (1948); Gyorgy Kepes, *The Language of Vision* (Chicago: Paul Theobald, 1944); C. G. Mueller et al., *Light and Vision* (New York: Time-Life, 1966).

For a description of such a study, see "How Does Light Affect Color?" *Architectural Forum,* January 1949.

Discussion

In view of the fact that although the eye looks, it is the mind that sees, we have undertaken this analytical exercise to heighten your awareness and perception of both the quantitative and qualitative color characteristics of a given environmental scene. How, for example, would you describe the quantitative color characteristics of the room you now occupy . . . and of another room with which you are familiar? Could you make an approximately central tendency plot on hue-value/chroma diagrams of these spaces? Having done this, do you think that the corresponding hypothesized qualitative characterizations of "temperature feeling" and "mood feeling" apply to these spaces? In any event, you should realize that these hypotheses must not be taken as set formulae, but rather only as first approximations necessarily subject to empirical verification, and that above all color attributes are sensitive to context.

A most instructive series of experiments may be performed to demonstrate this last point (as a continuation of the visual illusions shown in Problem 1). Not only are the apparent hue, value, and chroma of a given color area modified by the color of the surrounding or adjacent areas, but also are its apparent size, and apparent advancing or receding position relative to the surface. To investigate this, prepare a 10″ x 15″ illustration board with six equal 5″ x 5″ areas colored respectively black, white, red, green, blue, and yellow. Then place six 1½″ squares, cut from the same piece of colored paper, in the center of each of these larger squares, and compare their apparent differences in hue, value, and chroma, as well as in relative size, and in position behind or before the surface. Repeat this experiment with another set of squares cut from paper of another color.

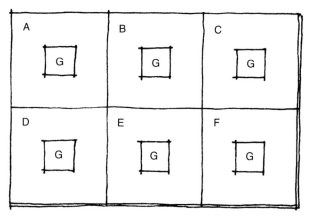

Since "color is how you light it," you should inspect the work under several different sources of light: for example, sunlight, incandescent light, fluorescent light, and daylight from a northern exposure. Better still, prepare the original experiment in duplicate, and compare results side by side under two different, separated light sources. This would make an excellent collaborative project.

In these experiments you are being encouraged to look closely at specific color areas in situational terms, and to become aware of the changes in their appearance when seen in different contexts and under different illuminations. Ordinarily we do not do this and are inclined to unconsciously see so-called "local colors" as preserving the same identity under all conditions and in all circumstances. This tendency is one of the well-known "perceptual constancy" phenomena in which we neglect the momentary and transitory effects of a situation, drawing instead on our memories of essential invarient characteristics and our personal affective associations. But, as you will readily appreciate once you try it, this alternate way of seeing colors adds a richer and wider dimension to your visual world—and your professional competence. Some people spend their whole life transcending the constancy of local color, discriminating and enjoying the mutual interactions of light and color, and developing and exploiting its signification.

As a matter of fact, despite the vast amount of work that has been done, the whole subject of color is still pretty much an unknown territory, with continuing explorations and many widely divergent theories—to say nothing of the subject of synesthesia, or that phenomenon in which sensations in one mode produce impressions in another (as in colored sounds or flavors).

Having convinced yourself now that you *are* capable of carefully discriminating color nuances, and that you *are* able to mix and match pigments to closely match the colors you observe, how about trying some further challenges?

For example: arrange and mount a collection of small two-dimensional examples of differing surface qualities (specular, glossy, matte, luster, and iridescent), and also of differing *physical* textures (sandpaper, wood, fur, glass, crinkled aluminum foil, etc.) on a panel, and then render them, full size, as exactly as possible on an adjacent panel. Try subtractive color mixing, and additive color mixing.

Or: set up a still life of three-dimensional objects of wood, glass, metal, paper, cloth, and ceramic, and try rendering it, using small pieces of torn colored paper, both transparent and opaque, rubber-cemented to a gray panel.

Or: select one of your favorites from your collection of multicolored natural objects—shells, leaves, polished rocks, tree bark, fruits, or vegetables—and render it as exactly as possible, perhaps double its actual size. Then reproduce its color BPAs in an adjacent rectangular array with their areas in the same proportions as in the original. Finally, prepare two or more identical rectangular arrays with the color areas interchanged, as a way of investigating the effects of differing proportions of the same colors.

The traditional term "local color" is rather misleading, since it refers to the "normal" name of a color (as a conceptual abstraction) and *not* to the specific appearance of a given color area (as a carefully observed perception). "Local color" identifies the perceptually constant class name of a color without reference to its variable optical appearance in different surroundings; and the term "situational color" is used here to denote the carefully discriminated appearance of a given color area as modified by its particular surrounding and previously seen colors, its direct or reflected illumination, and the atmospheric conditions.

See J. Albers, *Interaction of Color* (New Haven: Yale University Press, 1963); and Gyorgy Kepes, "Design and Light," *Design Quarterly 68* (Minneapolis, Minn.: Walker Art Center, 1967).

For example, see Ralph Evans, *The Perception of Color* (New York: John Wiley and Sons, 1974); E. H. Land, "The Retinex Theory of Color Vision," *Scientific American,* December 1977; and L. E. Marks, "Synesthesia: The Lucky People with Mixed-Up Senses," *Psychology Today,* June 1975.

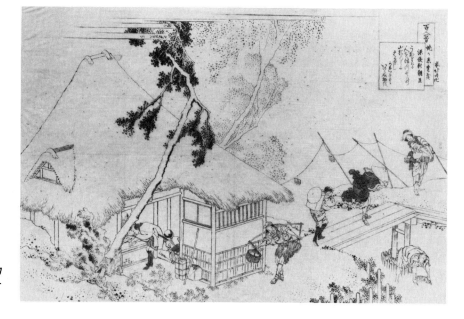

Katsushika Hokusai (1760-1849), *Drawing for an unpublished print*. Courtesy of the Museum of Fine Arts, Boston

"Primary colors designate strong emotions. Young children appear to have little interest in mixed or impure colors apparently because they denote ambiguities that lie outside their experience. Among chromatic colors, red is the most dominant and its meaning is the most widely shared by peoples of different culture. Red signifies blood, life, and energy. Since Upper Paleolithic times red ocher has been used in burials. Greek, Etruscan, and Roman sarcophagi bear traces of red paint in their interior, and the red shroud has been in use for interment down to the present, although the practice is now limited to the burial of a pope. In China, red is the color used in weddings for it symbolizes life and joy. On the other hand, a red sky means calamity and warfare. Here is no contradiction: red is the color of blood and blood is life, but spilt blood leads to death. Red also symbolizes energy and action—action aimed at life though it may result in death. The red flag is the flag of revolutionary fervor.

"All peoples distinguish between black and white or darkness and light. Everywhere these colors carry powerful symbolic reverberations; only red among chromatic colors matches them in importance. Black and white have both positive and negative meanings, thus:

Black: (positive) wisdom, potential, germinal, maternal, earth-mother. (negative) evil, curse, defilement, death.

White: (positive) light, purity, spirituality, timelessness, divine. (negative) mourning, death.

"Nonetheless the chief associations of white are positive, and those of black negative. The two colors symbolize opposed and yet complementary universal principles: analogous pairs are light and darkness, appearance and disappearance, life and death. These antinomies are different ways of saying the same thing. They are the necessary halves of a total reality: one merges into the other in space and evolves out of the other in time. In rituals, myths, and philosophical synthesis, the complementarity of black and white is emphasized. In isolation, however, these terms often appear to represent irreconcilable values. It is well known that in the Western tradition black stands for all the negative values of curse, evil, defilement, and death, whereas white signifies joy, purity, and goodness. But similar interpretations are given in a large number of non-Western cultures. For example, to the Bambara—a west African negro tribe—white is a regal color, representing wisdom and

Color Expression

In the previous problem we introduced some hypotheses relating the frequency distributions of color areas to the "temperature feeling" and "mood feeling" of the overall color patterns. Here we continue our study of the affective qualities of color with a further consideration of color associations and symbolism. You will be challenged to apply new insights in the expressive communication of some of your own experiences, and you will also have an opportunity to consider some further aspects of the 1,200-year-old aesthetic culture of Japan, in which the natural landscape and human life are related in ways often complementary to many western modes.

For this problem you are asked to recall two different environmental scenes and two different situational events, each connected with a strong personal experience which remains in your memory with a particular vividness. Examples of such environmental scenes might be springtime in Paris, morning at Big Sur, Times Square on New Year's eve, or sunset in the desert; and examples of situational events might be re-reading old letters on a rainy day, Friday night at the singles bar, a honeymoon in Tahiti, or the funeral of your child.

purity of spirit. The dark tones of indigo, on the other hand, are identified with sadness and impurity. To the Nupe tribe of Nigeria, black signifies sorcery, evil, and frightening prospects. Among the peoples of Malagasy (Madagascar) the word black is associated with inferiority, evil, suspicion, and disagreeableness; the word white with light, hope, joy, and purity. Examples can be multiplied easily. A reason for the negative response to black may lie in the child's horror of the night—a time of isolation, disturbing dreams, and nightmares, when invisibility of the familiar encourages fantasy to run wild. There is also the fear of blindness.

"White, black, and red thus appear to be colors of universal significance. According to Victor Turner, they are among man's earliest symbols. Turner believes that these colors are important to man because they represent products of the human body whose emission, spilling, or production is associated with a heightening of emotion. The human individual is caught by sensations beyond the normal range; he is possessed by a power the source of which he posits outside of himself in nature and society. Thus the symbol, a superorganic cultural product, is intimately connected with organic bodily experiences in its early stages. The phys-

iological events associated with the three colors are also experiences of social relationships, which may be summarized as follows:

White = semen (man and woman tie).
= milk (mother and child tie).

Red = bloodshed (war, feud, social discontinuities).
= obtaining and preparing animal food (male productive role; sexual division of labor).
= transmission of blood from generation to generation (index of membership in corporate group).

Black = excreta (bodily dissolution; change from one status to another—mystical death).
= rainclouds, fertile earth (shared life-values).

"Almost every language has special words for black and white. Among chromatic colors red occupies a special position. The term for red is usually one of the oldest color terms in a given language; as a rule it is a native word. Yellow in many respects follows the pattern of red. Like red, a special term develops for it which is old in the color vocabulary. Next come green and blue. Unlike red, for which comparison is readily

made with blood, neither yellow, nor green, nor blue is the outstanding color of any ubiquitous phenomenon in nature. In China, yellow dominates because it is perceived to be the color of earth and of the center; but this attribution is not widespread. The evident object of comparison for green is given in plants, and in the great majority of languages the term for green is related to the words for plants and growth. In English, 'green,' 'growth,' and 'grass' are derived from the Germanic root *gro* which probably meant 'to grow.' It would seem natural to associate the color blue with the sky; yet the influence of sky on the development of terms for blue has not been as great as one might expect. Almost everywhere, blue is the last of the color primaries to be indicated by a special term. In many languages there is no word for blue at all. Brent Berlin and Paul Kay believe that basic color terms evolve through stages: first, black plus most dark hues and white plus most light hues; then red, orange, and yellow; then green and blue; then brown."

—Yi-Fu Tuan, *Topophilia* (Englewood Cliffs, N.J.: Prentice-Hall, 1974). See also the tabulation of color associations in Henry Dreyfus, *Symbol Sourcebook* (New York: McGraw-Hill, 1972).

You are to communicate your feeling about each of your chosen scenes and events by means of a color composition in the form of a short mosaic "poem." For examples of similar succinct expressions of feeling, but in a different mode of communication, consider the following Japanese *haiku* for each of the four seasons:

Spring

Summer

Yes, spring has come;

This morning a nameless hill

Is shrouded in mist.

—Basho

A hoe standing there

No one to be seen,—

The heat!

—Shiki

Spring rain;

Raindrops from the willow,

Petals from the plum-tree.

—Shoha

The short night;

Between the reeds flows

The froth of crabs.

—Buson

The brush wood,

Though cut for fuel,

Is beginning to bud.

—Boncho

The wind-bell is silent:

The heat

Of the clock.

—Yayu

Autumn **Winter**

The moon in the water

Turned a somersault

And floated away.

—Ryota

They spoke no word,

The host, the guest,

And the white chrysanthemum.

—Ryota

From R. H. Blyth, *Haiku* (Tokyo: Hokuseido, 1960). The *haiku* is a traditional verse form in three lines of five, seven, and five syllables respectively, and including a word suggestive of the season for which the poem was written.

Ah, grief and sadness!

The fishing-line trembles

In the autumn breeze.

—Buson

The winter rain dyes

The letters on the grave-stone:

Sadness.

—Roka

The morning dew:

The pampas grass is drooping,

The bush-clover lies prostrate.

—Chora

The old pond;

A straw sandal sunk to the bottom,

Sleet falling.

—Buson

Along the same lines, the traditional Japanese dwelling may also be seen as a sort of poem. Here are some comments to this effect by Antonin and Noemi P. Raymond, from *Antonin Raymond: His Work in Japan, 1920-1935* (Tokyo: Johnan Shoin, 1935):

"An architect working in Japan has the advantage of seeing materialized before him in Japanese architecture and civilization, fundamental principles the rediscovery of which is the goal of modern architecture. Occidentals, hampered as they are by deep-rooted materialism, have not yet realized these principles in all their purity, for this would demand a spiritual outlook.

"These principles express themselves with great clarity in Japanese domestic architecture.

"The Japanese does not wallow in matter for the love of it. It is at all times subservient to an idea. For him matter exists only as a symbol of spiritual truth and to use it unconscious of the truths which it expresses is what constitutes bad taste.

"Life is actually a drama or a landscape in which he seeks some hidden meaning. Living for this quest, or trying to express in his living the truths he understands, the maximum of comfort is not the aim of his constructions.

"He plans a shelter against inclemency at its worst, using it as one more means of manifesting the subtleties of the spirit which he sees vitally expressed in all forms of life. The problem of Function, Form and Matter with which we struggle ponderously is solved with incomparable ease for it is seen in its right perspective, the exteriorization of an idea.

"A Japanese house resembles the evolution of a natural form. At every point it is related to an inner motive for which it has found an exact and fitting solution, not only practical but expressive of a profound understanding of the real values of life.

"Compared with the Japanese our love for Nature is very superficial. For him she is the very key to the secret of existence. His concern not to betray her has been his safeguard throughout the ages, and at all times he turns to her as the infallible guide. He chooses materials which speak for her. Wood in its natural state, straw under foot, sand on the walls. And his only architect up to recent years has been the carpenter, deft in handling them, and respectful of their intrinsic qualities.

"Yet the word rustic cannot be applied in any way to Japanese architecture, for nothing in it is the result of chance nor of an artificial mimicry in the manner of the XVIIIth Century, but of an urgent need to lose one's self in nature. Likewise the word 'decorative' is falsely applied to the art of the Japanese. It happens only that his ideas take a harmonious form. In the place of the framed picture which belongs nowhere he incorporates in a whole the idea which moves him. It is none the less as real, as true, as the oil painting of a cow hung above the drawing room couch, because that is the only wall space.

"To the contrary, that which you note as decorative, is the outcome of a necessity: the variety of rectangular planes playing one into the other; the silhouette of the indispensable skeleton of the paper win-

dows, the rectangles drawn by the borders necessary to the mats, the variable openings on the garden. There is a symbol in the interplay of geometrical forms and natural forms which deeply moves the Japanese.

"He understands the quality of the eternal that is why he does not attach himself to permanence in things. The cherry blossom, glory of a single day, is the emblem of the soldier. He does homage to the Eternal by setting forth the frailty of the temporal. With the exception of the walls of the castle moat (the castles themselves are very light constructions) the Japanese prefers to a strong wall giving no trouble for years to come, a neatly made bamboo-fence for the renewal of which he will later be obliged again and again to call his gardener whom he likes to see at work.

"A beautiful old house may be admired but to it is preferred the immaculate purity of the new one like clarity in water and freshness in a flower. A Shinto shrine must be rebuilt every 20 years.

"The fury of the elements peculiar to Japan, strong winds, heavy rains, cold, burning sun, earthquakes, typhoons, have helped to make him understand the frailty of things, to appreciate the quality

which heightens by contrast the immutable grandeur of the spirit.

"The house, the objects, have no intrinsic value in Japan. There is nothing monumental in art as for example in China. Everything serves a precise purpose and is only satisfactory relatively to that purpose. The highest satisfaction which a Japanese experiences is to be found in the harmony which he perceives between the idea, the act and the material, space and time.

"Is there any other civilization for which beautifying means elimination? It is through increased simplicity and elimination that the man of taste finds elegance. The home of the master and that of the labourer differ only in that the former shows a greater concern for the clarity of construction and plan. All is the direct result of a necessity, be it material or spiritual. Nothing is ever sufficiently clear, sufficiently pure. It would seem that by dint of trying to eliminate all that which is not essential, of clearing the void, of seeking the essence of things, at last, in the silence thus created one hears the voice of form, substance and space.

"Occidental architecture in its entirety appears shockingly gross by comparison. Even our greatest epochs have a barbaric

aspect. As for modern times, the concern over purely exterior appearances and the excessive seeking after comfort offer a still greater contrast.

"The doing away with all but essentials, discipline, are at the basis of Japanese charm. A Japanese room is empty, without chairs, and one takes out low tables and other necessities from a closet when needed. On one side a Kakemono is hung on the wall and a few flowers or an object appropriate to the season are set at the base. Nothing "furnishes" or "decorates" or conceals the void odious to an occidental. Nothing veils the sharpness of the openings. The room is occupied only by space, and the thoughts of its inhabitant. When I speak of sharpness or purity, I do not mean that insistence on exactitude, on finish, which is the seal of the bourgeois of any nation; that emphasis put on perfection in the object for its own sake, be it a house, a chair, or a garden, which is the joy of the proprietor. Like Nature herself the Japanese like to express perfection in creation and also a certain carelessness and detachment which like that found in the dried grasses and shrivelled leaves of autumn give things their poetry . . . .

"When entering, one takes off one's shoes and puts on slippers, the floor be-

ing something sacred and not to be soiled by the dust from outside. The visitor is never admitted into the intimacy of the family. A separate impersonal reception room is required for meeting guests. It must be situated near the main entrance and allows no views of the interior. The ancient Japanese entrance leading to the left and right was often blocked by a partition which created an aspect of imposing reserve . . . .

"The Japanese house possesses a wonderful flexibility. During the night and in winter it is a box hermetically closed to the exterior, divided into rooms inside. In summer, away with the shutters, the paper windows, doors and partitions, the house becomes nothing more than a pavilion open to all the winds. The 'Sudare,' delicate blinds made of rush or bamboo, swinging to the slightest breath of wind, shade the interior.

"The Japanese clings to old-fashioned customs. He still loves to sit on the mats in the simplicity and inimitable poetry of the Japanese room . . . .

"Also the Japanese woman still dresses the more often in Kimono. For which she must have a special room provided with chests of drawers wherein to keep her Kimono and sashes which must be folded on mats. For the children too we arrange rooms having mats, soft to the tread, on which they can sleep in numbers; the beds are put away in deep closets after having been aired . . . .

"From ancient times in Japan the bath has been considered as much a pleasure as a necessity. At the natural hotsprings people spend most of the time in the water. The country people often set their bath tub in the middle of the courtyard. In private houses the bath is fitted up very sumptuously. From the ante-room used for undressing, one steps down into the large and well ventilated bathroom where one must soap oneself, rinse and shower before entering into the bath. The latter is usually of natural white wood emitting a good odour; it is deep and when one is seated in it the very hot water comes up to the neck. People go to the bath together. It is a very cheerful place . . . .

"There is also the 'Kura.' It is a kind of sublimated store-house. The family treasures are kept in it. That is to say, the Kakemonos, rare porcelains, family swords, etc.

"It is made of two constructions, one within the other. Externally incombustible, giving protection against moisture and insects, internally of wood. There are treble windows with shutters of iron, of glass, and of wire-mesh to keep out insects. The inner construction resembles a library. There are shelves of wood on which are ranged the white wooden boxes tied with green cord in which the treasures are kept wrapped up in cotton-batting and silk. The Japanese have in this way preserved for centuries pictures on silk and paper and fine porcelains. Each box is numbered and catalogued. The steward or the mistress of the house keeps the key and the catalogue . . . .

"Now arises the question of orientation which is of great importance considering the climate. There is to be found here the maximum of moisture and of dryness in sudden transition. Shoes get covered with moss during a damp summer night, wood cracks during a dry winter. Now a dry bitter cold, then the burning sun and the rains. The principal winds blow from the north in the winter and from the south in summer.

"The Japanese house faces the south and is entirely open on this side, that is to say that the house is nothing more than apertures and pillars, engulfing the cool breezes in summer, and the sun in winter, which is the only way of heating. Apertures necessary for ventilation are

Illustrations are of the building exhibited by New York's Museum of Modern Art in 1954. The design, in the *shoin-* style, is based on sixteenth and seventeenth century prototypes, and might have been built by a scholar, a government official, or a priest. Photos by Ezra Stoller, © ESTO

made on the north side without which everything would become musty, and also to give a view onto the shady side of the garden. Our plans are orientated according to these traditions which are perfectly logical.

"The Japanese loves nature ardently, more than we do, and he shows it by making for her sacrifices which we do not make. The garden and the house are one whole. The garden enters into the house and the house creeps through the garden as a snake in the grass. The cube style of house set on the ground in the western manner is impossible here.

"There must be exits everywhere. The idea of looking for a door would be unbearable. Neither would it suffice to commune with a distant horizon from the second floor. Even though it were no longer larger than a pocket-handkerchief, a Japanese must have a bit of mossy ground with a stone, and a few leaves from which he can see the rain drops trickling. This must be arranged in such a manner as to allow him to make distant journeys while sitting all the time on the straw matting in the middle of his room. After a trip to the Occident one comes back convinced that the Occidental fears contact with the exterior. Very

often he must go over to the window to find out what the weather is like, if he is at all interested in it. He rarely concerns himself about the seasons except to change his dress.

"When shall we hang on the wall a picture of a mountain torrent to refresh the friends who will come to see us on a summer's day?

"The Japanese, on the contrary, rearranges his home and changes his picture to keep in accord with all the aspects of nature . . . .

"There is still one more important thing peculiar to the Japanese home, the 'Kimon,' or the science of conciliating the household gods. When the plans are sketched, the architect and the client must consult a scholar in this science who will tell them whether the various parts of the house, entrances, W.C.s, bed rooms, kitchen, etc. are auspiciously situated in reference to the center of the house or if it is probable that disaster and ill-health will befall the unfortunate occupant. We may have to push a certain room towards the east, or see that the fountain be not placed due south, or sometimes even completely abandon the project. The date of starting the construction as well as the moving in of the family must be fixed on favourable dates.

The modern Japanese does not lack in humour when speaking of the Kimon, but for nothing in the world would he live in a house without having consulted a seer. We have noticed that the advice given often had a foundation of good sense, no matter what reasoning had been followed to obtain it."

For a native's comments on some related aspects of the Japanese aesthetic, see Junichiro Tanizaki, *In Praise of Shadows,* translated by Thomas J. Harper and Edward G. Seidensticker (New Haven: Leete's Island Books, 1977). See also the essay on "Japanese Aesthetics" in Donald Keene's *Landscapes and Portraits* (Tokyo and Palo Alto: Kodansha International, 1971) and the special issue of *House Beautiful,* August 1960.

For further information on the Japanese house, see Teiji Itoh, *The Elegant Japanese House: Traditional Sukiya Architecture* (New York: Walker/Weatherhill, 1969); the same author's *The Classic Tradition in Japanese Architecture: Modern Versions of the Sukiya Style* (New York: Weatherhill/Tankosha, 1972); Heinrich Engel, *The Japanese House: A Tradition for Contemporary Architecture* (Rutland, Vt.: Charles E. Tuttle, 1964); and Edward S. Morse, *Japanese Homes and Their Surroundings* (New York: Dover, 1961).

Materials

1   20″ x 30″ white illustration board in vertical format

Paint set

Old magazines

Rubber cement

Procedure

Review some of the more momentous events of your life, in which you were conscious of a strong emotional response. Select two of them involving social situations, and two based on environmental scenes. Jot down some of the key words (perhaps taken from the adjacent list) that best characterize your feelings on each of these occasions. Then develop a short, haiku-like poem suggesting the nature of each scene and situation, using two or three of these words to indicate your emotional responses to each scene and situation.

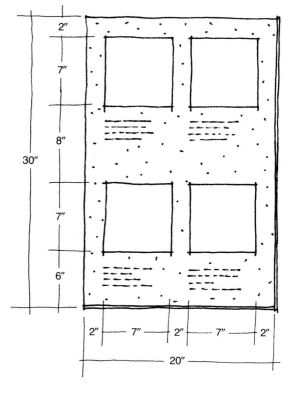

Next, lay out the illustration board in accordance with the accompanying diagram. Using 1″ painted squares in two cases, and 1″ (approximate) squares of colored paper torn *freehand* from magazine illustrations in the other two cases, develop four 7″ by 7″ abstract, nonrepresentational mosaics in colors that express your feelings about each scene and situation.

In each 7″ x 7″ mosaic all the forty-nine tesserae are to be different; that is, no single color is to be repeated. Also, each tessera is to be uniform in color and without texture. And, just as the seventeen syllables of the Japanese *haiku* represent the jewel-like distillation of the poet's strongly felt emotions, so also should the overall effect of the forty-nine tesserae of your mosaics convey a richness representing the depths of your feelings.

The reason for these constraints, of course, is to minimize the potential expressive contribution of position, form, size, direction, number, texture, and surface quality, so as to emphasize the expressive role of the colors you have used.

Under each mosaic, letter in your poem in a size that will be readable from a distance of five feet. Please underline the two or three key words characterizing the emotions your colors are meant to express. And check the specifications for freehand lettering in Problem 2, so that this part of the work will be a convincing demonstration of your lettering capability.

ambiguous	dusky	gay	lurid	piquant	somber
agitated	discordant	gruesome	luminous	pathetic	sordid
animated	delicate	gloomy		poignant	strident
awesome	desolate	gaudy	melancholy	pensive	savage
	dreary	glad	mean		solemn
bland	dreadful	glacial	morbid	quiet	squalid
brilliant	delightful	grim	moribund	quizzical	splendid
boisterous			musty		spontaneous
blissful	elegant	happy	morose	radiant	
benign	exuberant	harmonious	mysterious	restful	tranquil
	enervated	heavy	murderous	resplendent	tender
clean	ethereal	horrible	murky	raw	tragic
confused	ecstatic	hygienic		rich	tense
clear	elated	hopeless	nebulous	revolting	turgid
cool	euphoric	hateful	noxious	refreshing	
clamorous			noble	restless	vivacious
cheap	frosty	inert	nostalgic		vague
calm	flamboyant	insipid		sprightly	vulgar
carefree	feminine	inactive	ominous	serene	vapid
cloying	forlorn		obscure	stately	
crisp	fusty	joyful	opulent	sober	warm
crude	frigid	jocular	optimistic	still	wan
chic	friendly			showy	wild
	fresh	lively	peaceful	sumptuous	weary
depressing	felicitous	lavish	playful	sad	
dull	forboding	light	pale	stark	zestful

Discussion

In the characterization of the environmental *scene* one might attempt to reproduce the essential colors found in the scene in approximately the same proportions, or, to use color to suggest one's personal feelings about the scene (which might depend on the environmental colors as only one element among many). Which approach does the problem call for?

In the characterization of the *situational* event there is perhaps less likelihood of a mechanical transcription of environmental colors and a greater possibility for the use of color as an expression of feeling. This brings up the question "Is it possible that the scenic colors themselves serve as an adequate indication of one's emotional responses?" Is there perhaps a higher level of objectivity involved here? What do Kepes or Arnheim have to say on this matter?

How about the validity of the hypotheses on color "mood feeling" and "temperature feeling" presented in the previous problem? Can you see any correlation between "aesthetic quality" and the central tendencies of the hues in the form of definite analogous or complementary relationships? Try plotting hue and value/chroma frequency distributions for each of your mosaics to help you answer these questions.

Along these lines you may now be interested in experimentally testing the theory that color harmony results when one of the three attributes of color—hue, value, or chroma—is held more or less constant, and the others are varied. This may be checked with another set of 7″ x 7″ mosaics using 1″ squares on a new illustration board. Thus:

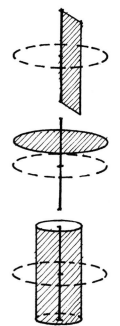

using the same hue and varying value and chroma, you have a monochromatic arrangement of colors limited to one vertical plane in the Munsell color solid;

when value is held constant, and hue and chroma vary, you use only those colors on one horizontal plane of this color solid;

and when chroma is fixed and hue and value change, you are working with only those colors on a vertical cylinder of the Munsell solid.

Still stronger, if simpler, relationships result if two color attributes are restricted, and only the other varies. In this case the colors range along a line on one of the three surfaces described above.

In this problem you used two different media: painted squares and pasted torn paper. In the first case the color areas met each other directly along a uniform straight edge; while in the latter case they were separated by an irregular white border (as occurs in the case of stone or glass tesserae bedded in white mortar). Did you notice any difference in color effect? Can you describe this difference? What would be the effect of using a *black* border (regular or irregular) between tesserae? This of course occurs in the case of stained glass windows. Perhaps you could investigate this with the aid of a transparent acetate overlay.

The effects resulting from these two different treatments have been described by Van Bezold and Rood before 1900. See Ralph Evans, *An Introduction to Color* (New York: Wiley, 1948), for a discussion.

This problem asked you to use uniform and textureless color elements. Do you think texture and/or color gradations within some tesserae might have an expressive potential? One way to study this would be to repeat one of your mosaics using texture or gradations or both, again perhaps by means of a transparent overlay.

By now you have recognized that in this problem the use of color has been quite different from its role as an adjunct in the mundane presentation and representation of forms and objects. Instead of using local or situational colors for the denotation or recording of known or perceived environmental relationships, the present problem has been concerned with the use of what may be called "expressive" color, as a means for the communication of feelings and attitudes.

The gradual liberation of color, from its matter-of-fact use in imitative recording to an expanded role in the untrammeled realm of subjective expression, may be followed in the history of Western painting. We can start with Leonardo da Vinci, who formulated some fifteenth century precepts on the use of color as a secondary means to depict form and shape in three-dimensional objects. The work of the Renaissance and subsequent academic painters reveals extraordinary skill in this mimetic rendering of textures and surface qualities, as embellishments to the modeling of forms by light and shade. But with the changing social and environmental conditions of the nineteenth century, these academic canons were challenged by artists with a new interest in recording their impressions of the momentary and fleeting color-effects of light, air, and space in the natural world; as well as by others such as Gauguin and Van Gogh who went beyond this naturalistic "Impressionism" to pioneer the final emancipation of color as a vehicle for the communcation of emotion. This movement, known as "Expressionism," numbered Matisse, Vlaminck, Munch, Kirchner, and Kandinsky as its leading members. Abandoning the conventional connection of a particular color with a given object or environmental surface, they freed the elementary sensory quality of color to function at a higher objective level, as an independent agent for the evocation of emotion.

For additional comments and illustrations, see John Russell, *The World of Matisse* (New York: Time-Life Books, 1969); Gyorgy Kepes, *The Language of Vision* (Chicago: Paul Theobald, 1948); and Gyorgy Kepes, "Design and Light," *Design Quarterly 68* (Minneapolis, Minn.: Walker Art Center, 1967).

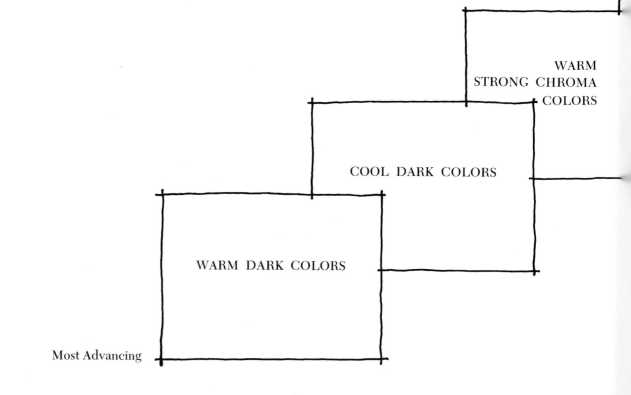

WARM
STRONG CHROMA
COLORS

COOL DARK COLORS

WARM DARK COLORS

Most Advancing

Color and Space

Earlier we made reference to the presumed advancing and receding properties of color. Now we present a formulation of these properties *as applied to their use on environmental surfaces.*

"When the color area occupies the total peripheral field like the walls of a room, black and dark red are the most advancing and light blue and white the most receding. Thus:

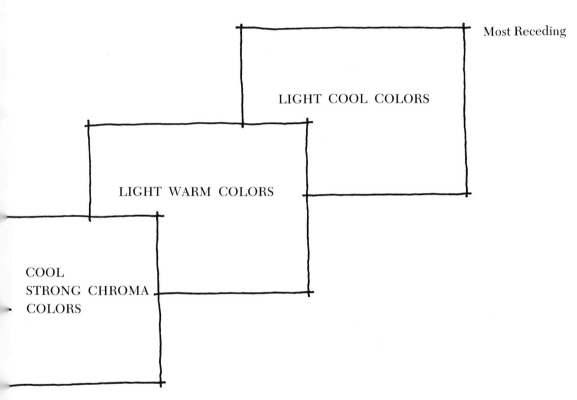

Most Receding

LIGHT COOL COLORS

LIGHT WARM COLORS

COOL
STRONG CHROMA
COLORS

"Strong chromas mixed with black tend to advance, making a room seem smaller. Strong chromas mixed with white tend to recede, making a room seem larger. Conspicuousness through contrast should not be confused with the tendency to advance. Contrast can easily counteract the sense of position in space."

Adapted from "Color and the Use of Color by the Illuminating Engineer," *Illuminating Engineering,* vol. 57, no. 12 (December 1962)

In this problem you and your classmates will have an opportunity to collectively evaluate this conventional wisdom with the aid of three-dimensional models. Your model will represent two adjacent and physically identical spaces of the same "temperature feeling" and "mood feeling," and you will try through the use of color to make these spaces appear to be of different sizes or proportions.

Materials

1 15″ x 20″ white illustration board

Additional white illustration board

Paint and drafting gear

Casein cement

Colored paper

Procedure

Your first step is to prepare the model out of white illustration board as specified in the adjacent diagram, exercising your best craft skills. Then you are to select one suitable "floor" or "carpet" color to be used for both spaces and the corridor between them; and next, the different wall colors for the interior surfaces of the two rooms. Your objective is to achieve a set of conditions assigned by your instructor, including:

1. Color "temperature feeling": warm, neutral, or cool.

2. Color "mood feeling": A, spontaneity and gaiety; B, depression and dullness; C, lightness and cleanliness; or D, richness and quality.

3. Apparent differences in the size or proportions of the space of the two rooms: I, one space larger than the other; or II, one space longer and narrower than the other.

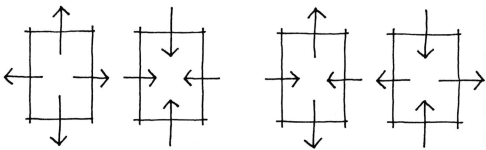

To simplify the problem, and to facilitate comparison with your classmates' work, each wall is to have only one color, and it should be patternless. Different walls may of course have different colors. It is suggested that you first try out your color hypotheses on ready-made colored paper, and then on specially painted paper. To make it easier for the viewer to relate to the environmental scene simulated by your scale model, please provide identical six-foot "scale figures" at the same location in each space. It is important that these clues to the relative size of the spaces be carefully made in true adult proportions, and that they are recognizable as human figures.

Be sure to include your name, and a diagram of your assigned conditions (space size/proportion change, "temperature feeling," and "mood feeling") along the bottom 15″ edge of the board.

Since the model you constructed for this problem will be reused later, in connection with the texture and space studies of Problem 17, you are well advised to photograph it now so as to have a record of your work on this problem.

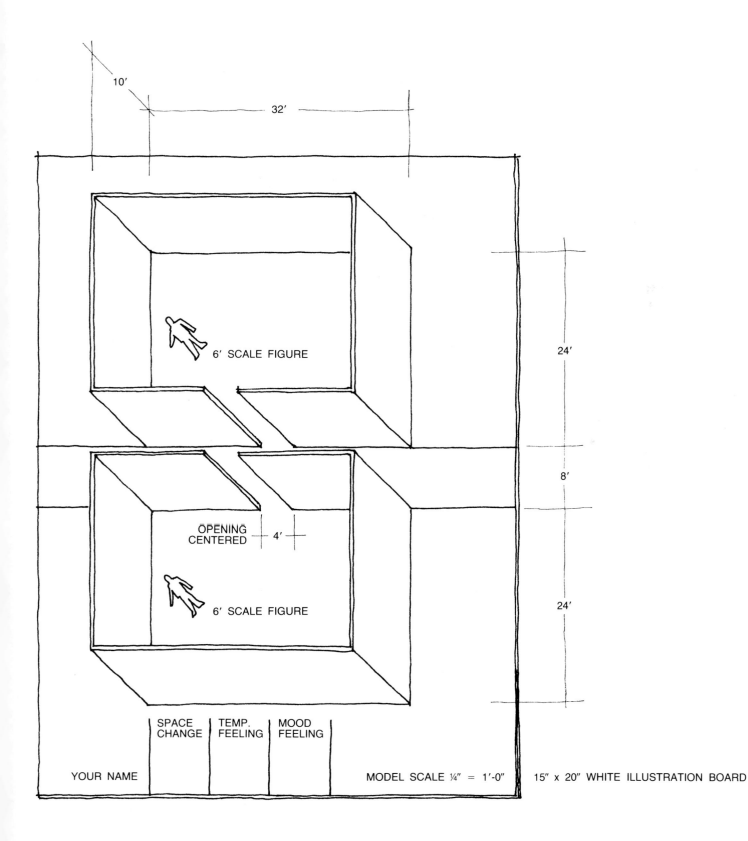

10′

32′

24′

6′ SCALE FIGURE

8′

OPENING
CENTERED   4′

24′

6′ SCALE FIGURE

SPACE CHANGE	TEMP. FEELING	MOOD FEELING

YOUR NAME   MODEL SCALE ¼″ = 1′-0″   15″ x 20″ WHITE ILLUSTRATION BOARD

208

Discussion

The spatial effects of color investigated in this problem represent yet another mode of color use. In the present problem we have employed color on environmental surfaces as a means for the modeling of space in two or three dimensions. Once again we can find a precedent for this use of color in the work of the pioneering painters. The studies of Paul Cézanne present the most convincing demonstrations of the use of color, on the two-dimensional surface of a canvas, to produce effects of three-dimensional form modeling and differing distances in space. Here color is not used as an adornment of form, or as a vehicle for the conveyance of feeling, but as a "building material" for the construction of visual space.

See Richard W. Murphy, *The World of Cézanne* (New York: Time-Life Books, 1968)

There is a good chance that this design problem presented you with a situation in which each requirement entailed a solution in conflict to some degree with those implied by the other requirements. Welcome to the real world!

This is a common characteristic of most design situations, and is perhaps the greatest challenge in the "art" of design decision-making. One way of handling this situation is to review and reformulate the conditions (refer to the top feedback arrow in your flow chart of the design process). Additionally, a reasonable procedure is to seek a creative compromise in which something less than an optimal solution in terms of each individual condition is accepted in exchange for the best overall solution in terms of all the conditions.

In this connection you might also question the particular means of simulation used in this problem for evaluating your design hypotheses (refer here to the fourth arrow in the feedback cycle of your design process flow chart). Obviously a full-size space would be ideal, but time and cost factors usually exclude this possibility. What alternative means can you imagine? (What about using a ¼″ scale *two*-dimensional plan-oblique simulation, as in the diagram for the model? Would this be better? Why? Or why not?)

Did you notice how the colors in your model changed, depending on whether they were in shadow or under full illumination? Would this happen in a two-dimensional simulation? Is this effect a loss or a gain in simulation?

Here we interject a practical note of caution in connection with the matter of judging color effects by means of small color areas (occupying a small part of the visual field) in comparison with the effect of the same paint used on environmental surfaces (and occupying most of the visual field). As you might expect, the expansion in color area results in a "stronger" impression, and the conventional caution is to reduce the chroma of the color found satisfactory in the small-scale simulation to achieve the intended effect in the full-size space.

Note that the conditions assigned in this problem by no means exhaust the range of factors involved in determining the specification of colors for use in environmental spaces. Some of the other experiential factors to be considered include the orientation and exposure of the windows of the space, the physical temperature, the noise level, the activity carried on in the space, the nature and type of artificial illumination, the preexisting forms and textures, and other factors connected with the users of the space themselves.

These factors are incorporated in the following step-by-step procedure for the determination of "suitable" interior colors, excerpted and adapted from "Color and the Use of Color by the Illuminating Engineer," *Illuminating Engineering,* vol. 57, no. 12 (December 1962).

"This system lists, step by step, many of the factors which should be considered in determining suitable colors for interiors. By considering all the known factors such as warmth, spaciousness, excitement level, etc., it is possible to determine the most suitable dominant color as well as the degree of contrast . . .this procedure is best suited to places where public taste is the criterion. The system indicates only the dominant color for the largest areas. A sense of color relationships must be used to choose the other colors for smaller areas. . . .

Step I

"This step helps decide *value,* that is, how light or dark the color scheme should be. If a high level of illumination is necessary, colors with a high reflectance should be used. Dark color combinations tend to produce brightness ratios that are unsatisfactory for efficient seeing.

"The *IES Lighting Handbook* lists tasks or rooms with their recommended levels of illumination. As light reflected from wall surfaces is an important part of illumination, a wall color reflectance closely related to the level of illumination is indicated . . . ."

Step II

"This step helps decide the 'color temperature [feeling].' The number of points favoring warm and cool colors should be checked, allowing that some points have more weight than others.

"Use Warm, Exciting, Advancing Colors *if:*
Room has northern exposure
Temperature is cool
Noise element is low
Room size is too large
Texture is smooth

Physical exertion is light
Time exposure is short
Stimulating atmosphere is desired
Lamps are fluorescent (cool).

"Use Cool, Restful, Receding Colors, *if:*
Room has southern exposure
Temperature is warm
Noise element is high
Room size is too small
Texture is rough
Physical exertion is heavy
Time exposure is long
Restful atmosphere is desired
Lamps are incandescent or fluorescent (warm)."

Step III

"This step helps to decide the *chroma.* Pure colors, that is colors of strong chroma, are primarily used for advertising, display, accents and food merchandising. Grayed colors, colors of weak chroma, are primarily used for fashion areas, general interiors and merchandising.

"Use Pure Color *if:*
Time exposure is short
Responsibility is low
Bright and lively atmosphere is desired
Noise level is low
Sense of taste or smell is unimportant.

"Use Grayed Color *if:*
Time exposure is long
Responsibility is high
Atmosphere of restraint and dignity is desired
Noise level is high
Sense of taste or smell is important."

Step IV

"This step helps decide the amount of contrast. Contrast is obtained by using light with dark, gray or low chromas with high chromas, and one hue with another. When colors of complementary hues are employed, one should usually be of stronger chroma than the other. This color will normally occupy the smaller area. The opposition of small areas gives small contrasts while the opposition of larger areas gives a sense of stronger contrast. In interiors small contrast is obtained with trim and usually with furniture, equipment, etc., which are beyond the colorists' control. Probably the strongest contrast is obtained by painting different walls of the same room in complementary colors."

"A pattern which is large and strong in value contrast makes a room seem smaller. A pattern which is small in size and gentle in contrast makes a room appear larger. The absence of pattern can give the illusion of maximum space.

"Strong color contrast and strong pattern contrast have almost the same effect. In corridors, places of entertainment, entrance halls, etc., where people spend a short time, contrast is stimulating and is good practice. In a public washroom or a quick-lunch counter, where it is desired that people spend a short time, contrast is stimulating and effective. Strong contrast makes people restless and makes time seem longer. Gentle contrast is restful and makes time seem shorter. Wherever people are meant to spend a long time, gentle contrast in both pattern and color is the best practice."

"Consider Little or No Contrast *if:*
Time exposure is long
Room size is small
Atmosphere of restraint and dignity is desired
Wall surfaces are textured.

"Consider Strong Contrast *if:*
Time exposure is short
Room size is large
Lively and exciting atmosphere is desired
Wall surfaces are flat."

To the above we might also add the suggestion that in most cases it is advisable to use the highest possible value for the color of any wall containing windows, as a means of reducing annoying or even disabling brightness contrast.

" 'A person of fair complexion standing between a green bush and a red brick wall has certainly a face green on one side and red on the other, and if the sun shines on his forehead it may be at time intensely yellow. Still, we are, or at least were, not accustomed to depict these eminently realistic traits. We rather concentrate our attention upon what is permanent in the individual complexion as seen in the ordinary diffused daylight. We are accustomed to see the accidental momentary lights weakened in favor of the permanent impression.' Color appears to reside in the objects entirely independent of illumination.

"From the memory also comes another kind of association. Seeing an object means more than placing it in a frame of reference of the three-dimensional world. Even while one is seeing color as substance, one also sees it as cold or warm, bright, gay, sad, depressing, irritating, pleasing, crude, refined, wild, tame, exciting, relaxing, dirty, clean, rich, and possessed of innumerable other feeling qualities. These associations have their origin partly in the neuromuscular process, but partly also in sum total of the dominant other sensations connected with the color seen. The red of the flower, the blue of the sky, the white of the snow bring back feelings one already has for these things. When one says he sees cold water or a burning red, he is saying that his perception is an intersensory blend, a fusion of two or more sensory experiences."

—Gyorgy Kepes, *The Language of Vision* (Chicago: Paul Theobald, 1944)

You will find it worthwhile now to repeat this problem, this time incorporating some arbitrary combination of conditions from this longer list of factors as the "givens" in the problem. Again we offer the caveat that the appended suggestions for handling these other factors should not be taken as sure-fire formulae, but only as first approximations, subject to modification for intentions and contexts other than those explicit and implicit in these suggestions, and, as always, also subject to your own empirical verification.

At this point let us enlarge on the matter of the influence of the light sources on the appearance of surface colors. A given space may be illuminated by one or more sources of light, including such natural sources as zenith skylight, north skylight, overcast sky, sunlight plus clear sky, and direct sunlight (all of which vary with the time of day), and such artificial sources as incandescent lamps, the many different fluorescent lamps, and the several high-intensity discharge lamps. The *physical differences* between these *light sources* can be described by means of a "spectral energy distribution curve" showing their relative energy at each wavelength in the range of visible spectrum. In a similar manner the *physical differences* in *environmental surfaces* may be characterized by the relative amount of energy they reflect at each wavelength in the visible spectrum. This can be described by means of a "spectral reflectance curve," and is a fundamental property of the material involved, independent of the incident light. Thus, when a given environmental surface is illuminated by light from a given source, the light reaching the observer's eyes from that surface is the unique consequence of the properties of that surface and that light, as described by these two curves. The accompanying diagram illustrates several aspects of this situation.

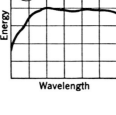

In an example and diagram adapted from Ralph Evans, *An Introduction to Color* (New York: Wiley, 1948) we can show how the light reaching the eye from an object has been selectively modified. Thus, in the case of viewing a yellow flower in front of a red brick wall:

"The course of events is as follows: daylight, which has the spectral-energy distribution given by curve A, strikes both the red brick wall whose spectral reflectance curve is given by C and the yellow flower whose reflectance curve is given by D. The light reflected after selective absorption by the wall has the energy distribution as shown in B. Part of the light from the wall strikes the flower, is selectively absorbed by it, and again reflected. This is additively mixed with the daylight which has reached the flower directly, been selectively absorbed, and reflected again. The additive mixture of these two which strikes the eye is given in E. The action of the wall makes this radiation slightly orange, whereas it would have appeared yellow had the flower been isolated from the wall."

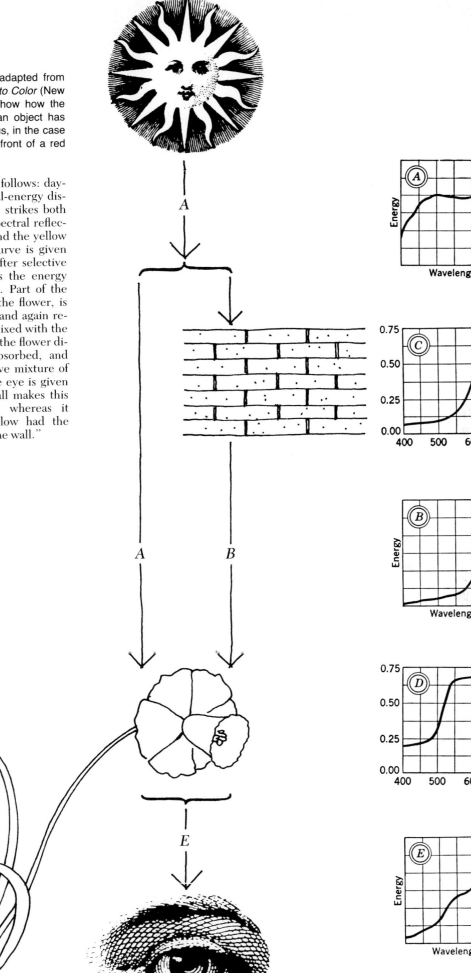

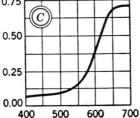

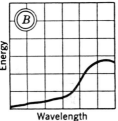

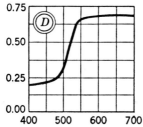

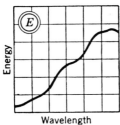

From the brochure *Color Is How You Light It*, published by GTE Sylvania Incorporated

Note that our previously introduced characteristic of "color temperature *feeling*" refers to a subjective impression of the relative warmth or coolness of surface colors, and should not be confused with the term "color temperature," which is an objective measure in degrees Kelvin applying to natural and incandescent light sources.

Light *sources* and their effects on the appearance of the colored surfaces they illuminate are often described in terms of their "color temperature" or "correlated color temperature," and the "color rendering index." A good description and definition of these terms is as follows:

"It is common to speak of 'cool' colors, such as blue and green, and 'warm' colors, such as red and yellow. Light sources can also be cool or warm or in between. It is useful to have a way of giving numbers to the degree of coolness or warmth, and to indicate the color-rendering ability of a source.

"Lighting engineers and photographers know the concept of color temperature; and it is helpful for others to understand it because of its relationship to color rendering index.

"Let's discuss color temperature first. When the old time blacksmith heated a piece of iron, or when great grandmother's kitchen stove lids got very hot, the iron started to glow a deep red. As it got hotter it became a bright red and, finally, 'white hot.' The easiest way to describe the color of a glowing metal is to give its temperature, because any two glowing pieces of a given metal having the same temperature will always have the same color. Those who have seen neither a blacksmith's forge nor a kitchen stove can think of an electric range element, although this is not allowed to become white hot.

"The tungsten of an incandescent lamp filament behaves in the same way; and the color of its emitted light is always directly related to its temperature in Kelvin degrees. These are degrees above absolute zero, which is 273 degrees below zero on the Centigrade (Celsius) scale. The color temperature of a household incandescent lamp, for example, is a little less than 3000°K. Strictly speaking, color temperature applies only to natural sources such as the sun and the sky, and to *incandescent* metal sources. The scale of degrees Kelvin goes on upward beyond the melting point of tungsten, into bluer colors such as the light from the sky.

"Now, let's analyze correlated color temperature. When it comes to sources such as fluorescent, mercury, and other gaseous discharge lamps, correlated color temperature is the proper term to use. When we say that a fluorescent lamp has a correlated color temperature of 3000K we mean that its color looks to the normal human eye more like that of a 3000K incandescent lamp than it does like an incandescent lamp of any other color temperature. This does not mean that it will illuminate colored objects in just the same way, however . . .a fluorescent lamp does not have the smooth output curve of an incandescent lamp so its color temperature is only an apparent one. To take an extreme example, it would be possible to make a fluorescent lamp which had all its output in two very narrow bands of blue light and yellow light . . .and the colors could be balanced so that it looked just the same to the eye as another lamp having a curve with all colors represented. A red object would look 'natural' under the second source, but would appear to be black or dark gray under the first one because it emits no red light to be reflected from the red object. Thus two lamps which look alike when lighted, and therefore have the same correlated color temperature, can render colors quite differently.

"What we need is some way of describing how well a light source renders colors; and this is provided by the color rendering index. It is a measure, on a scale of 100, of how a source compares with a natural one at that correlated color temperature. This cannot be emphasized too strongly, because any source can give a cool cast to colors if its correlated color temperature is high, or a warm cast if it is low.

"There is no point in saying that an incandescent fluorescent lamp (2700°K) having a color rendering index of 90 is better than a deluxe cool white lamp (4100°K) with a color rendering index of 86. Both are good sources, but the question is whether we want a warm source or a cool source for the particular application. Color rendering index should never be used without tying it to the correlated color temperature of the lamp in question.

"Putting it still more simply; correlated color temperature is what the lamp is trying to be; color rendering index shows how well it is succeeding . . . ."

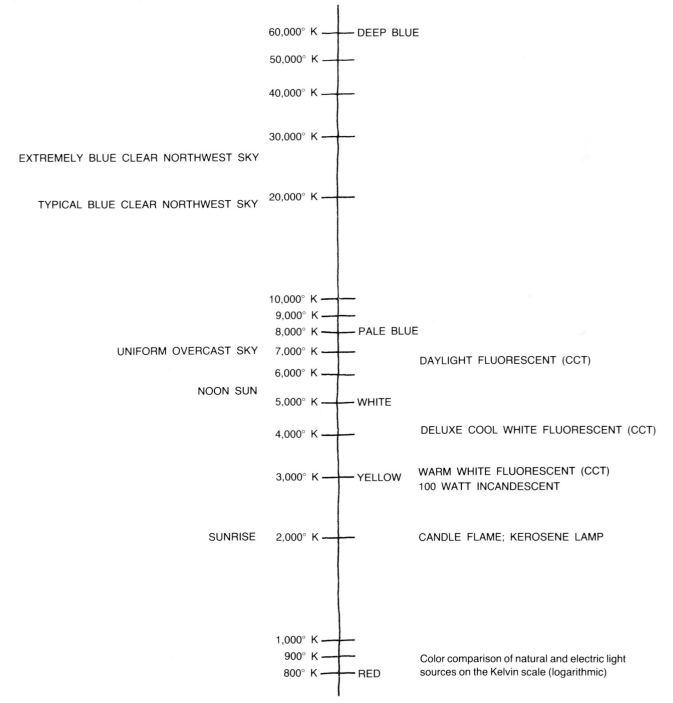

Color comparison of natural and electric light sources on the Kelvin scale (logarithmic)

Problem 14

For an example, here is how one shipyard color codes the hard hats of its employees:

"**White hats** means salaried people . . . **Light blue** hats indicate hourly, nonunion people . . . Below is a list of further hat colors and the people they top:

Blue—shipfitters, welders (welders' hats sometimes have a white stripe).

Black—machinists (a yellow and black target indicates a maintenance machinist).

Pale blue with a red stripe—warehousemen, warehouse clerks, and drivers.

Brown—painters . . . With an **orange stripe**—scalers and sandblasters.

Gray—sheet metal (white circles indicate temporary ventilation) . . . With a **red stripe**—boiler operator.

Light green—pipefitters.

Yellow—electricians (a yellow and black target indicates maintenance.

Cream with blue stripe—electronics.

Fluorescent red with yellow stripe—riggers.

Dark green with a white stripe—shipwrights (a white circle in front indicates an insulator).

Powder blue—with **target**, engineers . . . With **red triangle** in front—government engineer . . . With **black square** in front—quality assurance.

Gold with black stripe—test and trial people, operators.

Purple—Yard clerks.

Gold—Whirley, mobile, magnetic crane operators.

Red—Guards.

Beige—Production control.

Orange—Visitors.

Gray and yellow—Navy personnel.

Yellow with a magenta stripe (so-called 'radiation' colors)—Radiographers.

A, T, L, F, S letters on hats indicate apprentice, trainee, leadmen, foreman, or superintendent, respectively."

For further examples see: Department of the Navy, Naval Facilities Engineering Command, *Color for Naval Shore Facilities*, NAVFAC P-309 (Washington, D.C.: Government Printing Office, 1971).

Color Coding

"When particular stimulus patterns, e.g., formal properties, colors, textures, lighting, are systematically paired with particular behaviors leading to a reinforcing consequence (finding a physician when one is ill, social interaction, reaching a friend), the stimulus pattern itself comes to reinforce the behavior. For example, color is often applied to certain surfaces in designed environments. If the topography of these stimuli is carefully integrated with a particular behavioral topography, they will come to exert an influence via stimulus control. If the patterning of the color surfaces is random with respect to the behavioral goals, it is called decoration."

Raymond G. Studer, "Behavior Manipulation in Designed Environments," *Connection,* Fall, 1967 (Graduate School of Design, Harvard University)

Some examples of the designed use of color in the environment as a means of facilitating social interaction and enhancing public convenience are seen in the color coding of mailboxes, fire alarm signal boxes, traffic signs, parking indications, service uniforms, piping systems, machinery controls and guards, operating zones in industrial plants, emergency vehicles, and so on. Undoubtedly color could be used much more extensively than it is, not only to enrich our daily environment but to make us feel more at home in it. In this problem you will have an opportunity to explore one of these ways.

Assume that you have been retained to design a color coding system for the doors to the various rooms of a large complex of differentiated spaces in a building or group of buildings, such as a school, a hospital, or an industrial plant. In these circumstances a possible pattern of space classification might be as follows:

Division 1. (Administration)

Section A

Section B

Section C: Department a, b

Division 2. (Operations)

Section A: Department a, b, c

Section B: Department a, b, c, d

Section C: Department a, b

Division 3. (Services)

Section A (washrooms): men, women

Section B (janitorial): Department a, cleaning; Department b, maintenance

Section C (food service): Department a, b

Section D (supplies): Department a, b, c, d

Section E (building engineering): Department a, regular; Department b, hazardous

Given the above classification, your problem is to select door colors which:

(1) as far as possible express the nature of the use of the space; and

(2) in their similarities and differences also imply the organizational relationships; and, furthermore,

(3) can be easily discriminated by people not particularily sensitive to color nuances.

Assume that the doors will be identified with only one solid color, and nothing else, and that the corridor walls are painted a light warm gray.

Present your proposal in a clear, logical format, readable from a distance of ten feet and capable of being easily implemented and maintained by the people in Division 3, Section B, Department b.

Materials

1 15″ x 20″ board in vertical format

1 10″ x 15″ white illustration board in horizontal format

Paint set

Drafting gear

Rubber cement

Procedure

In this problem you should consciously simulate the procedures you expect to follow in your future professional life. Your finished design is to be presented on one 15″ x 20″ board in vertical format for approval and acceptance by the people in Division 1, Section A. As mentioned above, this design is to be implemented and maintained by another group of people, and of course it is to be *used* by still another and presumably larger group. You should consider all aspects of your work from the possibly quite different viewpoints of these several groups. How will it look to each of *them?*

Your skill in distributing your time between the conflicting demands of several classes and a number of extracurricular activities is analogous to that required in the "real world" of design practice. With a payroll to meet, or a budget to keep within, there is a similar practical challenge to establish priorities, estimate requirements, assess capabilities, assign responsibilities and schedule time-sharing; then to monitor performance and to adapt flexibly to various emergencies and exigencies. This is the price of professional survival. Art may be long, but life is short; and "practical" creativity requires many types of competence.

We will also use this problem to demonstrate your competence in the planning and management of your time—a vitally important aspect of your professional capabilities. One hour after the first class meeting on this problem please submit a memorandum breaking down the stages of the problem and the time you estimate you will spend on each (no doubt by now you are in the habit of doing this). At the end of the problem please submit along with your design proposal a summary of your time record on the 10″ x 15″ board using the format shown here. This will also serve as another demonstration of your proficiency in freehand lettering.

Furthermore, since by this time you are also in the habit of surveying the literature relevant to each new problem to discover the current "state of the art" and to learn of any existing conventions which may prove useful, you are also asked to include a bibliography. This should be presented on the same board, and should list all the pertinent references you have found that shed light on the issues of the problem.

Time Estimate, Schedule, and Record

JOB BREAK-DOWN AND SEQUENCE	DAYS I		II		III		IV		(etc.)	SUBTOTALS EST.	ACT.
HOURS	0 12	24	0 12	24	0 12	24	0 12	24			
PHASE A (describe) EST. ACT.											
PHASE B (describe) EST. ACT.											
PHASE C (describe) EST. ACT.											
PHASE D (describe) EST. ACT.											
(etc.)											
GRAND TOTALS											

References Consulted (alphabetically by author, n the following format):

JOURNALS AND PERIODICALS

author's last name, initials (coauthors, if any)

title of article (in quotes)

title of journal or periodical (underlined)

volume, number, date, page numbers

BOOKS

author's last name, initials (coauthors, if any)

title of book (underlined),

place of publication, publisher, date

page numbers

Discussion

A large part of the responsibility of professionals is their concern for the quality of their work. Although they take great pleasure in doing good work, they are constantly raising their standards as to what "good" means, and thus they are always intensely critical of and generally dissatisfied with their performance. With this attitude they continue to grow and develop in competence all their lives. Since they are well aware that hell is paved with good intentions, they scorn the easy escape of "But I did the best I could," and waste no time in bleeding and bleating about intentions and extenuating circumstances. No professor is standing by to evaluate their work for them by assigning them a grade. Rather than salving their conscience and bolstering their ego, they are more concerned with broadening their awareness and improving their capabilities.

Some of the characteristics of creative people are: (a) that they keep *all* their experience accessible for use, and (b) that they develop a facility in *applying* that experience. Recently we discussed the mutual effects of colors: the phenomenon of simultaneous contrast. This would of course be a factor in the case of door colors. What assumptions did you make in your design studies (and illustrate in your communication of your design proposal) about the color of the walls adjacent to these doors?

Creativity exists only in the degree that it is communicated to others. Your intentions may be very clear—to yourself—but unless the users are equally well informed, your efforts come to nothing. How well have you communicated to the maintenance personnel? Do they have a *large,* clear color swatch of each color? Did you *clearly* identify each with its intended use (applying the previously discussed criteria for good lettering)? Did you key it with one or more paint manufacturers' identification codes? Or with the Munsell identification (applying your previous experience in color classification)? Is your overall arrangement simple, logical, and understandable, and will it also be durable in use?

Comprehending a problem demands the ability to simulate actual operating conditions. Two color swatches side by side may be easily seen to be somewhat different. But how easily will they be discriminated as different when separated in time and distance? Did your design assume that all the users will be extraordinarily gifted in color sensitivity and color memory?

There is a systematic hierarchy implicit in the relationships of the divisions, sections, and departments of the given institution. Have you expressed these relational similarities and differences with your colors? (Refer to the typology of color relationships presented in Problem 10.) Is your design systematic, or is it arbitrarily decorative? Culturally determined color associations and institutionally standardized color codings exist as potential advantages and resources for this problem. Have you availed yourself of them by reference to your library catalogue and conference with your librarian?

What about that minority of the general population who are color blind? What might be done to serve their interests in this area (beyond the arbitrary limitations imposed in this problem)? Can you think of any precedents?

In this connection, note E. J. McCormick's *Human Factors in Engineering and Design* (New York: McGraw-Hill, 1976), which quotes two sources indicating that "normal observers" can identify about nine surface colors, varying primarily in hue; and that, with training, people can make up to twenty-four such discriminations of nonredundant combinations of hue, value, and chroma.

The facade of a traditional Japanese merchant's house shows a rich variety of rhythmic patterns.

Rhythmical Organization

We have already considered the use of proximity, similarity, continuance, and closure in the spatial structuring of the elements of the visual field. With this problem we take up a means of organizing these elements on a higher order: in terms of their rhythmical patterning. Kepes writes:

"Rhythmical patterning of the picture surface can exist on as many levels as the differentiations of the visual field. If a surface permits any subdivision that repeats its own shape or size in a smaller form, a simple geometrical order is achieved. This subdivision implies sizes, positions, directions and intervals. On this level there can be rhythm through regular alternating or orderly repeating shapes, positions, length, angles, curves, directions, intervals. When the orderly measure of the optical units is related to their virtual movement from and to the picture-plane a higher level of rhythm is reached. We have then a rhythm of the plastic forces, a regular change of sensation of spatial movements of colors and values; advancing, receding, expanding, contracting, moving up, down, left and right. Finally we might have orderly changes or repetition of more complex configurations of visual experience; rhythmic order of tension and repose, concentration and rarefaction, harmony and discord. Rhythm may be simple, restricted to one or another metre of the optical differences. It may also be compounded, as two or more lawfully varying metres existing simultaneously. Rhythms may correspond with and amplify each other, or they may oppose each other, causing a higher level of rhythmic configuration."

Gyorgy Kepes, *The Language of Vision* (Chicago: Paul Theobald, 1948)

222

Our experiments with rhythm will be in terms of linear patterns developed by the systematic procedures shown in Norman McLaren's notes on the canon (see opposite page). This problem will also provide an opportunity for an exercise of your freehand ability with a pencil.

Materials

1 10″ x 40″ white illustration board (cut from a 30″ x 40″ sheet)

Architect's sketch paper

Pencils, drafting gear

Procedure

Using two or three elements such as straight lines and circular arcs, invent a number of simple linear "motifs." Combine one or two of these motifs and/or their inversions and/or their reversals in a linear "melody" exactly 10″ long. Do all this work freehand and full size.

Select one of these 10″ melodies and using a soft pencil or a felt-tip pen, carefully trace it freehand, end-to-end, four times in a row on one piece of tracing paper more than 40″ long. Prepare three more such identical strips: then you will have the four "voices" of your canon.

Use these strips to study the ways in which they can be combined in simple canon form (without augmentation, diminution, inversion, or retrogression). The first voice will consist of the melody repeated four times (the full 40″ length of the board); the second voice will enter from the left at the octave, the fifth, etc., above or below the first voice (or wherever you choose); the third voice will then enter relative to the second voice *exactly* as the second entered relative to the first; and so on. The second, third, and fourth voices will bleed right. By shifting the position of the overlapping separate pieces of tracing paper on which you have traced the identical melody you can easily explore a multitude of possibilities in a very few minutes. In doing this try to develop linear continuances from the lines of one voice to those of another, and to create unexpected new shapes from the juxtaposition of the voices. To help keep the voices in alignment draw a series of light horizontal lines on the illustration board.

Please note that it is almost impossible to predict which melodies will combine well in canon form from an inspection of a melody by itself. To achieve the best results within a given amount of working time, it is important that you work full-size from the very start, with separate strips of tracing paper.

When you have serendipitously discovered a good combination in canon, trace it off freehand on a superimposed piece of tracing paper and put it up on the wall.

Repeat this process for a number of different melodies, one at a time, and when you have developed, displayed, and discussed a good number of successful alternatives, carefully trace off your most promising one on the board for presentation, doing all the work *entirely freehand in pencil*, and using a line of uniform weight.

CANONCANONCANONCANON

A CANON IS A STRICT AND CONTINUOUS IMITATION BETWEEN SEVERAL IDENTICAL PARTS WHICH ENTER, NOT SIMULTANEOUSLY, BUT ONE AFTER THE OTHER.

MOTIF

REPETITION

In music, the canon astonishes us. Just think! a single theme is used to accompany itself, two, three or four times; it need only be staggered or overlapped in relation to itself, and, according to the method used, we get a network full of surprises!

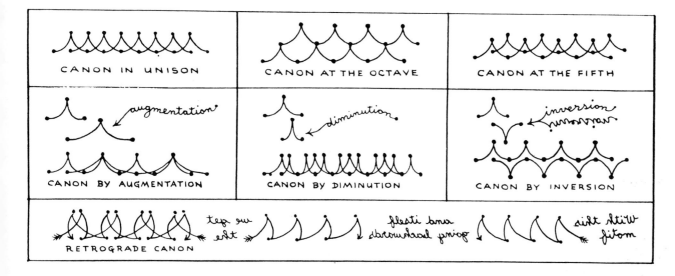

CANON IN UNISON

CANON AT THE OCTAVE

CANON AT THE FIFTH

augmentation

CANON BY AUGMENTATION

diminution

CANON BY DIMINUTION

inversion

CANON BY INVERSION

RETROGRADE CANON

Everybody knows "Frère Jacques": it is an example of a successful canon. Here is a graph of its melody.

Now we need four voices to sing it. The first starts alone, and the others follow at regular distances. If no one gets out of step, here is the kind of "scaffolding" they put into the air:

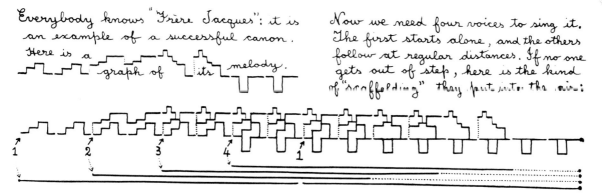

1   2   3   4   1

There is nothing to stop us from combining the different kinds of canon. But, be careful! Not every melody can be "canonized", and the inventor who discovers one that can be

deserves a halo.

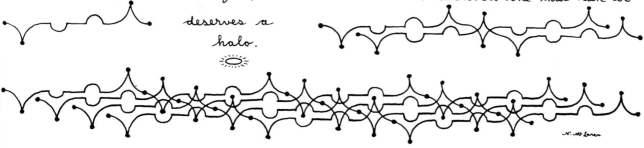

224

adagio	slow, leisurely
agitato	excited, restless
allegro	cheerful, quick, lively
andante	moderate speed
animato	animated, spirited
con brio	with vigor, spirit
dolce	sweet, soft
fluchtig	hurried, casual
flussig	flowing
giocoso	joyful
grave	very slow, solemn
largo	slow and expressive
lento	slow tempo
lustig	cheerful, merry, gay
machtig	powerful, intense
maestoso	majestic
pesante	heavy, firm
presto	very fast
prestissimo	as quickly as possible
rubato	varied in tempo
ruhig	serene, calm
sanft	soft, smooth
scherzando	lively
sforzando	sudden accent
staccato	short and disconnected
teneramente	tender, gentle
vivace	quick, lively, vivacious
zart	delicate, fragile, tender

Discussion

When your work is displayed along with that of your colleagues (vertically, with the start of the canon at the bottom, and the bleeds at the top) it will no doubt be very apparent that each work has quite a different rhythmic style. Can you find any words on the adjacent list of musical terms which appropriately describe the character of your work; or any terms in the adjacent diagram of semantic space which adequately describe the movement? Please select two or three from each list, and letter them, with your name, along the bottom of the board.

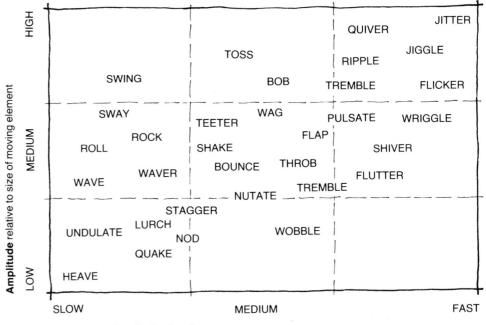

How would you characterize the rhythmic feeling of the patterns of this facade?

226

For examples, see Marthe and Maurice Blackburn, *An Audio-Visual Experiment* (Montreal: Jeunesses Musicales du Canada, 1967). The mathematically inclined may be interested to compare this exercise with a Fourier analysis, in which any periodic function may be expressed as the sum of sine and cosine functions.

In the present problem, as in all the others in this program, we employ fairly rigorous constraints as a means of focusing your attention on a few specific issues. Once these issues have been illuminated, it is appropriate that you relax, or modify, the constraints and explore the further potentials of the subject on your own. For instance, you might now care to investigate musical analogies other than the canon, or alternately, less systematic, quasi-canon forms.

Similarly, in this problem we have explicitly required a uniform weight of freehand pencil line as evidence of your control of that tool. But you will appreciate that "control" can also be exercised to produce other kinds of line work, and that again each particular line quality has its own expressive potential.

Perhaps you have also noticed in Problem 5 how the dynamic impulse of some edges of the triangles sets up a movement through the assemblage, thus relating these triangles into a larger form? We can generalize this (as another example of the law of continuance) by saying that the kinetic continuity of the outlines of a number of basic pattern areas will act to organize these subelements into a larger whole.

Perhaps now you are also aware of similar rhythmic—and expressive— patterns in the examples you have developed in your work on the collateral problem in texture (Problem 3: Texture Archetypes)? Does this suggest anything about the "organic" visual qualities of natural forms?

The work of the painter Piet Mondrian (1872-1944) illustrates a lifelong effort to distill and document this rhythmical essence of our visual world. For example, here are some of his tree studies, made over a three-year period, in which he successively eliminates the representational aspects and extracts the underlying rhythmic patterns. The culmination of his work is seen in his last paintings, in which the dynamic rhythms of the urban grid of Manhattan are transcribed into an abstract visual harmony.

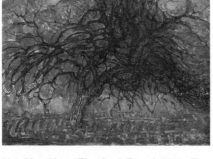  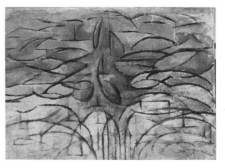

Piet Mondrian, *The Red Tree* (1909), *The Gray Tree* (1911), *The Flowering Apple Tree* (1912). Collection of the Haags Gemeentemuseum, The Hague

See also Michel Seuphor, *Piet Mondrian: Life and Work* (New York: Abrams, n.d.); and Richard P. Lohse, "Standard, Series, Module: New Problems and Tasks of Painting," in Gyorgy Kepes, ed., *Module, Proportion, Symmetry, Rhythm* (New York: Braziller, 1966).

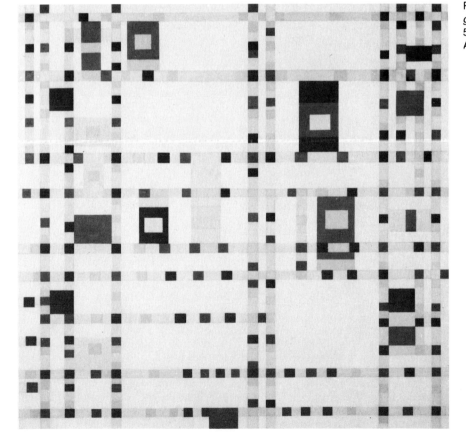

Piet Mondrian (1872-1944), *Broadway Boo-gie-Woogie* (1942-43), oil on canvas, 50″ x 50″. Collection of The Museum of Modern Art, New York (given anonymously)

228

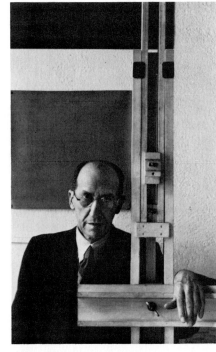

Photograph © Arnold Newman

"In the photographs that survive from his last years, Piet Mondrian's own head began to verge on geometrical abstraction. The domed skull had its remaining hair brushed flat, each strand meticulously parallel to its neighbor; the two neat creases on the pale forehead; the paired circles of his spectacle frames, and the thin mouth joined with utmost precision to his beak of a nose by two engraved lines. It was the face of no compromise—austere and possessed by a forbidding moral rectitude. No artist ever looked more like his own work.

"Mondrian was one of the great lawgivers of modern art. He was born just short of 100 years ago, at Utrecht in 1872; he died in New York in 1944. To mark his centenary, the Guggenheim Museum has assembled a retrospective which later goes to Bern's Kunstmuseum in Switzerland. The show is a reminder of what 'high seriousness'—a quality notably absent from most recent art—can mean in the hands of a master.

"Mondrian's influence on art and design in the past 50 years has been so huge that it tends, if anything, to obscure his own work. He is the father of asymmetrical design, and his progeny are legion. Bastard Mondrians, with their printed grids of black lines and their rectangles of primary blue, red and yellow, turned up on every flat surface that industry made—from tea towels to Courèges dresses, from cigarette packs to apartment façades.

"Art needs stamina to survive that kind of diffusion. Mondrian survived triumphantly, though at some cost. The characteristics of industrial reproduction—flatness, harshness, gloss and repetition—became wrongly linked to his work. The idea that Mondrian was a kind of machine painter, all sensuousness barred, is one of the many illusions that the Guggenheim's exhibition will dispel.

"The son of a strict Calvinist schoolteacher, Mondrian began his art studies in Holland. In the Guggenheim show, we first meet him around 1890, painting talented but not remarkable brown Netherlands landscapes and still lifes. Though Mondrian came to detest nature, the flat horizons punctuated by vertical poplars and crisscross windmills gave him a set of predilections about form which survived through his career—immeasurably refined and philosophized.

"The blocks and dabs of red and blue pigment that pulsate across the surface of an early figurative Mondrian like *Church at Zoutelande* (1909-10), record the same reflective delight in the rhythm and energy of particles that he must have felt when painting his last, unfinished canvas, *Victory Boogie-Woogie* (1943-44). The ethical and mystical concerns that underlie Mondrian's abstracts had become apparent earlier still in such paintings as *Passion Flower* (1901). This Art Nouveau-flavored image had a curiously mundane origin: Mondrian suspected that his model had VD, and painted her face contorted into a St. Teresalike truance of meditation and repentance.

"A few years later, Mondrian became an enthusiastic convert to Theosophy; he was very much struck by Philosopher Rudolf Steiner's belief that 'occult influences. . .can be awakened by devotional religious feelings, *true* art, music.' But what was 'true' art? Mondrian was sure that art got truer to the extent that it provoked meditation and devotion. 'In aesthetic contemplation,' he wrote, 'the individual is pushed to the background, and the universal appears. The deepest purpose of painting has always been to give concrete existence, through color and line, to this universal which appears in contemplation.'

"Hindsight makes it seem inevitable that Mondrian, believing this, should move

away from objects. But in its period, Mondrian's road toward total abstraction was as audacious as it was lonely. In 1911, he first saw cubist paintings by Picasso and Braque at a show in Holland. His pictorial intelligence could not resist the challenge. But the concrete, specific nature of cubist painting hindered him. Thus Mondrian's paintings after 1911 show him wrestling to keep the integrated pattern of Cubism while dispensing with solid form. *Tree* (1912), with its sober tones of gray, green and brown, preserves the rhythm of branches in its arabesque of lines but remains as flat as a stained-glass window.

"In 1912, Mondrian moved to Paris, where he changed his life and his art. The 'real' image gradually sank. *Composition #7* (1913), still kept a few legible clues of the façades and city roofs; but by *Composition* (1916), even these had vanished, and a fully abstract dance of signs and patches replaced them. Not even these were stable enough; Mondrian wanted to achieve a Platonic essence of structure. He now pushed reduction almost to the limit—nothing but right angles and primary color. This lean scaffolding was to occupy him from the '20s until his death. His geometric abstracts are the most systematic investigation of flat pattern in all modern art, and they have the clarity and finality of laboratory proof. No print can do justice to paintings like *Composition with Red and Blue* (1939-41), for one of the startling characteristics of such work is its traditionalism as painting. Within the radical statement it makes, the warm, silky glow of the layered paint held in its finely adjusted grid is almost Vermeer-like.

"Had it not produced such interactions, Mondrian's austerity would have had its comic side. He hated green because it reminded him of nature. In restaurants, he would sit with his back to the window to avoid seeing any trees. His main pleasure was ballroom dancing, but according to one of his friends, 'he carried out his steps in such a personally stylized fashion that the results were frequently awkward.' His solitary rooms in Paris, and later in New York, were kept with fussy precision, down to the exact placement of ashtrays. His life was a masterpiece of sublimation in art's interest.

"Mondrian's intellectual tenacity remains startling. After the *volte-face* toward abstraction in 1911, there were no sudden switches in his work—only the steady, undistracted pursuit of the mathematical harmony that he glimpsed at the end of his experiences. Mondrian had fled to New York in 1940 to avoid the war and he was nearly 72 when he died there. But his great unfinished picture, *Victory Boogie-Woogie*, gathered all the dynamism and modernity that fascinated him in Manhattan into one comprehensive image. The blips of red, yellow and blue shuttling along the avenues of the grid, the slow blocks of gray, the orchestration of scale and pace—these constitute Mondrian's final answer to the critics who rebuked him for pushing art into 'sterility.' They were, of course, wrong: for Mondrian's work possessed that rich and exemplary gravity which only the puritan passions can release."

—Robert Hughes, "Pursuit of the Square," *Time*, 8 November 1971

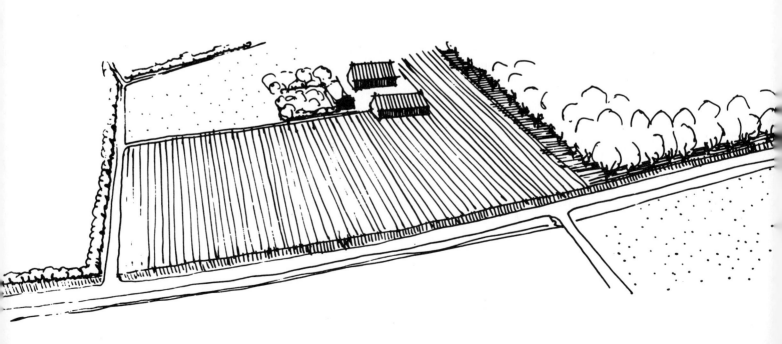

Rhythm and Modulation

In the previous problem we suggested that rhythm is an important means for the organization of elements in a visual field. Although a rhythmic patterning of the visual attributes of the basic pattern areas will serve to bind them into a higher order of relatedness, the mere repetition of such rhythms soon becomes predictable, and thus monotonous. Under these circumstances our attention shifts elsewhere; the field fades from our focus of awareness and becomes "boring" or "invisible."

Note that in some circumstances this may be advantageous. Can you think of any cases where this is so?

To hold our attention and provide the possibility for further levels of organization, it may be sufficient that the rhythmic patterns modulate: that is, that they undergo progressive changes or development. The resulting higher-order structure itself may be patterned in a variety of modes characterized as regular or irregular, formal or informal, romantic or classical, free or constrained; and of course various combinations of these patterns are possible.

These modulations, or superordinate virtual movements, may be created by progressive variations in any one or more of the visual attributes: position, size, shape, number, direction, hue, value, chroma, texture, or surface quality; and thus a practically unlimited richness of possibilities exists. In this problem we will explore a small part of this potential, limiting our attention to the use of variations in number, size, position, hue, value, and chroma to generate developments in rhythmic patterns.

Materials

1 10″ x 40″ strip of white illustration board

Paint and drafting gear

Black, white, and gray construction and colored paper

Procedure

Phase A

1. Lay out your board lightly in pencil as shown in the diagram, and prepare a supply of 1″ x 3″ black, white, light gray, and dark gray *elements* cut from construction paper.

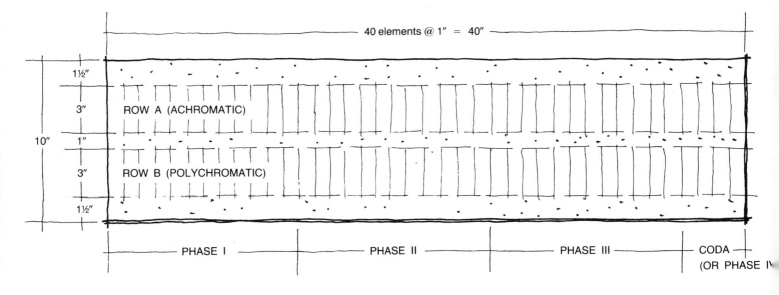

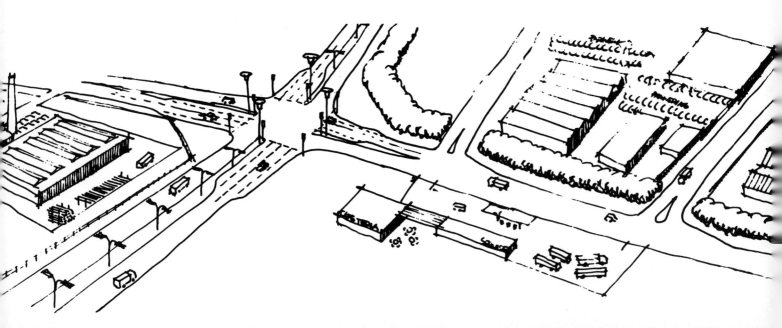

2. Starting at the left end of row A arrange any combination of two to four of these achromatic elements vertically, side by side, to form a simple *figure*.

3. Repeat this identical figure two times on row A. This forms your first rhythmic *phrase* of three figures.

4. Next to this phrase on row A arrange a variation of your original figure by "augmentation" (increasing the number of some or all of the elements but keeping them in the same order), "diminution" (reducing the number of some or all of the elements but keeping them in the same order), "retrogression" (reversing the order of the elements), or retrogression with either augmentation or diminution.

5. Repeat this modified figure twice on row A, as your second rhythmic phrase of three figures.

6. Repeat steps 4 and 5 with yet another variation of your original figure to form the third phrase.

7. Conclude your rhythmic composition in the remaining element spaces on the board with a *coda,* either by a restatement of your intitial figure, or with a new and different figure. Or, instead of this, you may choose to continue your (endless?) composition with a fourth phrase based on yet another variation of your original figure. (To make this work out you may have to go back and revise the number of elements in your figures, or the number of figures in your phrases.)

Review your design to see if it "reads" easily: that is, if the organization is readily apparent. This will be the case if you use black, gray, and white progressions in your figures, and/or strong contrasts in tempo from one phrase to another (e.g., slow, quick, quicker; or quick, slow, quicker; etc.).

8. When you have developed what you feel is a good forty-element rhythmic composition, cement the strips of colored paper to the board or, better, paint their equivalent on the board.

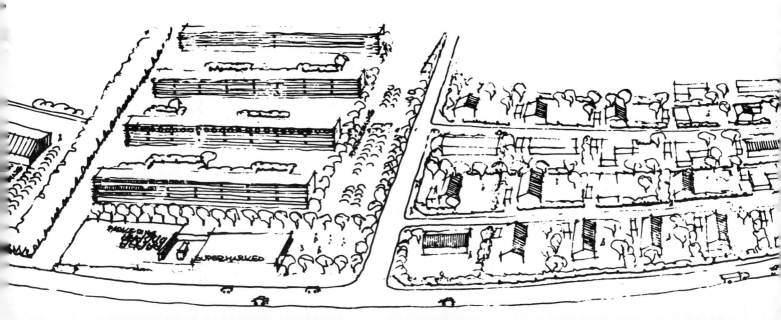

Phase B

Here your task is to use the rhythmic pattern of row A as the basis for a more complex color composition in row B. The additional attributes of hue and chroma enrich the possibilities, but must be carefully considered so as to contribute further levels of organization. For example, the value patterns of row A could be used in row B also, but the hues might progress analogously from phrase one to phrase two to phrase three: for instance, in row B phrase one could be values of green; phrase two, values of blue-green; phrase three, values of blue; etc. An alternate procedure would be to adopt a monochromatic hue for all of row B, but to increase the chroma from one phrase to the next. Many other arrangements are possible, of course, but it is strongly recommended that you start with one of these simpler schemes, as a first approximation, to gain a clear insight into the nature of the problem.

It will be useful to prepare a broad range of colored paper elements for your chromatic simulations. As you develop your ideas keep track of the color feelings and color moods of the different simulations. When you have painted your final design on the board, please letter some words descriptive of its color character in the board's bottom margin.

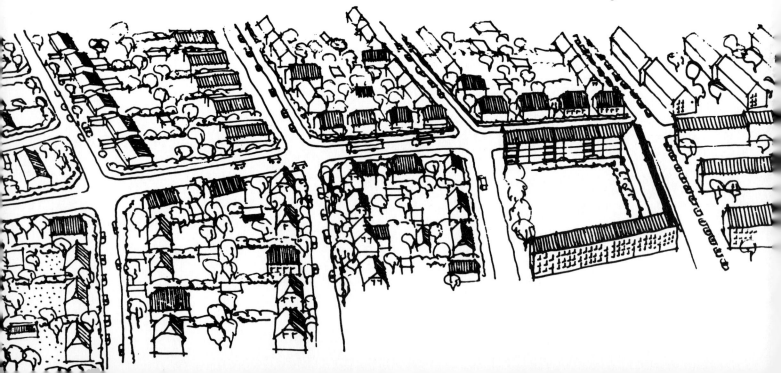

Discussion

What you have now could be thought of as the color layout for the opposite walls of a long corridor, to be executed in mosaic tile, or paint, or perhaps colored lights, and experienced while moving past at a given rate of speed. Or it might be seen as the score for the lighting of a stage play or a spectacle.

See "Rapid Transition" in *Progressive Architecture*, October 1972.

Although we imposed a number of constraints in this problem as a means of focusing your attention on specific issues, it is now appropriate and desirable that you formulate your own constraints for an enlarged version of this problem, which will challenge your ability to orchestrate a wider range of visual attributes. In addition to number and color, you should consider the use of size, shape, position, direction, texture, and surface quality.

This problem has presented only one illustration of the large category of sequentially structured visual patterns designed to be "discursively" experienced over an interval of time. Other examples include book design, dance and drama, cinema and television, and the environment itself, with many wonderful visual patterns dating from prehistory, and found in all parts of the world.

See Philip Thiel, "Processional Architecture," *A.I.A. Journal*, February 1964.

Let us consider the implications of rhythm and movement in the context of our experience of this larger environment. Madame de Stael once likened architecture to a "continuous and stationary music," while her contemporary, the philosopher Friedrich von Schelling, called it "music in space . . . a frozen music." No doubt they were thinking in terms of the rhythmic patterning of the formal elements of a facade. The historian Steen Eiler Rasmussen, in his essay "Rhythm in Architecture," shifts the analogy slightly, moving it from the context of a facade or a building to that of facades, buildings, spaces between buildings, and the environment in general. If one thinks of the natural and the built environment as a phonographic record or tape, then *we* must be the phonographic pickup whose motion through space realizes the inherent rhythms and latent expressive meanings of the environment. Rasmussen goes on to say:

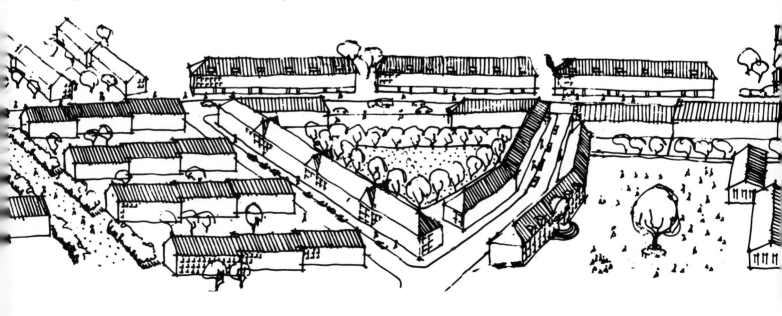

"People who live in the same country at the same time often have the same sense of rhythm. They move in the same way, they receive pleasure from the same experiences. When we see the costumes of an earlier age, we often wonder how anyone could have worn them. At one time those garments were the most natural thing in the world and now they seem cumbersome and hampering. This can only be explained by the fact that the people who wore them moved in a rhythm that was different from ours. There was intimate connection between the way those people conducted themselves and the things they wore and used, and it would take a great deal of coaching before the cleverest actor of today could give a perfect representation of a person of that period. In the same way the architecture of various periods must be looked upon as expressions of changing rhythms. In the Spanish Steps in Rome as depicted by Piranesi we have an illuminating example of this. The architect's problem was a simple one—to create a link between the low-lying Piazza di Spagna and the lofty Piazza della Trinità. The slope was too steep for a ramp; a flight of steps was necessary. Though Rome had many examples of monumental stairways—such as the long, straight flight leading up to Santa Maria in Aracoeli—the new one, when finished, was unique. With its bends and turns, its design seems to have been based on an old-fashioned, very ceremonial dance—The Polonaise—in which the dancers advance four by four in a straight line and then separate, two going to the right and two to the left; they turn, turn again, curtsy, meet again on the large landing, advance together, separate once more to left and right, and finally meet again at the topmost terrace where they turn to face the view and see Rome lying at their feet. The Spanish Steps were built in the seventeen-twenties when the farthingale was in fashion. Piranesi's engraving gives a faint idea of how the men and women of that day conducted themselves. They knew little about walking but so much the more about the very ceremonious dancing of the period, and therefore they could move gracefully on those steps which so closely resemble the figures of one of their dances—the men in high heeled shoes with toes turned out as they had learned from their fencing masters, the women in tight-laced bodices above their dipping and swaying farthingales. Thus, in the Spanish steps we can see a petrification of the dancing rhythm of a period of gallantry; it gives us an inkling of something that was, something our generation will never know.

"If we believe that the object of architecture is to provide a framework for people's lives, then the rooms in our houses, and the relation between them, must be determined by the way we will live in them and move through them."

Steen Eiler Rasmussen, *Experiencing Architecture* (New York: Technology Press and John Wiley and Sons, 1959)

The Spanish Steps, Rome. Detail of an engraving by Piranesi

A preliminary formulation of a taxonomy of these elements is presented in Philip Thiel, "Notes on the Description, Scaling, Notation, and Scoring of Some Perceptual and Cognitive Attributes of the Physical Environment," in H.M. Proshansky et al., eds., *Environmental Psychology: Man and His Physical Setting* (New York: Holt, Rinehart and Winston, 1970).

At this architectural and urban scale of design we are dealing with a whole new category of elements, such as:

spaces, in terms of their number, size, proportions, establishing elements, degree of explicitness, degree of enclosure, and form quality;

views, in terms of their number, position, size, direction and range;

objects furnishing the spaces, in terms of their number, position, type, size, direction, and movement;

finishes of all the environmental surfaces of the scene, in terms of their color and texture; and

effects such as light, sound, olfactory, and micro-climate.

In regard to the organization of such elements, Gyorgy Kepes comments:

"We have found that periodicity is an important factor in the perceptual structuring of our visual environment. Complex scenes, high buildings, high-intensity and low-intensity lighting, closed and open spaces are elements that recur. The recurrence of visual features in a structured sequence produces a textural rhythm that facilitates perceptual unification of the form of the city.

"Abrupt change and gradual change are the two basic units of periodic modulation. For example, the angles of streets may change in unison, bringing rhythmic order. Similarly, a gradual diminution or increase of the height of buildings, the width of streets, and the flow of traffic organizes a directional structure . . . .

"In our performance of so complex a task as the perception of our urban environment, periodicity has more intricate aspects. It combines regularly repeated configurations, such as dense traffic or arrangements of park benches. Part of the richness of the Paris scene is owed to the large number of small parks recurring at almost regular intervals. As activity must be punctuated by repose, so should the task of orientation be balanced by frequently recurrent opportunities for rest. In traveling through the urban environment there are a great number of periodic lulls such as traffic lights or bus stops. These directly underscore the rhythmic structure of the environment.

"It is important to have a variety of situations each with its rhythmic character, contrasting with one another, flowing into one another. The vitality of the cityscape depends on this. It is significant that some of the most sensitive and daring painters of our age have been occupied in reading and expressing the rhythm of the urban scene. Mondrian, one of the major figures in contemporary art, is obsessed with expressing the rhythmic richness of the metropolis. His *Broadway Boogie-Woogie*, a major opus of twentieth-century art, draws its stimulation and its expressive idiom from the pulsation of New York city traffic according to the beats and measures of streets and buildings. . . .

"In the total pattern of perception, both clear and distorted vision are esthetically important. A continuous chain of clear information may force us to break our attention if it does not give the necessary periodicity to the process of perception. Without the succession of activity and repose in our perception, the scene would be so dense with information that it would lie beyond our grasp. A world made continually illegible by overcomplexity or an extreme speed of impacts strains and irritates the observer. Artistic forms employ a periodicity of order and disorder to build up a total continuity through the proper sequence of these relationships."

Gyorgy Kepes, "Notes on Expression and Communication in the Cityscape," in L. Rodwin, ed., *The Future Metropolis* (New York: Braziller, 1960)

Georges Eugene Haussmann (1809-91), prefect of the Seine under Napoleon III, was responsible for a number of major transformations in Paris, including modernized water and sewage systems, monumental boulevards, and several large parks. A good description of his activities is given by Sigfried Giedion in *Time, Space and Architecture* (Cambridge, Mass.: Harvard University Press, 1967).

See Donald Appleyard et al., *The View From the Road* (Cambridge, Mass.: MIT Press, 1964); Yoshinobu Ashihara, *Exterior Design in Architecture* (New York: Van Nostrand Reinhold, 1970); and Amos Chang, *Intangible Content in Architectonic Form* (Princeton, N.J.: Princeton University Press, 1956).

Now you might like to consider the design of an imaginary urban environment, or study a Haussmann-like redesign of an existing portion of your environment, as encountered in the course of a ten to twenty minute path through it (the length of the path depending on your rate of movement: on foot, or in some vehicle). In this endeavor you will seek to organize these urban elements into a rhythmic structure, which modulates along the path, to produce an effective sequential experience.

Since it will now be apparent that design in terms of time-based sequential experience has many analogies with musical composition, or the "sculpture of time," you will be interested to read what Leonard Bernstein has to say about the art of conducting, and the work of Bach and Beethoven, in *The Joy of Music* (New York: Simon and Schuster, 1959).

Finally we may point out that the use of color investigated in this problem represents the fifth example of what we may now call the *modes of color use*. You will remember that in Problem 11 you were asked to mix pig-

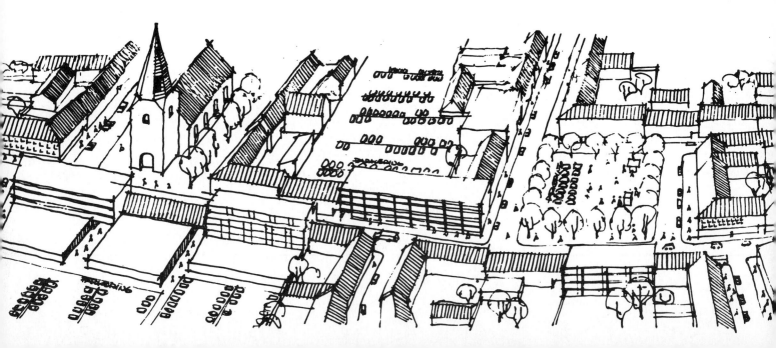

ments to match given basic pattern areas, and to "scale" or identify these colors in terms of the Munsell hue-value/chroma notation. In general, when local or situational color is used to record known or perceived color-attributes of objects and environmental surfaces we are using color in what may be called the *representational mode*. In Problem 12, however, we were involved with color as an agent for the communication of subjective feelings and attitudes. In this case color was used in the *expressive mode*. In Problem 13 we employed color on environmental surfaces as a means for the modeling of space in three dimensions. This may be called a use of color in the *spatial mode*. Next, in Problem 14, we used color systematically as a means to organize elements in a hierarchy: an example of what may be termed the *orientational mode*. Finally, in the present problem we have been concerned with the use of color as a means for the structuring of a number of elements in terms of rhythmic patterns of movement and development. This case constitutes a use of color in the *structural mode*.

Drawing of Danish road sequence by Karsten Jorgensen, architect

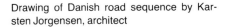

Texture Archetypes: Conclusion

Phase 4. From the many 8″ x 10″ prints you have made you are to select the quintessential example of each of the six archetypes and then present the six chosen prints, dry mounted, on one sheet of 20″ x 30″ white illustration board in vertical format (so that a group display of this work will require less wall space). Each print is to be exactly the same size (why?)—about 7½″ x 9½″—as trimmed from an 8″ x 10″ sheet; and each should be identified on the board with the name of its pattern.

How you lay out the prints, their captions, and your name is of course a design problem. Bear in mind that once again you are communicating: what is your message here? Watch out for "noise"—everything you put on the board *and* the way you display it should contribute to what you mean to say. Is it clear from your arrangement that there are two general categories of pattern: the linear and the nonlinear? Is it also clear that within each category there is an entropic order of the patterns? Is there any ambiguity about which caption goes with which print? Are you able to capitalize on any visual characteristics of the prints themselves in the organization of the presentation? (Perhaps you will want to review the principles presented in Problem 8 before starting work.)

Dry mounting is the preferred method of presenting photographs for display. It involves the use of special adhesive tissue and hot press equipment. The procedure, briefly, is as follows: starting with thoroughly dried prints, lightly outline in pencil the precise position of each print in your layout. Then "tack," or spot-adhere, a sheet of dry-mount tissue, slightly larger than the untrimmed print, to the center of the back of the print, using the electric tacking iron available for that purpose. When this is done, both the print and the attached tissue should be trimmed together to the required size (in our case all prints are to be trimmed to the same size). Be sure to trim off all the white borders of the prints. Next precisely position the print (with tissue attached) in the predetermined location on your board, and while maintaining the exact position, lift each corner of the print in turn and tack the corners of the tissue to the board. This prevents the print from shifting its position on the board during the next step—the insertion in the dry-mount press for full adhesion. The final step, on removal from the press, is to cover each print with a clean sheet of paper and to go over the surface with a rubber brayer or roller while the tissue cools to room temperature.

In connection with this matter of selection, read what Okakura Kakuzo wrote about the way the famous Japanese tea master Rikiu handled the problem:

"In the sixteenth century the morning-glory was as yet a rare plant with us. Rikiu had an entire garden planted with it, which he cultivated with assiduous care. The fame of his convolvuli reached the ear of the Taiko, and he expressed a desire to see them, in consequence of which Rikiu invited him to a morning tea at his house. On the appointed day Taiko walked through the garden, but nowhere could he see any vestige of the convolvulus. The ground had been leveled and strewn with fine pebbles and sand. With sullen anger the despot entered the tea room, but a sight waited him there which completely restored his humour. On the tokonoma, in a rare bronze of Sung workmanship, lay a single morning glory—the queen of the whole garden!"

—Okakura Kakuzo, *The Book of Tea* (New York: Duffield, 1925)

By thus ruthlessly eliminating the second-rate and the less-than-perfect, the tea master Rikiu was able to express the quintessence: the "queen of the whole garden," or that single example which summed up and thus most effectively communicated the innermost nature of the species. In a similar manner, if you have provided yourself with many examples of each of the six categories of texture, you may demonstrate your penetration to the heart of the matter and express most effectively its essential nature by selecting and presenting only the best example of each.

Discussion

At this point, having recorded or produced examples of each archetype, it may occur to you to test the hypothesis that all possible texture patterns can be made from combinations of the six archetypes. Can you find (or invent) some textural patterns that are *not* combinations of two or more of these archetypes? Another procedure would be to try to reproduce an existing texture pattern by synthesizing it in a multiple-exposure print, using two or more negatives of your archetype photographs. If you made photograms instead of photographs, you could use copy negatives made from your photograms, or copy them on 35 mm slides and combine them in projection.

In any event, now that you have developed new skills in light-sensitive media, it is a good time to consider the following comments on the larger implications of light in your professional life:

From Gyorgy Kepes, "Design and Light," *Design Quarterly 68* (Minneapolis, Minn.: Walker Art Center, 1967)

"Everything that is seen enters the human eye as a pattern of light qualities. We discern forms in space as configurations of brightness and color. The whole visible world, natural and man-made, is a light world. Its heights and depths, its great outlines and intimate details are mapped by light.

"When the artist or designer makes forms, he shapes light and the forms themselves become shapes of light.

"Any manipulation of a physical substance is inevitably a modulation of light. Paintings and photographic prints are surface patternings of reflected light. Lantern slides and motion pictures are surface patternings of light that are first transmitted and then reflected. When a sculptor models clay, leaving imprints of his fingers, he is actually modeling with light. Each impression of his hand and tool on the pliant substance directs the traffic of light and shade. The traces of pigment left by the painter's brush are devices to catch a certain part of the light that falls upon the canvas. When a painter spreads different pigments on his canvas, he creates areas of different light reflections and absorptions. These, in turn, arouse through our eyes sensations we call colors. The physiochemical microstructures of the pigments, through selective absorption, modulate the illuminating light into different wave lengths, which we sense as different color qualities.

"Every architectural form, every building or group of buildings, regardless of the practical purpose or expressive need that formed it—stability, comfort, economy or symbolic meaning—is a visible form built from differences of light qualities, created by the different hues, textures, opacities, and transparencies of its materials. Without our perception of these patterns of light, our distance sense, our appreciation of the qualities of our wider space would completely disappear and our space would shrink to the reach of our fingertips."

Buildings of similar functions in two different cultures and climates achieve their legibility by contrasting means: a chapel on Myconos modulates the brilliant, clear light of Greece by the differential illumination, shading, and shadows of its uniformly whitewashed surfaces; while a temple in Kyoto reveals its forms in the soft, muted light of Japan through the selective absorption and reflection of the naturally pigmented surfaces.

(Reproduced from post cards)

Putting it this way enables us to understand that the work of the visual designer is essentially as a manipulator of light sources and light modulators—by these means (and *only* by these means!) establishing both visual forms in space and visual space itself. Your new skills could now be directed, to your considerable benefit, to the following (collaborative?) series of studies:

1. Prepare a set of six white panels, about 30″ x 40″, each a tactile manifestation of one of the six archetypes. Then photograph the effect on each panel produced by variations in *light type* (direct sunlight, overcast sky, spotlight, floodlight, etc.), *number of sources* (one, several, many), and *direction of light sources* relative to the surface (perpendicular, parallel, oblique, etc.).

For an alternative study, prepare a supply of identical three-dimensional modular elements, such as small blocks of wood, as models of bricks or concrete blocks. Here the problem is to find a way to arrange these elements within a rectangular panel whose smallest dimension is at least twenty elements, so that when the panel is illuminated from each of three different directions ("morning," "noon," and "evening") it will produce in each case a rich pattern of highlights, shades, and shadows. For a start, compare the many traditional bonds used for masonry construction, and then go on from there, on your own. Photographically record your work in a systematic and comparative way.

2. Repeat the above exercise, this time incorporating both reflective and translucent material in the textural surfaces.

3. Using what you have learned from the preceding exercises, prepare a new tactile panel designed to demonstrate the richest possible variety of light effects when observed under a changing pattern of illumination. Your work for this study could be thought of as a model of a light-mural, intended for an exterior surface and illuminated by the sun and sky as they change from morning to noon to evening; or for an interior surface artificially illuminated by a programmed sequence of lights.

See for example "Rapid Transition," in *Progressive Architecture,* October 1970.

Light sources and light modulators in the articulation of form

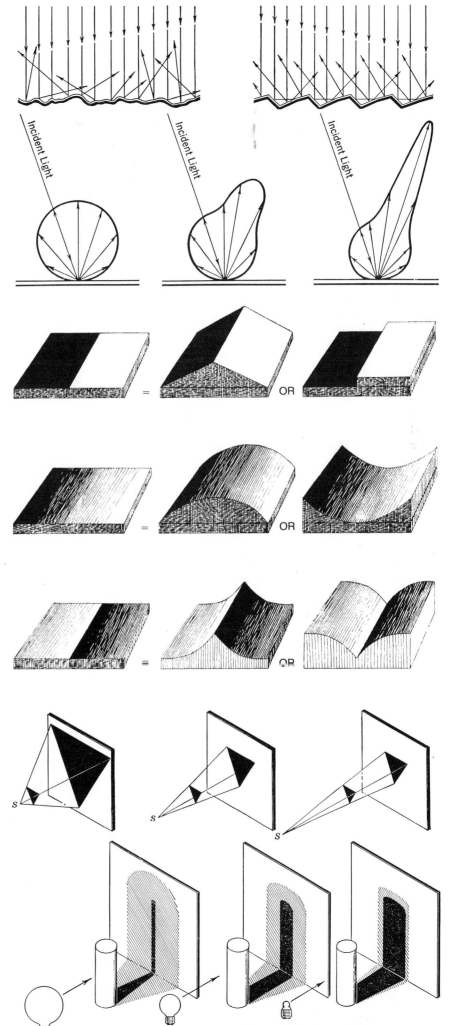

Surface Reflection

The directional pattern of light reflected from a surface depends on the degree of roughness of the surface, and on the pattern of that roughness. If a surface is rough, with micro-facets randomly distributed at all angles, the surface will reflect light in a *diffuse* manner. If there is some regularity in the arrangement of the micro-facets, the reflected light will be patterned. If the surface is smooth or mirrorlike, the light will be reflected at an angle equal to its angle of incidence, or in a *specular* manner. (Figures adapted from Ralph M. Evans, *An Introduction to Color* [New York: Wiley, 1948])

Light and Shade

At a scale larger than that of the micro-faceting of its surface, a three-dimensional opaque object directly illuminated by a source such as the sun will show a differential patterning of illumination on its surface. This distribution of light and shade, or *chiaroscuro,* is a consequence of both the positional relationship of the primary source of light and the object, and the three-dimensional form of the object. Thus those parts of the form facing the primary source are "highlighted"; while other parts, indirectly illuminated to a lesser degree by light reflected from adjacent environmental surfaces, (as secondary sources), are "shaded" to various degrees. In addition, the nature of the light-to-shade transitions between the directly and indirectly illuminated parts of the object correspond directly to the local form character of the object. Thus, curved surfaces show gradual transitions, and faceted forms are associated with abrupt changes. Note also that surface textures are best revealed by illumination at a low angle, or "grazing" the surface. (Figures adapted from H.B. Cott, *Adaptive Coloration in Animals* [London: Methuen, 1957])

Shadows

Shadows cast by opaque objects are clues for the perception of both the form of the object, and the conditions of illumination. The *silhouette* of the shadow represents a profile of the object, while the size of the shadow, and the relative size of the *penumbra* and *umbra* of the shadow, correspond respectively to the distance and size of the light source. Dappled or "broken" shadows denote screen-like objects, and multiple shadows result from more than one light source. (Figures from Ralph M. Evans, *An Introduction to Color* [New York: Wiley, 1948])

For precedents, see the work of such masters as Eugene Atget, Berenice Abbott, Ansel Adams, Matthew Brady, Wynn Bullock, Harry Callahan, Henri Cartier-Bresson, Walker Evans, Dorothea Lange, Laszlo Moholy-Nagy, Wright Morris, Man Ray, Aaron Siskind, W. Eugene Smith, Edward Steichen, Alfred Stieglitz, Paul Strand, Edward Weston, Minor White, and many others. At this point, because of your own struggles with the medium, you will better appreciate the achievements of these people, and find inspiration in their work.

Edward T. Hall, *The Silent Language* (Garden City, N.Y.: Doubleday, 1959)

For full details, see Philip Thiel, "Notes on the Description, Scaling, Notation, and Scoring of Some Perceptual and Cognitive Attributes of the Physical Environment," in Harold M. Proshansky et al., eds., *Environmental Psychology* (New York: Holt, Rinehart and Winston, 1970).

See Charles Morris, *Signs, Language, and Behavior* (New York: George Braziller, 1946).

A further challenge for your growing photographic capabilities lies in the exploration of some of the other types of environmental messages we are continuously sending and receiving, consciously or unconsciously, in our human use of and intentional, incidental, and accidental intervention in the environment. The selective viewpoint of the camera provides a useful discipline in focusing attention on the relationships that constitute the communicative essence of the visual scene, and your systematic documentation of some of them can only increase your awareness and enhance your understanding.

Since the environmental messages enveloping us are so numerous, varied, and complex, and because the use of any tool such as a camera implies some sense of a subject, locus, and objective, it will be helpful to refer to the following general catalogue of these factors, arranged as the main dimensions of a three-dimensional matrix and simultaneously interrelated. In this way, one may orient oneself and be able to deal comprehensively and consistently with a given aspect of the whole environment.

The **subject** ("who, what") may be taken to be some manifestation or evidence of an activity, human or otherwise. To categorize this we may adopt the pan-cultural, biologically based inventory of activity developed by Edward T. Hall. The list includes the ten "primary message systems" of interaction, association, subsistence, bisexuality, territoriality, temporality, learning, play, defense, and exploitation (use of materials).

The **locus** ("when, where") refers to that aspect of the visual environment which serves as the medium for the message. Here we may use a stage model of the environmental scene, organized in terms of "space," and its surfaces, screens, and objects as establishing elements; qualified as "place" by the furnishing properties, the surface colors and textures, and light effects; and conditioned as an "occasion" by the presence of men, women, and children in their various numbers, composition, and activities.

Finally, the **objective** ("why, how") concerns the purpose of your representations of a subject and locus. As communicative artifacts, your photographs may be said in general to show a relative emphasis on either the designative (documentary), appraisive (commentative), or prescriptive (persuasive) mode of signification.

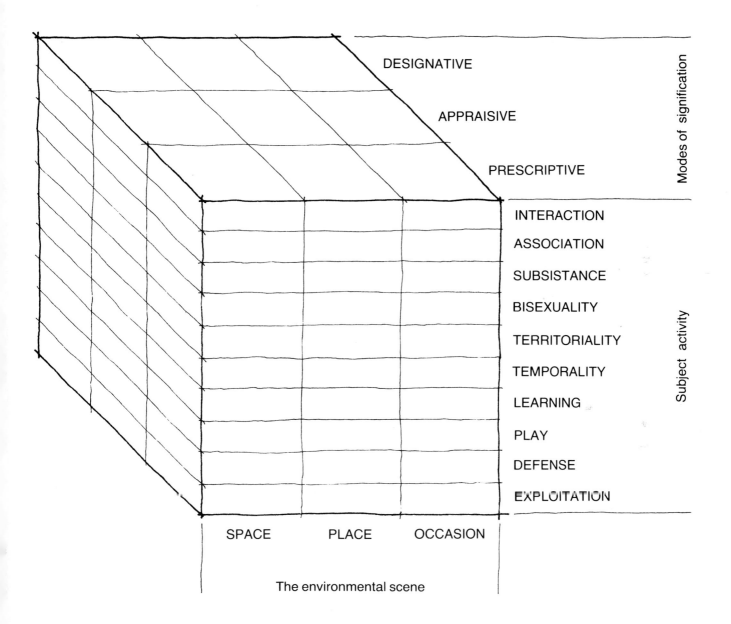

DESIGNATIVE

APPRAISIVE

PRESCRIPTIVE

Modes of signification

INTERACTION

ASSOCIATION

SUBSISTANCE

BISEXUALITY

TERRITORIALITY

TEMPORALITY

LEARNING

PLAY

DEFENSE

EXPLOITATION

Subject activity

SPACE   PLACE   OCCASION

The environmental scene

Texture, Space, and Scale

Having just completed and presented a photographic investigation of aleatory patterns in nature (Problem 3) you are very well acquainted with the texture attributes of trees, stones, sand, gravel, water, vegetation, wood, leaves, grass, and so on. Perhaps at the same time you also have become more aware of the textures of the manufactured surfaces in our environment? Underfoot there is asphalt, brick, carpet, concrete, cut stone, hardwood, linoleum, lawn, marble, mosaic, planks, steel gratings, terrazzo, tile, and wood decking; overhead there is acoustic tile, fabric, perforated metal, plaster (smooth or textured), plastic (molded or corrugated), and wood stripping or paneling; and on all sides we see brick, cloth, concrete, drapery, glass, marble, plywood, plaster, plastic, tile, wood siding, boarding and paneling, and wall paper in an infinite number of patterns. Each of these materials has its own characteristic texture-pattern, and just as colors can qualify the character of a space (as you discovered in Problem 13) so also can these textures affect our perceptions of an environmental scene.

In this final problem of the program you will have an opportunity to apply your present familiarity with the basic-pattern-area (BPA) attribute of texture to an investigation of its role in the qualification of various spatial characteristics.

For examples of the textures of traditional building materials in an English town, see Frederick Gibberd, "Wall Textures: A Local Study," *Architectural Review,* July 1940.

Materials

Scale model of two identical rooms from Problem 13

Unused prints from Problem 3

Rubber cement, "jumbo" paper clips

Knife, scale rule, etc.

Procedure

Here you are to try to achieve experimentally the same apparent changes in space that you were assigned in Problem 13, but this time using only achromatic, uniformly textured "wallpaper" instead of wall colors. The uniform texture patterns on this wallpaper may be differentiated in terms of the attributes of:

form type (as in Problem 3);

direction (horizontal, vertical, diagonal, directionless);

size (positive-negative basic-texture-element dimensions);

value (Munsell gray scale); and/or

contrast

With reference to value you will remember the hypothesis quoted in Problem 13 which suggested that in the case of surfaces establishing a space, those with lower (darker) values tend to advance and those with higher (lighter) values tend to recede.

The same source also hypothesized that a surface "pattern which is large and strong in contrast makes a room seem smaller. A pattern which is small in size and gentle in contrast makes a room seem larger. The absence of pattern can give the illusion of maximum space."

These observations provide a starting point for your study of the present issues. To proceed further, you may wish to keep value and pattern size constant and experimentally vary pattern direction and form type, one at a time, to discover the spatial effect (if any) of these attributes.

As a practical matter, if you pool your unused prints with your colleagues, you will then have a better supply of wallpaper with which to experiment. Large-size "jumbo" paper clips will be useful in temporarily holding wall-size pieces of these prints in place while you study their effect in the model.

Before you do this, you may want to take some color photographs of your model as a record of your work for Problem 13.

The final result of your studies should be demonstrated in your model, with the print wallpaper secured in place by means of a double coat of rubber cement. On the base of your model, you should letter a generalized statement about the spatial effect of each of the variables (form type, direction, size, value, and/or contrast). As before, be sure to include accurate and realistic identical "scale figures" in the same location in each space. And, as always, craft quality counts!

Discussion

From these studies you have gained some insight into the nature of the basic-pattern-area attribute of texture in qualifying the apparent dimensions and proportions of environmental space. For a given texture pattern, we find that contrast, value, form type, direction, and size each make their own contribution to the effect. For more on the matter of texture patterns, element sizes, and texture gradients in space perception, James Gibson's work is the classic reference, while Yoshinobu Ashihara provides a useful discussion from the standpoint of the architect and urban designer.

James J. Gibson, *The Perception of the Visual World* (Boston: Houghton Mifflin, 1950); and Yoshinobu Ashihara, *Exterior Design in Architecture* (New York: Van Nostrand Reinhold, 1970)

But there is more to "texture and space" than the perception of spatial form, size, and proportion. Just as we found (in Problems 11 and 13) that the basic-pattern-area attribute of color not only qualified our spatial perceptions but also influenced our responses to mood and affective quality, so also does texture qualify that subtle spatial attribute called "scale."

Scale is probably one of the most important higher-order attributes of the environmental scene, as well as one of the least well understood. But both Heath Licklider and J. W. Curtis have recently done much to clarify this matter, and we present here an approach to the subject based on their work.

J. W. Curtis, "A Functional Definition of Scale," *A.I.A. Journal,* February 1971; and Heath Licklider, *Architectural Scale* (London: Architectural Press, 1965

The comprehensive array of environmental surfaces visible at a given point in time and space may be represented in terms of the patterning of a "fish-eye" photograph, or a hemispherical projection. The adjacent figure shows such a hemispherical projection in which several basic pattern areas have been outlined and serially numbered, and in which the various texture patterns are also indicated.

With this we present an inventory of the basic-texture-element (BTE) patterns of these basic pattern areas (BPAs). Note that in this example several basic pattern areas are "smooth," and that one of the basic-texture-element patterns may be described as a combination of two simpler patterns. A textureless or "smooth" pattern area might be standardized as one whose texture elements are less than 0.0087" in size, which at "arm's length" (say 30") cannot be resolved with normal (20/20) vision.

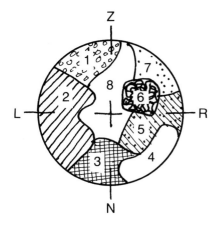

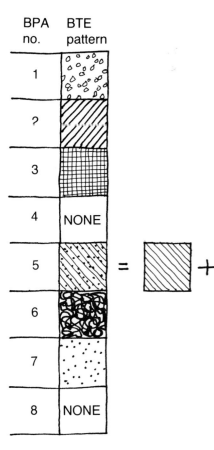

To size the basic texture elements we will use the *actual* linear dimensions that characterize their pattern. But what are the dimensions of a pattern? To clarify this situation, let us first remember that a basic texture element exists in terms of a figure-ground relationship within the basic pattern area: that is, the more-or-less regular optical differentiations constituting a textural pattern may be seen as smaller closed "figures" against a uniform "ground." Thus any basic-texture-element pattern will have a minimum of two measurable dimensions: the distance between contours on the figure, and the distance between contours on the ground. This simplest condition will occur for a regular polka-dot (granular) or a striped (linear) pattern. Other patterns (graded, mottled, matted, tangled) display a characteristic *range* of dimensions between contours. These actual dimensions, associated with the pattern of texture elements in a given basic pattern area, will apply over the entire surface of that area.

Thus the relative size of the basic pattern area (as a percentage of the total area of the hemispherical projection) indicates the relative "use" of these dimensions in a given scene. If we now summarize the relative use of each of the basic-texture-element dimensions over the whole hemispherical projection we will have a single characterization of the texture attributes of the surfaces of a given scene, as perceivable from a given point in time and space.

This summarization may be presented as a frequency distribution. For convenience we can use a logarithmic scale for the basic-texture-element sizes, ranging from 10^{-4} feet to 10^{+4} feet, in a polar format as the circumference of a circle. The ordinates designating the percentage of hemispherical projection area are the radii of the circle, with 0 percent at the circumference, and 100 percent at the center. Thus the circumference represents a "spectrum" of possible visible basic-texture-element pattern sizes, and the radial ordinates indicate *areal percentages* of these sizes; for a given scene as presented in the hemispherical projection.

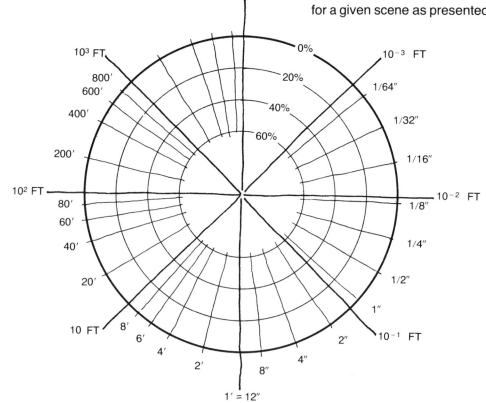

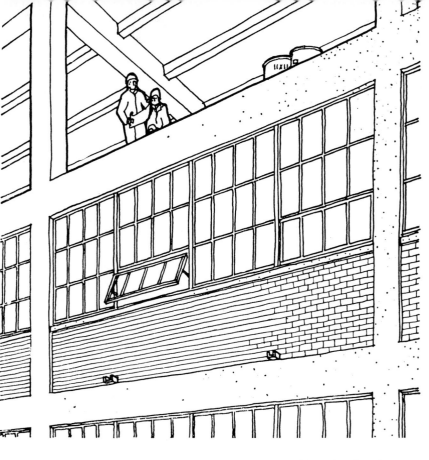

An illustration of some basic pattern areas of various sizes, each with different texture patterns of diverse basic-texture-element sizes. From Heath Licklider, *Architectural Scale* (London: Architectural Press, 1965)

At this point it should be noted that there is a second-level order of patterning in the hemispherical projection, in addition to that of the texture elements within each basic pattern area. This additional pattern is of the basic pattern areas themselves with reference to the hemispherical projection. As the number of basic pattern areas increases, the average percent area and the characteristic dimensions of the pattern areas decrease. To incorporate this second-level patterning in the frequency distribution, the characteristic actual dimensions of each basic pattern area are also included in the above tabulation.

To implement this notation the procedure is to set up a table listing the basic pattern areas and their percentage of the hemispherical projection area, followed by a scale of dimensions at convenient intervals (such as "smooth," 1/64", 1/32", 1/16", 1/8", etc.). Then, taking each pattern area in turn, the actual representative dimensions of its basic-texture-element (BTE) patterns are determined, and indicated on the table, as shown below. When this is completed the total percent area for each size is summed up, in turn, and plotted as the frequency distribution.

BPA no.	% HP area	BTE dimensions											
		S	1/64"	1/32"	1/16"	1/8"	1/4"	1/2"	1"	2"	3"	4"	etc.
1	10.1		✓	✓									
2	3.6					✓							
3	1.3			✓				✓	✓				
4	6.5							✓			✓		
etc.													

Osbert Lancaster, *A Cartoon History of Architecture* (London: John Murray, 1959)

To illustrate the use of this notation, consider two scenes differing greatly in their textural finishes, as suggested by two drawings from Osbert Lancaster. The basic pattern areas of the first are characterized by richly decorated surfaces, with basic-texture-element pattern dimensions ranging from coarse textures to large patterns. The frequency distribution of these dimensions might plot about as shown in the associated size-spectrum notation. The second scene, in contrast, is composed of basic pattern areas with mostly smooth surfaces, but including some fine-scale textures. Here the frequency distribution is considerably different, as indicated in its appended size-spectrum notation.

This then provides us with a succinct means of objectively characterizing the texture-pattern attribute of an environmental scene, as perceivable from a given point in time and space. It should be noted, however, that subjective human responses to the same scene may be quite varied. Curtis suggests that the situation in the first scene might be described as being "warm" and "cozy" by some people, or, on the other hand, as "fussy" and "cluttered" by others. Likewise, the scene suggested by the second case could be called "clean" and "crisp," or, alternately, seen as "cold" and "sterile." Thus we are again reminded that environmental perceptions are a function of individual human characteristics as well as specific environmental form.

What words can *you* find to describe your perceptions of the expressive qualities of your two texture-qualified scale-model spaces?

What might be the possible responses to an environmental scene with a frequency distribution showing a central tendency intermediate to these somewhat extreme cases? Or the responses to a *uniform* distribution over the whole range? Here we have another frontier in visual design and environmental perception; and here the frequency distribution of the basic-pattern-area and basic-texture-element sizes, as an objective description of a fundamental visual characteristic of a given scene, offers a new tool for the exploration of this frontier.

We have now considered the role of texture as a factor in the perception of spatial size and proportion, and as an element in the qualification of environmental scale. These may be termed the *spatial mode* and *expressive mode,* respectively; exactly analogous to the modes of color use (summarized in Problem 16). As in the case of color, we also find the *orientational mode,* and the *structural mode* of texture use.

The use of texture in the orientational mode is most commonly seen in the floorscape, as a means of cuing access and usage. A great variety of texture-rich materials are available for these purposes: flagstones, cobbles, setts, mosaic, gravel, grass, asphalt, stone slabs, and poured concrete in broomed, exposed aggregate and several other finishes. Gordon Cullen illustrates the uses of many of these materials in coding and clarifying the proper behaviors and special privileges of pedestrians and motorists in their common use of the ground surface. In some cases this may be adapted for use by the blind.

Gordon Cullen, *Townscape* (New York: Reinhold, 1961)

DRIVEWAY

CROSS-RIPPLED TEXTURE AT CORNER

RIPPLED CONCRETE

COARSE EXPOSED AGGREGATE CONCRETE AT ENTRIES & BUS STOPS

TEXTURED CROSSWALK

"Tactile Paving Signs for the Blind," from Michael Southworth and Kevin Lynch, "Designing and Managing the Strip," working paper number 29 (Cambridge, Mass.: Harvard-MIT Joint Center for Urban Studies, October 1974)

Larger-scale "urban textures" exist in terms of the building as the basic texture element, with a given precinct being characterized by a common pattern of building forms, sizes, and spacing. In many older cities there is little variation in the characteristics of these elements, and their relatively small size and uniform pattern produce a "fine grain" texture. Contemporary cities, however, with a greater functional differentiation of parts into residential, commercial, industrial, educational, recreational, civic, and service districts, usually show a greater variety of larger-scale textures, and may be said to have a "coarser grain."

See Kevin Lynch, "The Form of Cities," *Scientific American*, April 1954.

The use of such urban-scale textures in the structural mode is suggested by Gyorgy Kepes, who comments:

Gyorgy Kepes, "Texture and Rhythm," from "Notes on Expression and Communication in the Cityscape," in L. Rodwin, ed., *The Future Metropolis* (New York: Braziller, 1960)

"Textures as qualities of living surfaces are significant in the rhythmic structuring of the cityscape. In a complex environment like ours, the architectural spatial order is becoming less and less dominant and the textural play of buildings in sequence increasingly noticeable. To bring the vibrating, changing surfaces into a perceivable order, certain regularities among them have to be emphasized. One is the grain or density; another is the inherent direction. In the esthetic organization of the urban scene, both aspects of texture can be utilized. Regular changes from finely to coarsely grained surface textures bring their own type of order. The direction of textural qualities can best be illustrated by simple examples. When seen from a distance, roof patterns whether made from tile or shingle vary in their apparent directional alignment according to the movement of the eye, thus producing an oscillating surface texture. A tree whose leaves are wavering before a brick wall shows two textural surfaces, different both in grain and in mobility. The flutter of the leaves is important to the esthetic quality perceived.

"Our city scenes are made up of a rich combination of such textural characteristics; stable and mobile textures with different intensities and different directions are woven into a common fabric. At this moment, all the threads are accidental and, in an esthetic sense, uncontrolled. Although there is very little chance to control completely the textural range of the environment, an awareness of some of its effects could be a guide to those who are charged with the tasks of city planning."

For examples of such scale-model simulations, see Harry E. Rodman, "A Simulation Method for Study of Lighting Design," *International Lighting Review*, vol. 26, no. 3-4 (1975).

In preparation for this, it is suggested that you first familiarize yourself with the comments of Gyorgy Kepes in "Design and Light," in *Design Quarterly 68* (Minneapolis, Minn.: Walker Art Center, 1967); and the concepts of "ambient luminescence," "focal glow," and "play of brilliants" used by lighting expert Richard Kelly, as presented in Arnold Nicholson, "Mr. Kelly's Magic Lights," *Saturday Evening Post*, 5 July 1958. Also, see John E. Flynn and Arthur W. Segil, *Architectural Interior Systems* (New York: Van Nostrand Reinhold, 1970).

At this point, with your new competence in photography and your recent experience in simulating the spatial effects of color and texture, you are in an excellent position to combine these skills and undertake some advanced experiments in light/space design through the use of scale modeling and the photographic recording of the results.

As a preliminary step you should perform, with one or two colleagues, the advanced studies suggested in Problem 3 on the interaction of light and texture, and those on the effects of various light sources on color appearance mentioned in Problem 11.

Following this preparatory experience you are ready to construct some scale model "movie sets" (1″ = 1′ minimum), to be illuminated by a wide variety of light sources and types, and photographed from a given position at scale eye-level with color-slide film and a wide-angle or fish-eye lens. When the resulting slides are projected and viewed in pairs, you will have a very flexible means of simulation for the investigation of the role of light in determining and qualifying the visual perception of space.

The model should be surrounded by large white reflective panels to provide a source of even "fill-in" light (as from the sky). This of course may be supplemented as necessary with a main directional source (as from the sun) and by miniature local sources (as from light fixtures). If you photograph an exterior setting with a fish-eye lens you should use a translucent plastic dome over the model, to provide a sky dome, again with fill-in and directional light sources. As always, scale figures are essential in the set, and here you may try proper-size magazine cutouts mounted on cardboard for greater verisimilitude. Note that top-quality craft skills are necessary in all this work, to maintain a convincing illusion of "reality." Finally, when using a non-fish-eye lens be sure to use the smallest possible lens opening for the greatest depth of field.

It is suggested that, given a simple, generally rectangular space-form ("O-type") comprising one or more subspaces within one primary space, and one or more views to external spaces, you proceed with a series of controlled experiments as follows:

Series A. All environmental surfaces are to be white and "smooth," or textureless; and the illumination is to be colorless, or "white." The independent variables are to be light type, size, number, position, and direction; and the dependent variables will then be the apparent or perceived denotative character and connotative quality of the space, as a consequence of the illumination.

Series B. This will be the same as Series A except that the environmental surfaces are to be *colored* according to each of the hue-value/chroma hypotheses discussed in Problem 11. This series integrates the effect of light and color on space perception.

Series C. This will be the same as Series A except that the environmental surfaces are to be *textured.* Here several different patternings of textures and the same patternings of illumination will provide an opportunity to discover the effects on space perception of interactions of light and texture.

Series D. In this case both *color and texture* are combined on the environmental surfaces, with the same patterning of "white" illumination.

Series E. The illumination should now be systematically varied in *color temperature and light level,* with the same colored and textured surfaces of Series D. This provides an opportunity to study the effect of the color and amount of spatial illumination on spatial mood.

Following these scale-model simulations, your local theater group may provide you with further opportunities to study light/space effects at full scale, in the design and lighting of their stage sets.

Further details on the anatomy of space may be found in Philip Thiel, "Notes on the Description, Scaling, Notation and Scoring of Some Perceptual and Cognitive Attributes of the Physical Environment," in Harold M. Proshansky et al., eds., *Environmental Psychology* (New York: Holt, Rinehart and Winston, 1970).

You should by now be aware that the reason we make a simulation is to find an "answer" to a "question," and that the effectiveness of such a procedure is increased if both the questions and answers are formulated as explicitly as possible. Here the questions concern the role of the attributes of environmental light, color, and texture, singly and in combination, on the perception of spatial form and character; and the answers involve the varieties of user responses to these patterns of the environment. In our case the questions are explicit in the specifications for the independent variables of the model surfaces and their illumination. The corresponding dependent responses to the simulated conditions may be organized in terms of the denotative issues of spatial number, size, shape, position, explicitness, and enclosure; and the connotative factors of color mood feeling, scale, and the Kruithof theory relating level of illumination and illumination color temperature to impressions of temperature feeling and naturalness of color rendering.

Postscript

Consider, for example, the attitude of the great painter Paul Cézanne, who wrote at age sixty-seven, one month before his death in 1906:

". . . now it seems to me that I see better and that I think more correctly about the direction of my studies. Will I ever attain the end for which I have striven so much and so long? I hope so, but as long as it is not attained a vague state of uneasiness persists which will not disappear until I have reached port, that is until I have realized something which develops better than in the past. . . . So I continue to study.

"I am always studying after nature and it seems to me that I make slow progress. . . . But I am old, ill, and I have sworn to myself to die painting. . . ."

—letter to Emile Bernard, Aix, 21 September 1906, in John Rewald, ed., *Paul Cézanne's Letters* (Oxford: B. Cassirer, 1976)

The equally famous Japanese artist Katsushika Hokusai (1760-1849) wrote:

"From the age of six I had a mania for drawing forms of things. By the time I was fifty I had published an infinity of drawings, but all I have produced before the age of seventy is not worth taking into account. At seventy-five I learned a little about the structure of nature—of animals, plants, and bees, birds, fishes and insects. In consequence when I am eighty I shall have made a little more progress. At ninety I shall certainly have reached a marvelous stage, and when I am a hundred and ten, everything I do— be it but a line or a dot—will be alive."

Paul Cézanne: photographed in his thirties. Courtesy of John Rewald

Katsushika Hokusai: *Self-Portrait as an Old Man,* sumi sketch on paper, circa 1840

A Valediction

So here you are, seventeen problems later, having abandoned comfortable prejudices, normative stereotypes, facile assumptions, and familiar procedures in an intensive experience of self-transformation. And now that you have challenged yourself in the uncomfortable process of self-discovery, made agonizing reappraisals, persisted beyond the point of exhaustion, and thought the unthinkable, you have come to realize that you are much stronger and more capable of growth than you ever thought possible.

At this point you and your colleagues will find it rewarding to reinforce your sense of growth and self-accomplishment by recapitulating your recent experiences through the collaborative preparation of an exhibition of your work, with several examples selected for each of the seventeen problems. At the same time, bear in mind that the real significance of your accomplishment is not in these tangible artifacts, but rather in the intangible changes that have taken place within you in the course of producing them. The material on display is only a symptom of this process: in reality it is you, "before" and "after," that is on display. This is also a good time to reread your True Confessions, to gain a sense of how your ideas, feelings, and standards have evolved over the past weeks.

You understand, of course, that in all this work you have only scratched the surface: each problem has provided only a glimpse of a vast territory, and there are many areas we have not even mentioned, much less considered. The Discussions have touched on some of these other issues, many of which offer a lifetime challenge.

What would be the parameters of such an exhibition? Consider the following suggestions:

Purpose (Indicate achievement? Public relations?)

Audience (You and your classmates? Other design students? The general public?)

Location (Space? Lighting? Access and security?)

Content (An equal number of projects from each student? One or more examples of each project?)

Organization (Chronological sequence? Themes and variations?)

Time and Budget (Time available? Funds required?)

264

But now that you have achieved a measure of proficiency in design—that is, you are concerned with social purposes and ecological ramifications, aware of superordinate and subordinate contexts, responsible for all parameters, fluent in the generation of alternatives, adept in several modes of simulation, perceptually sensitive and sensuously involved, competent in managing your time, and never completely satisfied with your results—we might well review the circumstances in which you will operate and the values you might serve with your growing skills in visual communication and expression.

As an environmental designer, you will work in the public arena, and your contributions will take their place among those of many others of the past, present, and future, becoming a part of that ever-present and all-pervasive series of messages "to whom it may concern" which is the visual environment.

Because any sizable intervention in the environment requires the expenditure of a considerable amount of muscular and/or financial power, your message will to some degree be subject to the control of those who provide that power, and representative of their values. To the extent that a particular intervention requires collaboration with other individuals and groups in the decision-making process, the message will reflect this collective origin.

Given these pluralistic contexts and operational constraints, what then are your opportunities and responsibilities as an "artist," in our contemporary circumstances of increasing social interdependence and accelerating change in a "global village" of finite resources?

First of all let us remind ourselves that vision, as the faculty or sense of sight, is our major mode of environmental perception and knowledge. It is the ongoing cognitive process by which we interact with the constant stream of light signals available in the external environment to orient ourselves in that environment: to relate to it and to understand it so that we may operate purposefully within it. The continuing flux of this (and to a lesser extent) other external sensory data is the raw material from which we construct our personal "view of the world": those internal representations of "reality" we summarize in the form of our private images. These mental artifacts and "re-presentations" are the means we use to coalesce and focus our actions, feelings, and thoughts as ongoing experiences in terms of memories of the past, significations of the present, and plans and hopes for the future.

The adequacy of these images, and the "reality" of their implicit personal world, are tested in the comparison of our percepts and concepts with those of others. As Heinz Von Foerster suggests, the logical structure of the concept "environment" depends on the existence of such shared knowledge or consciousness.

For a review of the nature of these messages, see Introduction A: Vision and Environment.

For further disquisitions on the subject of "The Image," see the books of this same title by Kenneth E. Boulding (Ann Arbor: University of Michigan Press, 1956) and Daniel J. Boorstin (New York: Penguin Books, 1962). Charles W. Rusch also provides a lucid description of the role of the image in a model of the mental process, in "On Understanding Awareness," in *The Journal of Esthetic Education,* vol. 4, no. 4 (October 1970).

"Stop to think for a moment what you would answer if I asked you, 'What is the environment?' Most probably you would retort with a counter question, 'Environment of what?' When we use the concept 'environment' we tacitly assume an 'environmentee' or that which is surrounded, or acted upon, by the environment. A cockroach who stands in line with me at the box office to 'La Dolce Vita,' although he occupies almost the identical spatio-temporal neighborhood as I do, certainly has an entirely different environment. He may be looking forward to relishing a batch of old noodles which are, alas, protected by my foot, while I may be looking forward to Anita Eckberg's antics. Thus, if we are able to specify the environmentee, then at the same time, we have defined its environment. Clearly, this is a highly subjective affair, as you can see from the cockroach example. On the other hand, it might be conceivable that, by appropriate specification and enumeration of certain objective features, one may establish an appropriate environmentee. However, this is rarely done, as we have seen at this conference where the environmentee was always implicitly or explicitly given.
. . .

"Assume that a relationship 'environment-environmentee' will indeed describe adequately the situation under consideration. Under these circumstances it can be argued that the whole environment does not exist at all in reality, but that it is the sole product of the environmentee's imagination. In other words, we may insist that introspection does not permit us to decide whether the world as we see it is 'real,' or just the result of our dreams, an illusion of our fantasy. However, by looking around in our dreamworld, which perchance may be this conference, we cannot deny that our imaginary universe if populated with apparitions that are in many respects similar to us. Consequently, we have to grant them the privilege to insist that they are the sole reality and everything else is only a concoction of their imagination. On the other hand, they cannot deny that their fantasies will be populated by apparitions—and some of them may be we!

"With this we have reduced our original assertion to an absurdity, because if I assume I am the sole reality, it turns out that I am the imagination of somebody else, who in turn assumes that he is the sole reality. Of course, this paradox is easily resolved by postulating the reality of our environment in which we all happily thrive.

"I hope that the crucial point of my argument has become sufficiently clear, namely that, for the establishment of the logical structure of the concept 'environment' there must be at least two elements observing this environment, and they must be sufficiently alike in order to serve as mutual witnesses for any objective event. In other words, that which can be witnessed can claim to be real and to be part of our environment. Again, to put it differently, only knowledge that can be shared belongs to our environment. Thus, it turns out that the logical structure of 'environment' is that of a 'triadic relation' because it involves the relationship of three entities: an observer, A; a witness, A*; and that which is witnessed, B. Environment can be called 'together-knowledge' which in English undoubtedly sounds awkward. However, in Latin there is a splendid expression for exactly this term, namely **conscientia** from which, of course, our word 'consciousness' is derived. It probably was the triadic logical structure of this concept that gave all philosophers over the last three thousand years difficulty when they tried to resort to a simple true-false, two-valued, Aristotelian logic, where at least a three-valued logic is required. You may at this point argue that consciousnes is, by all means, a single man's affair and that you do not need a witness in order to be conscious. This seems, at first glance, to be true. However, closer inspection shows that our consciousness is produced by the 'together-knowledge' of the rapport of our different sensory modalities. The ear is witness to what the eye sees; the eye is witness to what touch reports; and so on. In order that these senses may compare their various experiences, it is necessary that they translate these into the same language."

—Heinz Von Foerster, "Logical Structure of Environment and Its Internal Representation," in R. E. Eckerstrom, ed., *International Design Conference Aspen 1962* (Zeeland, Michigan: Herman Miller, 1963) ·

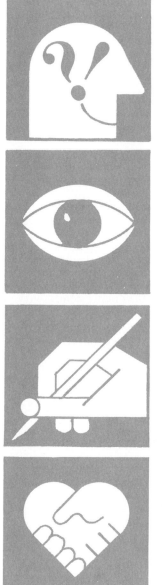

"The artistic image—the work of visual art—is the created image in its highest form, a significant message delivered simultaneously to our senses, our feelings, and our minds. At every stage of history men have looked for images that would keep them oriented in the world, that would tell them what the world was like, how sweet and rich it was, how good or bad, and what was their own place in it. Artistic images have served to bring their outer and inner worlds into correspondence, providing them with means for inducing inner pictures of the outer environment—pictures shaped with sympathy, with the joys and sorrows, fears and hopes in the heart of man. And above all the work of art has sustained man with visions of a felt order. It has returned understanding to the indispensable eye, the foundation of our thought and feeling, the core of experience.

"The common denominator of artistic expression has been the ordering of a vision into a consistent, complete form. The difference between a mere expression, however intense and revealing, and an artistic image of that expression lies in the structure of the form. This structure is specific. The colors, lines, and shapes corresponding to our sense impressions are organized into a balance, a harmony or rhythm that is in an analogous correspondence with feelings, and these in turn are analogues of thoughts and ideas. An artistic image, therefore, is more than a pleasant tickle of the senses and more than a graph of emotions. It has meaning in depth, and at each level there is a corresponding level of human response to the world. In this way, an artistic form is a symbolic form grasped directly by the senses but reaching beyond them and connecting all the strata of our inner world of sense, feeling, and thought. The intensity of the sensory pattern strengthens the emotional and intellectual pattern; conversely, our intellect illuminates such a sensory pattern, investing it with symbolic power. This essential unity of primary sense experience and intellectual evaluation makes the artistic form unique in human experience and therefore in human culture. Our closest human experience is love, where again sensation, feeling, and idea compose a living unity.

"The essential unity of first-hand percept and intellectual concept makes artistic images different from scientific cognition or simple animal response to situations. To repeat, it is the unity of the sensory, emotional, and rational that can make the orderly forms of artistic images unique contributions to human culture. The meaning of the artistic experience is impoverished if any one of these areas of experience takes undue preponderance.

"Images deriving solely from a rational assessment of the external world, without passion of the eyes, are only topographical records. Images of emotional responses without real roots in the environment are isolated graphs of a person's inner workings: they do not yield symbolic form. And the most beautiful combinations of color and shape, the most exquisitely measured proportions of line, area, and volume, leave us where they find us if they have not grown out of rational and emotional participation in the total environment. Each of these visions is a fragment only."

—Gyorgy Kepes, Introduction to *The Visual Arts Today* (Middletown, Conn.: Wesleyan University Press, 1960)

It is, of course, in the establishment and expansion of this shared knowledge and consciousness that those *created* visual images we call works of art—exemplary messages of order, mobilizing "all the strata of our inner world of sense, feeling, and thought" in a living unity—play a key role. These tangible visual images, subliminally integrating all components of human consciousness, serve a basic social need by publicly displaying an inner individual vision for contemplation by others, and by this means providing an opportunity for the testing, challenging, expansion, and confirmation of others' private visions. In this externalization of hidden assumptions, art facilitates the growth of a vital collective consciousness and a greater human commonwealth.

The social role of the artist may be understood as illuminating what is before us, but out of awareness; and articulating what could be, but is not yet. By expanding human consciousness and suggesting possible goals, in wholistic terms and at transcendental levels, art serves society as a medium for personal growth and social development, and as an early-warning system of changing contexts and values. Art is thus a social means for coping with uncertainty, optimizing resources, and realizing latent human and social potentials. Although we cannot predict the future, we can with the aid of the arts domesticate the ever-changing present and conceive preferable future alternatives. But what about the practical aspects of art as visual expression and communication in environmental design practice? What are the pragmatic realities of operation as a design professional?

"The American designer is at once a central figure in what I am going to call the cultural apparatus and an important adjunct of a very peculiar kind of economy. His art is a business, but his business is art and curious things have been happening both to the art and to the business—and so to him. He is caught up in two great developments of twentieth-century America: One is the shift in economic emphasis from production to distribution, and along with it, the joining of the struggle for existence with the panic for status. The other is the bringing of art, science and learning into subordinate relation with the dominant institutions of the capitalist economy and the rationalist state.

"Designers work at the intersection of these trends; their problems are among the key problems of the overdeveloped society. It is their dual involvement in them that explains the big split among designers and their frequent guilt; the enriched muddle of ideals they variously profess and the insecurity they often feel about the practice of their craft; their often great disgust and their crippling frustration. They cannot consider well their position or formulate their credo without considering both cultural and economic trends, and the shaping of the total society in which these are occurring. . . ."

—C. Wright Mills, "The Man in the Middle," *Industrial Design*, November 1958

"To do work of integrity the artist must have the courage to fight for what he believes. This bravery may never earn him a medal, and it must be undertaken in the face of a danger that has no element of high adventure in it—the cold, hard possibility of losing his job. Yet the courage of his convictions is, along with his talent, his only source of strength. The businessman will never respect the professional who does not believe in what he does. The businessman under these circumstances can only 'use' the artist for his own ends—and why not, if the artist himself has no ends? As long as he remains 'useful,' the artist will keep his job, but he will lose his self-respect and eventually give up being an artist, except, perhaps, wistfully on Sundays."

—Paul and Ann Rand, "Advertisement: Ad Vivum or Ad Hominem?" in Gyorgy Kepes, ed., *The Visual Arts Today* (Middletown, Conn.: Wesleyan University Press, 1960)

See also Anne Karpf, "Professional Revolutionaries," *Architectural Design*, September 1976; and Victor Papanek, *Design for the Real World* (New York, Bantam, 1976).

A cynic might suggest that environmental art today consists of either an ego-tangled, star-spangled glamour scene, in which designers compete for editorial notice and building commissions on the basis of fashionable novelty, capricious theories, and emotional exhibitionism; or a grubbier, déclassé world of cocktail-lounge or accounting-office design serving bottom-line, short-term financial interests, where aesthetic values are implicitly involved only as a pathetic form of investment insurance, or are explicitly pandered to the public in the form of a token "one percent for art."

The alternative to this Scylla of meretricious status and Charybdis of art prostitution is, of course, the development of your own convictions and the courage to fight for them. These convictions are best based on a recognition that your design is only a means to an end, and that the end or purpose can only be a fuller and richer life for all those who experience your work. In the case of architecture, for example, the building is not the "picture": the building is the *frame* for the picture, and the picture is life. This is only to make the point that, at a more general level, design must be life-enhancing in the broadest of terms and deepest of senses: recognizing life's complexity and contradictions; acknowledging its diversity and plurality; respecting its continuity in time and space; affirming the interdependence of all humanity as well as its unity with nature; and celebrating life's sensory richness and poetic potential.

What is implied here is that a vital design can only come from a vital designer: the creative act must be grounded in a comprehensive sensitivity to the personal, social, and ecological relationships that pattern our presence on planet Earth; and the creative impulse must be sparked by a strong sense of the difference between what is and what could be, and a passion to make manifest a new vision. In completing the program of this present course you have acquainted yourself with a method of approach appropriate to engaging these issues, and you are now well qualified to continue your preparation for a most challenging career. The author salutes you, and wishes you many happy comparisons of adjacent alternatives.

"Our individual and our common life both begin with a happy oneness with our surroundings. There are dim, half-buried collective memories of oneness that we yearn to recapture without any expectation of success in doing so. But, in addition to this unattainable and almost forgotten happy land, we have more easily revived individual memories of oneness with our surroundings.

"We are all acquainted with rare moments when meaning swells into double meaning or many meanings and the world manifests itself not as separated territories but as a living whole. These are moments in which single feeling takes over and we seem to dissolve into the world around us. Children who are allowed to be children sometimes reach such happy complete involvement. . . .

"Inevitably, most of us lose the marvelous capacity we had as children to sense life in its fullest whole. Present adult civilized life is systematically cut up, scheduled, and parceled out. We live by timetables and maps. We can recount the year, day, and hour in which something happened, and place it in the right house, street, and country, but we forget its taste and color. The capacity for sensing our belongingness, which gives living its color, richness, and, really, its justification, is drained out of most of us.

"What we have lost we sometimes miss, discovering the difference between life as it is and life as it could be. With shock and terror, we see how empty we are. And, unwilling to acknowledge the fact that we have turned into cornered beasts, we seek release by creating new foundation experiences that restore our confidence and enable us to reconstruct unity in the world. Artists, the men among us who retain the capacity to feel intensely, know how to build models of the missing quality of living and create experiences that are analogues of the richness that is missing."

—Gyorgy Kepes, "Kinetic Light as a Creative Medium," *Technology Review,* December 1967

Photograph by Jo Anne Rosen

Introduction

Redesigning Paradise (1971, color, 24 min.)
Producer: Weyerhaeuser Forest Products Co.
Distributor: Weyerhaeuser Audio-Visual Department, Tacoma, WA 98477

Problem 1: Form Perception

More than Meets the Eye (1971, color, 30 min.)
Producer: Time-Life Multimedia, Time & Life Building,
New York, NY 10020

Perception (1970, color, 15 min.)
Producer: Appleton-Century-Croft
Distributor: Prentice-Hall Film Library, Englewood Cliffs, NJ 07632

Light (1971, color, 10 min.)
Producer: American Federation of the Arts
Distributor: Films Incorporated, 1144 Wilmette Avenue, Wilmette, IL 60091

Shape (1971, color, 10 min.)
Producer: American Federation of the Arts
Distributor: Films Incorporated, 1144 Wilmette Avenue, Wilmette, IL 60091

Problem 2: Basic Pattern Areas

Communications Primer (1954, color, 23 min.)
By Charles and Ray Eames
Distributor: Pyramind, P.O. Box 1048, Santa Monica, CA 90406

Problem 3a: Texture Archetypes (Introduction)

Discovering Texture (1979, color, 17 min.)
Distributor: BFA Educational Media, 2211 Michigan Avenue, P.O. Box 1795, Santa Monica, CA 90406

Photography and the City (1969, color 15 min.)
By Charles and Ray Eames.
Distributor: Encyclopaedia Britannica, 425 North Michigan Avenue, Chicago, IL 60611

The Daybooks of Edward Weston
Part 1: How Young I Was (1965, 30 min.)
Part 2: The Strongest Way to See (1965, 30 min.)
Producer: Museum of Modern Art
Distributor: Museum of Modern Art, 11 West 53 Street, New York, NY 10019

Problem 4: Form Genesis

Art Sources in Nature (1960, color, 20 min.)
By Victor B. Sheffer
Distributor: Rarig Film Service, Inc., 834 Industry Drive, Seattle, WA 98188

Problem 5: Aleatory Form

Problem 6: Curvilinear Form

Japanese Calligraphy (1957, black and white, 17 min.)
Producer: Brandon Films
Distributor: Macmillan Films, 34 McQuester Parkway South, Mount Vernon, NY 10550

Discovering Line (1979, color, 17 min.)
Distributor: BFA Educational Media, 2211 Michigan Avenue, P.O. Box 1795, Santa Monica, CA 90406

Problem 7: Form and Content

Messages (color, 7 min.)
Distributor: International Typographic Composition Association, 2233 Wisconsin Avenue Northwest, Washington, D.C. 20007

The Alphabet: Mark of Man (1968, color, 20 min.)
Distributor: McGraw-Hill Films, 1221 Avenue of the Americas, New York, NY 10020

Problem 8: Visual Organization

Rain (1929, black and white, 15 min.)
By Joris Ivens and Mannus Franken
Distributor: Museum of Modern Art, 11 West 53rd Street, New York, NY 10019

Pacific 231 (1952, black and white, 10 min.)
By Jean Mitry
Distributor: Pyramid, P.O. Box 1048, Santa Monica, CA 90406

Go Slow on the Brighton Line (1955, black and white, 10 minutes)
Producer: British Broadcasting Company
Distributor: BBC Enterprises, Villiers House, The Broadway, Ealing, London W5 2PA, England

Film Program

Films are an integral and important part of this program. Shown for convenience on a regular schedule, in conjunction with the problem in hand, they dramatically supplement the presentation of the problem and enlarge upon its implications.

The following list includes those films available as of 1980. It will be noted that in some cases, alas, no pertinent films could be found. Since the rental film industry has a very volatile nature, with new (and sometimes better) films continually appearing, and old (and sometimes better) films continually being withdrawn, each instructor will find it necessary to develop and maintain his or her own version of this list.

Film previewing is a time-consuming process, and film selection (finding films that are both well produced and relevant to the program) is a demanding exercise of critical judgment. But this investment of time and energy on the part of the instructor will, in effect, bring to the students the services of the many gifted people who have researched, written, directed, photographed, edited, and scored those films that are shown. This, in turn, will enhance the effectiveness of the entire program.

Problem 9: Color Attributes

Discovering Dark and Light (1965, color, 18 min.)
By Paul Burnford, with Jack Stoops
Distributor: BFA Educational Media, 2211 Michigan Avenue, P.O. Box 1795, Santa Monica, CA 90406

Discovering Color (1979, color, 15 min.)
Producer: Film Associates
Distributor: BFA Educational Media, 2211 Michigan Avenue, P.O. Box 1795, Santa Monica, CA 90406

Color (1976, color, 16 min.)
Distributor: International Film Bureau, 332 South Michigan Avenue, Chicago, IL 60604

Problem 10: Color Scales

Georges Seurat (1971, color, 40 min.)
Distributor: Independent Television Corp., 555 Madison Avenue, New York, NY 10022

Color: A First Film (1979, color, 15 min.)
Distributor: BFA Educational Media, 2211 Michigan Avenue, P.O. Box 1795, Santa Monica, CA 90406

Problem 11: Color Analysis of Scene

Statistics at a Glance (1972, color, 26 min.)
By Robert Johnson and Lynne Hill
Distributor: The Media Guild, 118 South Acacia, P.O. Box 881, Solana Beach, CA 92075

Problem 12: Color Expression

Haiku (1974, color, 18 minutes)
Distributor: Paramount Communications, 5451 Marathon Street, Hollywood, CA 90038

Expressionism (1971, color, 26 min.)
Ditributor: International Film Bureau, 332 South Michigan Avenue, Chicago, IL 60604

Fauvism (1972, color, 17 min.)
Distributor: International Film Bureau, 332 South Michigan Avenue, Chicago, IL 60604

The Post-Impressionists (1970, color, 25 min.)
Distributor: International Film Bureau, 332 South Michigan Avenue, Chicago, IL 60604

Problem 13: Color and Space

Cézanne (1967, color, 16 min.)
Distributor: Universal Education and Visual Arts, 100 Universal City Plaza, Universal City, CA 91608

Problem 14: Color Coding

Problem 15: Rhythmical Organization

Rhythm and Movement in Art (1969, color, 19 min.)
By Paul Burnford, with Jack Stoops
Distributor: BFA Educational Media, 2211 Michigan Avenue, P.O. Box 1795, Santa Monica, CA 90406

Canon (1965, color, 10 min.)
By Norman McLaren
Distributor: International Film Bureau, 332 South Michigan Avenue, Chicago, IL 60604

Problem 16: Rhythm and Modulation

Movement (1971, color, 10 min.)
Producer: American Federation of the Arts
Distributor: Films Incorporated, 1144 Wilmette Avenue, Wilmette, IL 60091

Highway (1958, color, 6 min.)
By Hilary Harris, with music by David Hollister
Distributor: Film Images division of Radim Films, Inc., 17 West 60th Street, New York, NY 10023

Glass (1960, color, 11 min.)
By Bert Haanstra, with music by Pim Jacobs
Distributor: McGraw-Hill Films, 1221 Avenue of the Americas, New York, NY 10020

Problem 3b: Texture Archetypes (Conclusion)

This is Edward Steichen (1966, black and white, 27 min.)
Producer: WCBS-TV
Distributor: Carousel Films, Inc., 1501 Broadway, New York, NY 10036

Problem 17: Texture, Space, and Scale

Postscript: A Valediction

The River (1939, black and white, 32 min.)
By Pare Lorenz, with music by Virgil Thompson
Distributor: National Audiovisual Center (GSA), Washington, D.C. 20409

Appendix B

There are two unfortunate misconceptions held by many beginning design students (and some educators and professionals). The first is that design is essentially a matter of "intuition," or merely the materialization of a form following a tête-à-tête with one's muse. This elevation of process over content assumes that an unconscious creative operation need not be concerned with substantive knowledge, and indeed may actually be inhibited by such a burden. That this attitude also eliminates the troublesome task of becoming informed about a problem makes it all the more attractive.

The second sad misapprehension is the notion that the chief characteristic of a good design is its "originality," or lack of an apparent precedent. In this case, novelty is confused with creative insight, and mannerism is substituted for social and ecological responsibility. That this belief plays into the hands of the news-hungry fashion media is not lost on those who see professional success in terms of personal acclaim and as a matter of column inches of copy or square inches of photographs depicting stage sets devoid of people.

One might speculate that both these attitudes are a legacy of the worldwide influence of the competitive educational system practiced at the prestigious École des Beaux Arts in nineteenth-century Paris. There architectural students were required at regular intervals to generate design solutions to unfamiliar problems under pressure of limited time (the "esquisse" and "esquisse-esquisse") and in strict isolation ("en loge"), with no access to other persons or any reference material. The ostensible purpose of this system of instant and immaculate conception was to promote "originality" and to ensure "artistic freedom" by excluding all sources of external influence and information. Aside from the fact that the eventual consequence of solitary confinement and sensory deprivation is pathological hallucinations, it might also be noted that this competitive method of education engendered a star system within a professional elite dedicated to an aesthetic mythology.

See Jean Paul Carlhian, "The Ecole des Beaux Arts: Modes and Manners," in *The Journal of Architectural Education*, vol. 33, no. 2 (November 1979); and Peter Stringer, "The Myths of Architectural Creativity," *Architectural Design*, October 1975.

But if design has humanistic objectives, it can succeed only to the degree that it is based on an intimate understanding of the many categories of context that affect social signification, and on an extensive knowledge of the many factors which qualify ends and means. Since such omniscience is beyond the capabilities of any one person (limited, as we all are, by the constraints of one life and one body), the inescapable implication is that the responsible practice of design requires a collaboration with others and/or a reference to the knowledge and experience of others, as can be found in written material. Unless the designer is qualified with such other skills as the ability to walk on water, he or she has no option other than to transcend his or her limitations by consultation. The following list of references cited in this text constitutes only a small sample of the larger treasury of written resources which are the necessary adjuncts to a significant design education and design practice.

References

Adams, James L. *Conceptual Blockbusting.* San Francisco: W. H. Freeman, 1974.

Albers, Josef. *Interaction of Color.* New Haven: Yale University Press, 1971.

Alexander, Christopher. *The City as a Mechanism for Sustaining Human Contact.* Berkeley: Center for Planning and Development Research, University of California, 1966.

_____. "From a Set of Forces to a Form." In *The Man-Made Object*, edited by Gyorgy Kepes. New York: Braziller, 1966.

_____. "The City Is Not a Tree." *Design* 206 (February 1966).

_____, **and others.** *The Oregon Experiment.* New York: Oxford University Press, 1975.

Appleyard, Donald, and others. *The View From the Road.* Cambridge, Mass.: MIT Press, 1964.

Archer, L. Bruce. "An Overview of the Structure of the Design Process." In *Emerging Methods in Environmental Design and Planning*, edited by G. T. Moore. Cambridge, Mass.: MIT Press, 1968.

Architectural Graphic Standards. New York: Wiley.

Armour, Richard. "The Dictionary—Almost a Constant Companion." *The Christian Science Monitor,* 27 May 1975.

Arnheim, Rudolf. *Art and Visual Perception.* Berkeley: University of California Press, 1954.

_____. *Visual Thinking.* Berkeley: University of California Press, 1970.

_____. *Entropy and Art.* Berkeley: University of California Press, 1971.

Arnold, Edmund C. *Ink on Paper 2.* New York: Harper and Row, 1972.

Ashihara, Yoshinobu. *Exterior Design in Architecture.* New York: Van Nostrand Reinhold, 1970.

Banham, Reyner. "The Embalmed City." *New Statesman,* 12 April 1963.

_____. *Megastructure: Urban Futures of the Recent Past.* New York: Harper and Row, 1977.

Bayer, Herbert. *Herbert Bayer: Painter, Designer, Architect.* New York: Reinhold, 1967.

Beck, J. "The Perception of Surface Colors." *Scientific American,* August 1975.

Berlin, B., and **P. Kay.** *Basic Color Terms: Their Universality and Evolution.* Berkeley: University of California Press, 1969.

Bernstein, Leonard. *The Joy of Music.* New York: Simon and Schuster, 1959.

Berry, W. T.; A. F. Johnson and **W.P. Jasper.** *The Encyclopaedia of Type Faces.* London: Blandford Press, 1958.

Biegeleisen, J. I. *Art Director's Work Book of Type Faces.* New York: Arco, 1963.

Binyon, Laurence. *The Flight of the Dragon.* London: John Murray, 1911.

Blackburn, Marthe and **Maurice.** *An Audio-Visual Experiment: Six Classical Forms Explained Graphically and Illustrated Musically.* Montreal: Juenesses Musicales du Canada, 1967.

Bloomer, Carolyn M. *Principles of Visual Perception.* New York: Van Nostrand Reinhold, 1976.

Blyth, R. H. *Haiku.* Tokyo: Hokuseido, 1960.

Bonta, Juan Pablo. *Architecture and Its Interpretation.* London: Lund Humphries, 1979.

Boorstin, Daniel J. *The Image.* New York: Penguin Books, 1962.

Bothwell, Dorr, and **Marleys, Frey.** *Notan: The Dark-Light Principle of Design.* New York: Heinhold, 1968.

Boulding, Kenneth E. *The Image.* Ann Arbor: University of Michigan Press, 1956.

Boutourline, Serge. "The Concept of Environmental Management." In *Environmental Psychology,* edited by H. Proshansky and others. New York: Holt, Rinehart and Winston, 1970.

Brill, Michael. Discussed in "Structuring a New Vision." *Progressive Architecture,* July 1971.

Broadbent, Geoffrey. *Design in Architecture.* New York: John Wiley and Sons, 1973.

Bruner, J. S. "On Perceptual Readiness." *Psychological Review* 64 (1957).

Buhl, Harold R. *Creative Engineering Design.* Ames, Iowa: Iowa State University Press, 1960.

Burns, Aaron. *Typography.* New York: Reinhold, 1961.

Bynner, Witter, trans. *The Way of Life According to Lao Tsu.* New York: Capricorn Books, 1962.

Cancler, Leonard. "The Effect of the Application of Entropy on Your Life." *Northwest Professonal Engineer,* Summer /Fall, 1968.

Carlhian, Jean Paul. "The Ecole des Beaux Arts: Modes and Manners." *The Journal of Architectural Education*, vol. 33, no. 2 (November 1979).

Carpenter, Edmund. *They Became What They Beheld.* New York: Ballantine Books, 1970.

Catich, Edward M. *The Origin of the Serif.* Davenport, Iowa: Catfish Press, 1968.

Chang, Amos. *Intangible Content in Architectonic Form.* Princeton: Princeton University Press, 1956.

Chapelle, Howard I. *Yacht Designing and Planning.* New York: W. W. Norton, 1936.

Claiborne, Robert. *The Birth of Writing.* New York: Time-Life Books, 1974.

"Color and the Use of Color by the Illuminating Engineer." *Illuminating Engineering,* vol. 57, no. 12 (December 1962).

Color As Seen and Photographed. Kodak Data Book E-74H. Second ed. Rochester, N.Y.: Eastman Kodak Co., 1972.

Committee on Colorimetry, Optical Society of America. *The Science of Color.* New York: Thomas Y. Crowell, 1953.

Cook, J. W., and **H. Klotz.** *Conversations With Architects.* New York: Praeger, 1973.

Cott, H.B. *Adaptive Coloration in Animals.* London: Methuen, 1957.

Craig, James. *Designing With Type.* New York: Watson-Guptill, 1971.

Crosby, Theo; Alan Fletcher; and **Colin Forbes.** *A Sign Systems Manual.* New York: Praeger, 1970.

Cullen, Gordon. *Townscape.* New York: Reinhold, 1961.

Curtis, J. W. "A Functional Definition of Scale," *A.I.A. Journal,* February 1971.

Deasy, C. M. *Design for Human Affairs.* Cambridge, Mass.: Schenkman, 1974.

DeBure, Giles. "The Powerful Hum of Color." *Architecture Plus,* October 1973.

Diffrient, Niels, and others. *Humanscale.* Cambridge, Mass.: MIT Press, 1974.

Dreyfus, Henry. *Symbol Sourcebook.* New York: McGraw-Hill, 1972.

Drexler, Arthur, ed. *The Architecture of the Ecole des Beaux Arts.* New York: Museum of Modern Art, 1977.

Dubos, Rene. *So Human an Animal.* New York: Scribner's, 1968.

Durer, Albrecht. *Four Books on Human Proportions.* Facsimile ed. London: G. M. Wagner, 1970.

Ekman, Paul, and **W. V. Friesen.** "The Repertoire of Nonverbal Behavior: Categories, Usage, and Coding." *Semiotica* 1 (1969).

Emerson, Ralph Waldo. *Nature.* 1836. Reprinted in Brooks Atkinson, ed., *The Complete Essays and Other Writings of Ralph Waldo Emerson.* New York: Random House, 1940.

Engel, Heinrich. *The Japanese House: A Tradition for Contemporary Architecture.* Rutland, Vt.: Charles E. Tuttle, 1964.

Etiemble. *The Written Word.* New York: Orion Press, 1961.

Evans, Ralph M. *An Introduction to Color.* New York: Wiley, 1948.

_____. *The Perception of Color.* New York: Wiley, 1974.

Fathy, Hassan. *Architecture for the Poor.* Chicago: University of Chicago Press, 1973.

Faulkner, W. *Architecture and Color.* New York: Wiley-Interscience, 1972.

Ferkis, Victor C. *Technological Man.* New York: New American Library, 1969.

Fitch, James Marston. "Single Point Perspective." *Architectural Forum,* 1974.

Flynn, John E., and **Arthur W. Segil.** *Architectural Interior Systems.* New York: Van Nostrand Reinhold, 1970.

Fogden, M. and **P.** *Animals and Their Colors.* New York: Crown Publishers, 1974.

Gardner, John W. *Self-Renewal.* New York: Harper and Row, 1963.

Gardner, Martin. "Mathematical Games." *Scientific American,* December 1974.

"Mathematical Games." *Scientific American,* April 1978.

Gibberd, Frederick. "Wall Textures: A Local Study," *Architectural Review,* July 1940.

Gibson, James J. *The Perception of the Visual World.* Boston: Houghton Mifflin, 1950.

_____. *The Senses Considered as Perceptual Systems.* Boston: Houghton Mifflin, 1966.

_____. *The Ecological Approach to Visual Perception.* Boston: Houghton Mifflin, 1979.

Giedion, Sigfried. *Time, Space, and Architecture.* Cambridge, Mass.: Harvard University Press, 1967.

Gillam, Barbara. "Geometric Illusions." *Scientific American,* January 1980.

Gombrich, E. H. "The Image in the Clouds." In *Art and Illusion.* New York: Pantheon Books, 1960.

Goossen, E.C. *Ellsworth Kelly.* New York: Museum of Modern Art, 1973.

Grahame, Kenneth. *The Wind in the Willows.* New York: Charles Scribner's Sons, 1933.

Gregory, Richard. "Visual Illusions," *Scientific American,* November 1968.

Gregory, R. L. *The Intelligent Eye.* New York: McGraw-Hill, 1970.

_____. *Eye and Brain: The Psychology of Seeing.* New York: McGraw-Hill, 1970.

_____. and **Gombrich, E. H.,** eds. *Illusion in Nature and Art.* New York: Scribner's, 1975.

GTE Sylvania, Inc. *Color is How You Light It.* Danvers, Mass.: n.d.

Gump, Paul. "The Behavior Setting: A Promising Unit for Environmental Designers." *Landscape Architecture,* January 1971.

Habraken, N. *Supports: An Alternative to Mass Housing.* New York: Praeger, 1972.

_____. *Variations: The Systematic Design of Supports.* Cambridge, Mass.: Laboratory of Architecture and Planning at MIT, 1976.

Hall, Edward T. *The Hidden Dimension.* Garden City, N.Y.: Doubleday, 1966.

_____. *The Silent Language.* Garden City, N.Y.: Doubleday, 1969.

_____. *Beyond Culture.* Garden City, N.Y.: Doubleday, 1976.

Hanes, R. M. "The Long and Short of Color Distance." *Architectural Record,* April 1960.

Hayakawa, S.I. "The Revisions of Vision." In *The Language of Vision,* by Gyorgy Kepes. Chicago: Paul Theobald, 1947.

Heath, Thomas F. "The Algorithmic Nature of the Design Process." In *Emerging Methods in Environmental Design and Planning,* edited by Gary T. Moore. Cambridge, Mass.: MIT Press, 1970.

Hegener, Karen Collier, and **David Clarke,** eds. "The Nature and History of Architectural Education." In *Architecture Schools in North America.* Princeton, N.J.: Peterson's Guides, 1976.

Hess, John P. "French Nobel Biologist Says World Based on Chance Leaves Man Free to Choose His Own Ethical Values." *The New York Times,* 15 March 1971.

Homer, William Innes. *Seurat and the Science of Painting.* Cambridge, Mass.: MIT Press, 1978.

House Beautiful, August 1960.

"How Does Light Affect Color?" *Architectural Forum,* January 1949.

Hughes, Robert. "Pursuit of the Square." *Time,* 8 November 1971.

Huxtable, Ada Louise. "The Case for Chaos." In *Will They Ever Finish Bruckner Boulevard?* New York: Macmillan, 1971.

Inui, Masao. "Colour in the Interior Environment." *Lightning Research and Technology,* vol. 1, no. 2 (1969).

Itoh, Teiji. *The Elegant Japanese House: Traditional Sukiya Architecture.* New York: Walker/Weatherhill, 1969.

_____. *The Classic Tradition in Japanese Architecture: Modern Versions of the Sukiya Style.* New York: Weatherhill/Tankosha, 1972.

Itten, Johannes. *The Art of Color.* New York: Reinhold, 1961.

Ivens, Joris. *The Camera and I.* New York: International Press, 1969.

Johns, E. H., and **F. C. Sumner.** "Relation of the Brightness Differences of Color to their Apparent Distance." *Journal of Psychology* 26 (1948).

Jones, J. Christopher. *Design Methods.* London: Wiley-Interscience, 1970.

Kanizas, Gaetano. "Subjective Contours." *Scientific American,* April 1976.

Karpf, Anne. "Professional Revolutionaries," *Architectural Design,* September 1976.

Keene, Donald. "Japanese Aesthetics." In *Landscapes and Portraits.* Tokyo and Palo Alto: Kodansha International, 1971.

Kelly, Kenneth L. and **Deanne B. Judd.** *Color: Universal Language and Dictionary Names.* Washington, D.C.: Department of Commerce, 1976.

Kelly, Rob Roy. *American Wood Type: 1828-1900.* New York: Van Nostrand Reinhold, 1969.

Kepes, Gyorgy. "The Creative Discipline of Our Visual Environment." *College Art Journal,* vol. 7, no. 1 (Autumn 1947).

———. *The Language of Vision.* Chicago: Paul Theobald, 1948.

———. *The New Landscape in Art and Science.* Chicago: Paul Theobald, 1956.

———. "Notes on Expression and Communication in the Cityscape." In *The Future Metropolis,* edited by L. Rodwin. New York: Braziller, 1960.

———. "Kinetic Light as a Creative Medium." *Technology Review,* December 1967.

———. "Design and Light." *Design Quarterly 68.* Minneapolis, Minn.: Walker Art Center, 1967.

———, ed. *The Visual Arts Today.* Middletown, Conn.: Wesleyan University Press, 1960.

———, ed. *Education of Vision.* New York: Braziller, 1965

———, ed. *Module, Proportion, Symmetry, Rhythm.* New York: Braziller, 1966.

Knuth, D. E. "Algorithms." *Scientific American,* April 1977.

Koestler, Arthur. *The Act of Creation.* New York: Macmillan, 1964.

Kouwenhoven, John. "What's 'American' about America." In *The Beer Can by the Highway.* Garden City, N. Y.: Doubleday, 1961.

Lancaster, Osbert. *A Cartoon History of Architecture.* London: John Murray, 1959.

Land, E. H. "The Retinex Theory of Color Vision." *Scientific American,* December 1977.

Langer, S. K. "The Social Influence of Design." In *Who Designs America?,* edited by L. B. Holland. New York: Doubleday, 1966.

Lenclos, Jean Phillippe. "Couleurs et Paysages." *L'Architecture d'Aujourd'hui,* November 1972.

———. "Living in Color." In *Color for Architecture,* edited by Tom Porter and Byron Mikellides. New York: Van Nostrand Reinhold, 1976.

Lerup, Lars. "The Designer as Co-Learner." *Ekistics,* no. 216 (November 1973).

Lewis, H. R. and **G. H. Papadimitiou.** "The Efficiency of Algorithms." *Scientific American,* January 1978.

Lewis, John. *Printed Ephemera.* Ipswich, W.S. Cowell, 1962.

———. *Typography: Basic Principles.* New York: Reinhold, 1964.

Licklider, Heath. *Architectural Scale.* London: Architectural Press, 1965.

Life Library of Photography. New York: Time-Life, 1972.

Liggett, J. *The Human Face.* New York: Stein and Day, 1974.

Lohse, Richard P. "Standard, Series, Module: New Problems and Tasks of Painting." In *Module, Proportion, Symmetry, Rhythm,* edited by Gyorgy Kepes. New York: Braziller, 1966.

Luckiesh, Matthew. *Visual Illusions.* New York: Dover, 1965.

Lynch, Kevin. "The Form of Cities." *Scientific American,* April 1954.

———. *The Image of the City.* Cambridge, Mass.: MIT Press, 1960.

———. *What Time Is This Place?* Cambridge, Mass.: MIT Press, 1972.

McBride, Stewart Dill. "Boston Paint Mixer Leaves His Mark on City." *Christian Science Monitor,* 10 December 1975.

McCormick, E. J. *Human Factors in Engineering and Design.* 4th ed. New York: McGraw-Hill, 1976.

McKim, Robert H. *Experiences in Creative Thinking.* Monterey, Calif.: Brooks/Cole, 1972.

MacKinnon, Donald W. "What Makes a Person Creative." *Saturday Review,* 10 February 1962.

McLuhan, Marshall, and **Harley Parker.** *Through the Vanishing Point.* New York: Harper and Row, 1968.

Maertz, A., and **M. Rea Paul.** *A Dictionary of Color.* New York: McGraw Hill, 1950.

Maki, Fumihiko. *Investigations of Collective Form.* St. Louis, Mo.: Washington University School of Architecture, 1964.

———, and **Masato Ohtaka.** "Some Thoughts on Collective Form." In *Structure in Art and Science.* edited by Gyorgy Kepes. New York: George Braziller, 1965.

Mandelbrot, Benoit B. *Fractiles: Form, Chance, and Dimension.* San Francisco: W. H. Freeman, 1977.

Marks, L. E. "Synesthesia: The Lucky People with Mixed-Up Senses." *Psychology Today,* June 1975.

Markus, Thomas. "A Doughnut Model of the Environment and its Design." In *Design Participation,* edited by Nigel Cross. London: Academy Editions, 1972.

Meier, R. L. *A Communication Theory of Urban Growth.* Cambridge, Mass.: MIT/Harvard University Press, 1962.

Meinig, D. W., ed. *The Interpretation of Ordinary Landscapes.* New York: Oxford University Press, 1979.

Michaelides, Constantine E. *Hydra: a Greek Island Town.* Chicago: University of Chicago Press, 1967.

Mills, C. Wright. "The Man in the Middle." *Industrial Design,* Novemeber 1958.

"Modes of Participation," *Ekistics,* vol. 42, no. 251 (October 1976).

Moholy-Nagy, Laszlo. "Problems of the Modern Film." In *Cahiers d'Art,* vol. 7, nos. 6-7 (Paris, 1932).

———. *Vision in Motion.* Chicago: Paul Theobald, 1947.

Moon, P., and **D. E. Spencer.** "Area in Color Harmony." *Journal of the Optical Society of America,* vol. 34, no. 2 (February 1944).

Moretti, Luigi. "Colore di Venezia." *Spazio,* October 1950.

Morris, Charles. *Signs, Language, and Behavior.* New York: Braziller, 1946.

Morris, Desmond. *Manwatching.* New York: Abrams, 1977.

Morse, Edward S. *Japanese Homes and Their Surroundings.* New York: Dover, 1961.

Mueller, C. G., and others. *Light and Vision.* New York: Time-Life, 1966.

Mumford, Lewis. *The Culture of Cities.* New York: Harcourt, Brace, and World, 1938.

Munsell, A. H. *A Color Notation.* Baltimore, Md.: Munsell Color Co., 1967.

Murphy, Richard W. *The World of Cézanne.* New York: Time-Life, 1968.

Nelson, George. "We Are Here By Design." *Harper's,* April 1975.

———. *How to See.* Boston: Little, Brown, 1977.

Nicholson, Arnold. "Mr. Kelly's Magic Lights." *Saturday Evening Post,* 5 July 1958.

Nitschke, Gunter. "The Japanese Sense of Place." *Architectural Design,* March 1966.

O'Brien, J. F. *Design by Accident.* New York: Dover, 1968.

Okakura, Kakuzo. *The Book of Tea.* New York: Duffield, 1925.

Papanek, Victor. *Design for the Real World.* New York: Bantam, 1976.

"Participatory Planning and Design." *DMG-DRS Journal: Design Research and Methods,* vol. 9, no. 4 (October-December 1975).

Pearce, Peter. *Structure in Nature Is a Strategy for Design.* Cambridge, Mass.: MIT Press, 1978.

Perin, C. *With Man in Mind.* Cambridge, Mass.: MIT Press, 1970.

Portmann, A. *Animal Camouflage.* Ann Arbor: University of Michign Press, 1959.

Rand, Paul. "Design and the Play Instinct." In *Education of Vision,* edited by Gyorgy Kepes. New York: George Braziller, 1965.

———, and **Ann Rand.** "Advertisement: Ad Vivum or Ad Hominem?" In *The Visual Arts Today,* edited by Gyorgy Kepes. Middletown, Conn.: Wesleyan University Press, 1960.

"Rapid Transition." *Progressive Architecture,* October 1972.

Rapoport, Amos. "The Design Professions and the Behavioral Sciences." *Architectural Association Quarterly,* Winter, 1968/69.

Rasmussen, Steen Eiler. *Experiencing Architecture.* New York: Technology Press and John Wiley and Sons, 1959.

Ratliff, Floyd. "Contour and Contrast." *Scientific American,* June 1972.

Rauschenberg, Robert. Quoted in *Time,* 29 November 1976.

Raymond, Antonin and **Noemi.** *Antonin Raymond: His Work in Japan, 1920-1935.* Tokyo: Johnan Shoin, 1935.

Rehe, Rolf F. *Typography: How to Make It Legible.* Carmel, Ind.: Design Research International, 1974.

Reichek, J. "On the Design of Cities." *Journal of the American Institute of Planners,* vol. 27, no. 2 (May 1961).

———. "Questions Concerning Urban Design Principles." *Journal of the American Institute of Architects,* December 1962.

Rewald, John, ed. *Paul Cézanne's Letters.* Oxford: B. Cassirer, 1976.

Rodman, Harry E. "A Simulation Method for Study of Lighting Design." *International Lighting Review,* vol. 26, nos. 3-4 (1975).

Rogers, Carl R. "Towards a Theory of Creativity." *ETC.,* vol. 11, no. 4.

Rondthaler, E. *Alphabet Thesaurus.* New York: Reinhold, 1960.

Rosen, Ben. *Type and Typography.* New York: Van Nostrand Reinhold, 1976.

Rowe, Colin, and **Fred Koetter.** *Collage City.* Cambridge, Mass.: MIT Press, 1978.

Rudofsky, Bernard. *Architecture without Architects.* Garden City, N.Y.: Doubleday, 1964.

———. *Streets for People.* Garden City, N.Y.: Doubleday, 1969.

———. *The Prodigious Builders.* New York: Harcourt Brace Jovanovich, 1977.

Ruesch, Jurgen, and **Weldon Kees.** *Nonverbal Communication.* Berkeley: University of California Press, 1956.

Rusch, Charles W. "On Understanding Awareness." *The Journal of Esthetic Education,* vol. 4, no. 4 (October 1970).

Rushton, W. A. H. "Visual Pigments and Color Blindness." *Scientific American,* March 1975.

Russell, Bertrand. "How I Write." In *Portraits from Memory and Other Essays.* London: Allen and Unwin, 1965.

Russell, John. *The World of Matisse.* New York: Time-Life Books, 1969.

Safan-Gerard, Desy, "How to Unblock." *Psychology Today,* January 1978.

Sakanishi, Shio, trans. *The Spirit of the Brush.* London: John Murray, 1939.

Schwenk, Theodore. *Sensitive Chaos.* New York: Schocken, 1976.

Seuphor, Michel. *Piet Mondrian: Life and Work.* New York: Abrams, n.d.

Shannon, C. E., and **Weaver.** *The Mathematical Theory of Communication.* Urbana: University of Illinois Press, 1949.

Simon, H. A. *The Science of the Artificial.* Cambridge, Mass.: MIT Press, 1969.

Sitte, Camillo. *The Art of Building Cities.* New York: Reinhold, 1945.

Soby, James Thrall, ed. *Arp.* New York: Museum of Modern Art, 1958.

Sommer, Robert. *Design Awareness.* San Francisco: Rinehart Press, 1972.

———. *The Mind's Eye.* New York: Delta. 1978.

Spencer, Herbert. *The Visible Word.* New York: Hastings House, 1969.

Spiegel, J. P., and **P. Machotka.** *Messages of the Body.* New York: The Free Press, 1974.

Sprague, Chester L. "American Indian Communities: Toward a Unity of Life and Environment." *Technology Review,* July/August 1972.

Spreiregen, Paul D. *The Architecture of Towns and Cities.* New York: McGraw-Hill, 1965.

Steele, F. I. "Problem-Solving in the Spatial Environment." In *EDRA 1: Proceedings of the 1st Annual Environmental Design Research Association Conference,* edited by H. Sanoff and S. Cohn. Chapel Hill, North Carolina, 1970.

Steinberg, Saul. *The Labyrinth.* New York: Harper and Bros., 1960.

Stevens, Peter. *Patterns in Nature.* Boston: Litle, Brown, 1974.

Storr, Anthony. *The Dynamics of Creation.* New York: Penguin, 1976.

Stringer, Peter. "A Rationale for Participation." In *Design Participation*, edited by Nigel Cross. London: Academy Editions, 1972.

————. "The Myths of Architectural Creativity." *Architectural Design*, October 1975.

Studer, Raymond G. "Behavior Manipulation in Designed Environments." *Connection*, Fall, 1967 (Graduate School of Design, Harvard University).

Swedlund, Charles. *Photography.* New York: Holt, Rinehart and Winston, 1974.

Sze, Mai-Mai. *The Tao of Painting.* New York: Pantheon Books, 1956.

Tanizaki, Junichiro. *In Praise of Shadows.* Translated by Thomas J. Harper and Edward Seidensticker. New Haven: Leete's Island Books, 1977.

Teague, Walter Dorwin. *Design This Day.* New York: Harcourt, Brace and Company, 1940.

Thiel, Philip. "To the Kamaura Station." *Landscape,* Fall, 1961.

————. "An Experiment in Space Notation." *Architectural Review,* July 1962.

————. "An Old Garden, a New Tool, and Our Future Cities." *Landscape Architecture,* July 1962.

————. "Processional Architecture." *AIA Journal,* February 1964.

————. "Notes on the Description, Scaling, Notation, and Scoring of Some Perceptual and Cognitive Attributes of the Physical Environment." In *Environmental Psychology*, edited by H. M. Proshansky and others. New York: Holt, Rinehart and Winston, 1970.

Thom, Rene. *Structural Stability and Morphogenesis.* Reading, Mass.: W. A. Benjamin, 1975.

Thompson, D'Arcy Wentworth. *On Growth and Form.* Cambridge: Cambridge University Press, 1942.

Thomson, D. S. *Language.* New York: Time-Life Books, 1975.

Thorne, F. C. *Personality.* Brandon, Vermont: Journal of Clinical Psychology, 1961.

Time Saver Standards. New York: McGraw-Hill.

Tuan, Yi-Fu. *Topophilia.* Englewood Cliffs, N.J.: Prentice-Hall, 1974.

Tunnard, Christopher, and **Boris Pushkarev.** *Man-Made America: Chaos or Control.* New Haven: Yale University Press, 1963.

Vaccari, Oreste and **Enko.** *Pictorial Chinese-Japanese Characters.* Rutland, Vt.: Charles E. Tuttle, 1954.

Venturi, Robert; Denise Scott Brown; and **Steven Izenour.** *Learning from Las Vegas.* Cambridge, Mass.; MIT Press, 1972.

Von Foerster, Heinz. "Logical Structure of Environment and Its Internal Representation." In *International Design Conference, Aspen, 1962*, edited by R. F. Eckerstrom. Zeeland, Michigan: Herman Miller, 1963.

Waddington, C. H. "The Character of Biological Form." In *Aspects of Form*, edited by L. L. White. London: Lund Humpheries, 1951.

Wallas, Graham. *The Art of Thought.* London: Jonathan Cape, 1926.

Walter, Gerard O. "Typesetting." *Scientific American*, May 1969.

Wandersman, Abraham. "User Participation in Planning Environments." *Environment and Behavior*, vol. 11, no. 4 (December 1979).

Wang, William S-Y. "The Chinese Language." *Scientific American*, February 1973.

Wilder, G. D., and **J. H. Ingram.** *Analysis of Chinese Characters.* New York: Dover, 1974.

Wilson, Adrian. *The Design of Books.* New York: Reinhold, 1967.

Wilson, Forrest. *City Planning.* New York: Van Nostrand Reinhold, 1975.

Woodson, Wesley E., and **Donald W. Conover.** *Human Engineering Guide.* Berkeley: University of California Press, 1966.

Yee, Chiang. *Chinese Calligraphy.* Cambridge, Mass.: Harvard University Press, 1934.

Zeeman, E. C. "Catastrophe Theory." *Scientific American,* April 1976.

Appendix C

"As a parent, if I have done one thing, in addition to reading aloud to my children, it has been to encourage them to keep a dictionary at hand and to use it. By using it I mean reading everything the dictionary tells about the word being looked up; not only meaning and pronunciation but etymology and synonyms.

"I have especially encouraged my children to read what is said about the etymology of a word—its often fascinating source. Sometimes the origin of a word is not known, in which case the dictionary will indicate 'original unknown' or 'origin obscure.' That gives the reader a chance to do a little guessing.

"In school and in the home a child needs to be close to a good dictionary and to be prompted to use it until its use becomes habitual. And what is a good dictionary? I should say one that is complete and up-to-date. Sometimes it is not possible to find these two criteria in one dictionary. Though I have many dictionaries, I chiefly use two. One is a large dictionary, complete and unabridged. The other is not so large or complete but it is the very latest, containing new words and new pronunciations not in my larger but older dictionary.

"In our home we have not only the numerous dictionaries in my study but two dictionaries in the living room, one in the family room, and one in each bed-room. Looking up words, whether to make sure of the spelling, to check on someone's pronunciation, or to discover what may be an interesting and unexpected origin, can become a habit—not a bad habit but a good one.

"Words are the basis of both written and spoken communication; of both reading and writing. Use of the precise word, the best word, is important not only in conveying meaning but in projecting one's taste and personality. All the words are all in that inexhaustible book, the dictionary. . . ."

—Richard Armour, *Christian Science Monitor*, 27 May 1975

Quizzes

This program is as much concerned with the development of your conceptual awareness as with the growth of your perceptual sensitivity and craft skills. Since concepts and ideas are generally word-mediated, your comprehension of them clearly depends on your understanding of the words used to express them. Thus the development of your conceptual awareness is closely connected with a significant expansion of your working vocabulary.

The growth of your vocabulary, and the development of your understanding of new concepts, can be best indicated by your performance on the following quizzes. As always, good intentions and pious hopes count for nothing, and true competence is only demonstrated in the doing.

You may find the following procedure an effective routine for expanding your working vocabulary. In your first reading of the text, underline new and unfamiliar words as you encounter them. When you have finished your first reading, copy the underlined words in your notebook—*not* on miscellaneous scraps of paper! Using one or more collegiate dictionaries, and if necessary an unabridged or specialized dictionary, write out a full definition of each word, including its etymology. If several senses of the word are given, use only the one appropriate to the context in which it was used here. Add to these written definitions those of new and unfamiliar words you encounter as you read the supplementary references. In each case reread the material a second time with the definitions fresh in your mind. Once or twice a week, review *all* the words and definitions you have written out, and, whenever appropriate, try to use these words in your conversation.

Preface: A Word with the Instructor

1. Please define each word on the adjacent list, in the sense in which it is used in this section.
2. How many messages, in what categories, can you discover in the photograph on page 10?
3. What are some of the reasons for becoming visually literate?
4. In what ways is art similar to science?

anthology	literacy
artifact	manifest
cognitive	mediate
connotative	pious
constraint	premise
copious	proffer
denotative	regimen
etymology	replete
explicate	seminal
explicit	subliminal
inculcate	subsume
intervene	

Introduction A: Vision and Environment

afferent
agora
articulate
cataclysmic
caveat
cliché
coerce
commonwealth
cutaneous
enculturate
envisage
fetish
flux
habitué
haptic
implicit

irrevocable
isomorphism
milieu
mole
necropolis
neuron
nexus
nominal
noxious
olfaction
pervasive
physiognomic
poignant
proprioception
reciprocal
unanimity
visceral

1. Please define each word on the adjacent list, in the sense in which it is used in this section.
2. What evidence is there for the primacy of vision compared to the other senses?
3. What caveat does James Marston Fitch offer in this connection?
4. Give examples of ways in which the visual environment may cue behavior, express feelings, articulate attitudes, orient the visitor and habitué in time and space, and enculturate the young.
5. Discuss the role of images and symbols as a factor in the adaptation of the human species to the physical environment.
6. Give examples of how different cultural backgrounds and/or occupations may give rise to different perceptions of the same physical environment.

Introduction B: Design and Designers

abrogate
couturier
criteria
default
depot
empathy
empirical
ephemeral
expository
hypothesis
iconic
immaculate
inadvertent
iterate

kitsch
lineage
organic
pander
precedent
preponderance
pristine
proletarian
representation
schemata
sibling
simulation
stereotype
willy-nilly

1. Please define each word on the adjacent list, in the sense in which it is used in this section.
2. Define "design."
3. Draw the complete flow-chart diagram of the design process, labeling all parts clearly.
4. Name the five phases of design.
5. Compare environmental design with environmental management
6. Discuss the differences between "client" and "user."
7. C. Wright Mills suggests that we live in a "second hand world." What does he mean by this?
8. Describe three different role models for the environmental designer.
9. What are the necessary *and* sufficient conditions for design leadership?
10. Why has "participatory planning" become an important factor in environmental design?

Introduction C: Program and Procedure

alienate
atelier
blithe
chagrin
charrette
complacent
contingency
elite
facile
fluent
imperative
introspect
jargon

margin
mediocre
metaphor
normative
perfunctory
pesky
phenomenal
scenario
serendipity
signification
tentative
transcend
viable

1. Please define each word on the adjacent list, in the sense in which it is used in this section.
2. What is a major characteristic of a creative person?
3. What is the chief attitudinal difference between the novice and the professional?
4. Why does "nothing fail like success"?
5. Discuss the reason for the similarity between the experience of love and of an artistic form.
6. What is Hell paved with? Why?
7. What are the five steps in planning your design time?
8. What are the advantages of doing all your design work in the studio?
9. Why is "scratch work" inadvisable?
10. What is Murphy's Law?
11. Why should *you* take the responsibility for fully and explicitly evaluating your work?

Problem 1: Form Perception

1. Please define each term on the adjacent list, in the sense in which it is used in this problem.
2. In the event that you used a movie camera instead of a still camera on your evening downtown, would the implications be any different?
3. Please define perception. On what four conditions does it depend?
4. Why are there no absolute visual attributes?
5. On the basis of your understanding of the principles of camouflage, can you now formulate four principles of form *emphasis* or *display*?
6. What are the three magic words in visual design?
7. Please define "visual design" in terms of the material of visual perception.
8. Please distinguish between illuminated, shaded, and shadowed surfaces.

ascription
camera obscura
camouflage
epitome
modulate
probabilistic
saccade
somatolysis

Problem 2: Basic Pattern Areas

1. Please define each term on the adjacent list, in the sense in which it is used in this problem.
2. Draw a complete diagram of the general communication model, labeling all parts clearly.
3. Discuss the relationship of "redundancy" to "noise" in the communication process.
4. What are "basic pattern areas," and what are eight of their attributes?
5. Compare the visual world, the visual field, and the hemispherical projection: in terms of boundedness, extent, and gradient of clarity.
6. What are some real-life examples of the *ganzfeld*?
7. What is "Occam's razor"?
8. When in doubt as to whether to include an element in a graphic design, what is a good rule?
9. Please discuss the suggestion that "the greatest art is to conceal art."

aggregate
alphanumeric
anonymity
cardinal number
chaise longue
ganzfeld
idiosyncratic
introspection
iridescent
leading
lustrous
nadir
naive
ordinal number
periphery
phenomenal
redundancy
subtend
zenith

Problem 3a: Texture Archetypes (Introduction)

1. Please define each word on the adjacent list, in the sense in which it is used in this problem.
2. Name and describe six hypothetical archetypical texture patterns.
3. Distinguish between texture, form, tone, and pattern.
4. Which of the six archetypical texture patterns would you expect to see on a concrete block wall?
5. Who was the *original* Johnny Appleseed, and why was he famous?
6. Name and describe the two basic texture modes.
7. What are the characteristics of a "technically perfect" enlargement?
8. What factors determine whether surface textures are visible?

aleatory
archetype
collateral
emblem
gradient
hierarchy
photogram
pigment

Problem 4: Form Genesis

Apollonian
artificer
assimilate
blatant
bleed
brocade
calcareous
chide
dichotomy
Dionysian
exigency
fortuitous

impute
jetsam
latent
metamorphosis
metaphysics
peer
perspicuous
reasonate
satori
tentative
virtual

1. Please define each word on the adjacent list, in the sense in which it is used in this problem.
2. Discuss the role of the figure-ground dichotomy in the perceptual process.
3. Define and discuss what is meant by a "unity of opposites."
4. According to Lao Tse, "It is the non-existent in things which makes them serviceable." Explain this, and give examples other than those quoted in this text.
5. What do you suppose was the point of the anecdote about the proper way to sweep the garden path?
6. What reason does Waddington give for differences in form-quality between natural objects and human works of art? What are these differences?
7. Who were Janus and Lao Tse (or Lao Tsu)?

Problem 5: Aleatory Form

abashed
abeyance
accretion
algorithm
animism
antipodes
chaos
cosmos
determinancy
entropy
existentialism
facetious
immutable
indigenous
intrinsic

invariant
macroscopic
Marseillaise
nirvana
palatable
paleontology
plat
pluralistic
posit
prodigious
provenance
repugnant
stochastic
trajectory

1. Please define each word on the adjacent list, in the sense in which it is used in this problem.
2. What is entropy a measure of, as related to our form studies?
3. Please use all the following words in one or two sentences, in reference to the contemporary city: entropy, chaos, form, process.
4. Name and describe three typical approaches to urban collective form.
5. What is the implication of the use of the word "chaotic" with reference to a given situation?
6. Discuss Heinz Von Foerster's statement that an environment is defined by the kind and amount of order that can be discovered in it.
7. Who were Mozart, and Sisyphus?

Problem 6: Curvilinear Form

cuneiform
delineate
enigma
grotesque
homeostatic
ideograph
isobar
metabolism

morphological
nuance
opprobrium
panoply
phonogram
pictograph
trabecula

1. Please define each word on the adjacent list, in the sense in which it is used in this problem.
2. Identify four general categories of typefaces, and give examples.
3. Identify and discuss six separate areas in which proportion is an important consideration.
4. What is the length of the radius of curvature of a straight line?
5. Please discuss the significance of the concept of "line" in perception, and in graphic representation.
6. Discuss the influence of the writing instrument and surface on the development of "visible language," and give examples.
7. Prepare a flow-chart for the algorithm on page 133.

Problem 7: Form and Content

1. Please define each word on the adjacent list, in the sense in which it is used in this problem.
2. What is the "death-grip syndrome," and how may one overcome it?
3. Arnheim points out that "expression is an inherent characteristic of perceptual patterns" and suggests that "expression can be described as the primary content of vision." Why should this be so?
4. Discuss some of the arguments, pro and con, regarding the use of plastic or artificial flowers, and comment on the issues involved with such substitutions.
5. Who was Antaeus, and what was the Minotaur?

analogue	lyrical
anthropomorphism	meticulous
caprice	palpable
daunted	piquant
explicit	prolific
fawn	symbiosis
integrity	syndrome
intonation	synechdoche

Problem 8: Visual Organization

1. Please define each term on the adjacent list, in the sense in which it is used in this problem.
2. Identify four Gestalt laws of visual organization, and illustrate them with your own examples.
3. Describe the relationship between leading, measure, x-height, and readability.
4. What is a "law of Nature," according to Von Foerster?

ascender	leading
base line	letter spacing
bleed	light face
bold face	mean line
condensed face	measure
descender	myriad
discrete	pica
extended face	point
gutter	roman
heterogeneous	serif
indictment	superordinate
italic	x-height
justified	word spacing

Problem 9: Color Attributes

1. Please define each word on the adjacent list, in the sense in which it is used in this problem.
2. When you arranged the color chips on each Munsell chart, was the entropy of the chips increased or decreased?
3. Which color attribute(s) do the following have in common: pink, cerise, cherry, dusty pink, rose, scarlet, vermilion, crimson?
4. Draw a complete diagram of the three-dimensional Munsell color system, labeling all the parts and scales.
5. Name and illustrate three basic color attributes.
6. Why are the number and arrangement of color chips different on each Munsell hue chart?
7. Identify the five modes of color perception.
8. Describe the difference between the concepts of "lightness" and "brightness."

allusive	neutral
chroma	parameter
collage	saturation
conjure	swatch
hue	value

Problem 10: Color Scales

achromatic
additive mixing
alchemist
complementary
high key
indefatigable

low key
monochromatic
shade
solfeggio
subtractive mixing
tint
tone

1. Please define each term on the adjacent list, in the sense in which it is used in this problem.
2. Illustrate, in one diagram, the relationship between black, white, gray, hue, tint, shade, and tone.
3. Identify the additive and subtractive primary colors, and the secondary colors that result from their mixing.
4. Why do the flatly painted elements of your gray scale appear to vary in value from edge to edge?
5. Please explain the colored shadows that result when you intercept the colored lights in the demonstration of additive color mixing.

Problem 11: Color Analysis of Scene

affect
aggregate
ambient
central tendency
constancy
frequency distribution

histogram
local color
simultaneous contrast
situational color
synesthesia

1. Please define each term on the adjacent list, in the sense in which it is used in this problem.
2. When you matched the basic pattern area colors with the Munsell color charts, what was the purpose of the gray masks?
3. Describe the difference between "local color" and "situational color."
4. For each of the following combinations of value and chroma characterizing the colors of a given scene, please indicate the hypothetical characterization of mood: (a) high value, low chroma; (b) high value, high chroma; (c) low value, low chroma; and (d) low value, high chroma.
5. Diagram the value histogram for (a) a low key, (b) a high key, (c) a high contrast, and (d) a "technically perfect" black and white photograph.

Problem 12: Color Expression

anteroom
antinomy
auspicious
bourgeois
deft
fervor
gross
haiku
hermetic
immutable
inclement
inimitable
intrinsic

kakemono
mimetic
mosaic
mundane
posit
precept
sarcophagus
seer
sudare
tessera
tokonoma
trammel
ubiquitous

1. Please define each word on the adjacent list, in the sense in which it is used in this problem.
2. Antonin Raymond writes, "There is a symbol in the interplay of geometric form and natural form which deeply moves the Japanese." To what do you think this symbol refers?
3. According to Raymond, the Japanese prefer a perishable bamboo fence which requires constant repair, and thus symbolizes another aspect of the world in which we live. Please comment on the significance of this preference.
4. What is it, according to Raymond, that constitutes "bad taste" for the Japanese? And what, also according to Raymond, provides the "highest satisfaction"?
5. Why do young children "appear to have little interest in mixed or impure colors," according to Tuan?
6. Describe some simple ways to achieve color harmony.

Problem 13: Color and Space

1. Please define each term on the adjacent list, in the sense in which it is used in this problem.
2. List all the factors that may affect a color decision in connection with a given space.
3. Describe a "spectral energy distribution curve" and a "spectral reflectance curve," and indicate to what they refer.
4. Please indicate the apparent tint given a white surface by lamps of the following color temperature: 2,000° K; 2,800° K; and 3,400° K.

caveat
color rendering index
color temperature
correlated color temperature
criterion
modulate

Problem 14: Color Coding

1. Please define each word of the adjacent list, in the sense in which it is used in this problem.
2. What is a "good" number of design hypotheses?
3. Describe and discuss what is meant by the "decorative" use of color.
4. How are traffic signals arranged to cope with that minority of the public who are color-blind?
5. Please give some public examples of color coding in your community.

extenuating
pertinent
salve

Problem 15: Rhythmical Organization

1. Please define each word on the adjacent list, in the sense in which it is used in this problem.
2. Rhythm originates in repetition. What are some of the visual attributes involved in visual rhythm?
3. Who was Vermeer?

canon
Platonic
predilection
progeny
quasi-

retrospective
rigorous
sublimate
volte-face

Problem 16: Rhythm and Modulation

augmentation
coda
diminution
farthingale
modulate
orchestrate
petrification
retrogression
superordinate
taxonomy

1. Please define each word of the adjacent list, in the sense in which it is used in this problem.
2. Discuss the significance of modulation in the patterning of the elements of the cityscape, and give examples based on your own experience.
3. Name and describe the five modes of color-use.

Problem 3b: Texture Archetypes (Conclusion)

chiaroscuro
penumbra
quintessence
silhouette
specular
umbra

1. Please define each word on the adjacent list, in the sense in which it is used in this problem.
2. Describe the correspondence between gradations of shading and three-dimensional form.
3. Discuss the differences between the shadows cast by an object (a) in direct sunlight, (b) under an overcast sky, and (c) under a streetlight at night.
4. Discuss the relationship between the physical texture of a surface and the reflection of light from that surface.
5. What are the means used by the visual designer to establish and form space, and objects in space?

Problem 17: Texture, Space, and Scale

1. Please define each term on the adjacent list, in the sense in which it is used in this problem.
2. Name and describe the four modes of texture use.
3. What is the Kruithof theory?
4. Please give the approximate actual dimensions of *all* the basic-texture-element sizes that might be found in a concrete-block wall.
5. Please hypothesize the effect on the apparent size or proportions of a given space of the use of the following texture attributes on the vertical surfaces establishing that space: (a) form type, (b) size, (c) value, (d) direction, and (e) contrast.

basic texture element
scale
succinct
verisimilitude

Postscript: A Valediction

1. Please define each word on the adjacent list, in the sense in which it is used in this section.
2. Why is the "artistic form" unique in human experience, and in human culture?
3. What is Von Foerster's criterion for environmental knowledge?

adjunct
apparition
caprice
Charybdis
coalesce
concoction
credo
cynic
disquisition
déclassé
exemplary
lucid
meretricious

paradox
postulate
pragmatic
preponderance
rapport
recapitulate
retort
Scylla
tacit
tangible
trancendental
valediction

DATE DUE